"Dr. Gil deftly bridges the science and theology of sex and gender to provide an honest, refreshing, and faith-based perspective that also prioritizes the person. Here is a well-informed and compassionate guide for the Christian, whether a parent of intersex or transgender children, a pastor seeking information and guidance, or a gender-questioning individual. Central to the argument is the notion that God's kingdom is large enough to understand and embrace those who seek wholeness and acceptance in their lives."

—**Robert A. Mullins**
Azusa Pacific University

"How many times have I sat in my office wishing there was a good book that covers it all, gender questions to ask and answer, with Scripture, science, and life histories . . . well, here it is! This book moves us through the gauntlet with life histories and narratives of compassion that are biblically and scientifically grounded. Vince Gil provides practical tools for parents, pastors, lay leaders, while challenging us to create a more embracing, empathic, Christlike response to the gender moment. Look no further than this book!"

—**Erin (Bongiorno) Donovan**
Former Executive Director, HopeSprings

"There are books written by Christians that have never journeyed with transgender persons, or who speak of only prescriptives without understanding their histories. I thus wondered if Dr. Vince Gil would be one of those authors. He proved me wrong. Vince Gil goes to the heart of the issues without losing sight of the *person*. This is the first book I've read that rises to the occasion. Not only is the language accessible and direct in explaining the science, cultural and social understandings, theological views and challenges; it invites the reader to stop, reflect, and consider before cementing their response. There is novel information to further frame perspectives on the 'other'—intersex, transgender, non-binary—as well as on theological challenges. This book is an invitation to Christians to sit and reason together out of love for the 'other.'"

—**Lisa Salazar**
Author of *Transparently*

"Some Christians may wish for a return to simpler days when gender questions were ignored or brushed off with a quick application of a few Bible verses. But, if Christians are called to be salt and light in the world, and if we are called to love our neighbor as ourselves—and we are!—then it is crucial that Christians thoughtfully engage the difficult questions surrounding intersex and transgender. Happily, Gil provides a helpful guide to these labyrinthine issues. With an irenic spirit and an open mind, he helps us understand the questions better, and then steers toward helpful, workable answers that are biologically, theologically, and pastorally sound."

—**James Beilby**
Bethel University

A Christian's Guide through the Gender Revolution

A Christian's Guide through the Gender Revolution

Gender, Cisgender, Transgender, and Intersex

VINCENT E. GIL

Foreword by
JERRY CAMERY-HOGGATT

CASCADE *Books* • Eugene, Oregon

A CHRISTIAN'S GUIDE THROUGH THE GENDER REVOLUTION
Gender, Cisgender, Transgender, and Intersex

Copyright © 2021 Vincent E. Gil. All rights reserved. Except for brief quotations in critical publications or reviews, no part of this book may be reproduced in any manner without prior written permission from the publisher. Write: Permissions, Wipf and Stock Publishers, 199 W. 8th Ave., Suite 3, Eugene, OR 97401.

Cascade Books
An Imprint of Wipf and Stock Publishers
199 W. 8th Ave., Suite 3
Eugene, OR 97401

www.wipfandstock.com

PAPERBACK ISBN: 978-1-7252-8670-2
HARDCOVER ISBN: 978-1-7252-8671-9
EBOOK ISBN: 978-1-7252-8672-6

Cataloging-in-Publication data:

Names: Gil, Vincent E., author. | Camery-Hoggatt, Jerry, foreword writer.

Title: A Christian's guide through the gender revolution : gender, cisgender, transgender, and intersex / by Vincent E. Gil.

Description: Eugene, OR : Cascade Books, 2021 | Includes bibliographical references and index.

Identifiers: ISBN 978-1-7252-8670-2 (paperback) | ISBN 978-1-7252-8671-9 (hardcover) | ISBN 978-1-7252-8672-6 (ebook)

Subjects: LCSH: Gender identity—Religious aspects—Christianity | Gender nonconformity—Religious aspects—Christianity. | Christian transgender people. | Sex—Religious aspects—Christianity. | Transgender people—Identity. | Intersexuality.

Classification: LCC BR115.T76 G55 2021 (print) | BR115.T76 (ebook)

12/21/20

*To my wife and life coach, Dr. Magali (Mikki) Gil,
who can make anything possible through her forbearance,
wit, and unending love—this is for you.
And, to all those Christians who inspired me to write this book
to help traverse this "gender moment"—this is for you, too.*

Contents

Permissions | ix
Tables and Figures | xi
Foreword by Jerry Camery-Hoggatt | xiii
Preface | xix
Acknowledgements | xxv
Abbreviations and Acronyms | xxviii

1 The "Now" Of Gender | 1

2 The Language of Gender | 8

3 Portraits of Gender Today | 33

4 "Fearfully and Wonderfully Made" | 65

5 What Is a Parent to Do? | 88

6 Manipulating Biology in Children and Teens with Diagnosed Gender Dysphoria | 115

7 Christianity and the Gender Crucible | 137

8 Pastoral and Church Leadership Responses to the Gender Moment | 174

9 The Church and Transgender Activism | 194

  Conclusion | 216

Bibliography | 225
Index | 241

Permissions

Scriptures taken from the Holy Bible, New International Version®, NIV®. Copyright © 1973, 1978, 1984, 2011 by Biblica, Inc.™ Used by permission of Zondervan. All rights reserved worldwide. www.zondervan.com. The "NIV" and "New International Version" are trademarks registered in the United States Patent and Trademark Office by Biblica, Inc.®

Scripture quotations marked (NLT) are taken from the Holy Bible, New Living Translation, Copyright © 1996, 2004, 2015 by Tyndale House Foundation. Used by permission of Tyndale House Publishers, a Division of Tyndale House Ministries, Carol Stream, IL 60188. All Rights Reserved.

Permission to use Figure Differentiation of Reproductive System into Male and Female Organs granted under Copyright © Creative Commons Attribute 3.0 Unported. Original source is Connexions at http://cnx.org/content/col11496/1.6, 2013.

Internet addresses (websites, blogs, etc.) printed in this book are offered as a resource to you. These are not intended in any way to be or imply an endorsement on the part of Cascade Books, an imprint of Wipf & Stock Publishers, nor do we vouch for the content of these sites for the life of this book.

Permission to use relief block print "Les Miserables" on cover, Copyright Stephen Alcorn, Alcorn Studio and Galleries. Print is from Literary Classics Collection. www.alcorngallery.com.

Tables and Figures

TABLES

1. Charting Novel Gender Schemas | 22
2. Questions to Ask Therapists Who Treat Gender Conflicts | 113
3.1. Effects of Estrogen Therapies on MTF Transgender Patients | 134
3.2. Effects of Testosterone Therapies on FTM Transgender Patients | 135
3.3. Effects of Hormone Therapies on All Transgender Patients | 136
4. "Punch List" of Suggested Questions and Conversations on Sexuality and Gender the Church Should Address | 192

FIGURES

1: Differentiation of Reproductive System into Male and Female Structures | 86
2: Chromosome Contributions, Normal and Syndromes | 87

Foreword

> In times of change, learners inherit the earth; while the learned find themselves beautifully equipped to deal with a world that no longer exists.
>
> —Eric Hoffer

The writer of Ecclesiastes lamented what seemed then an explosion of books, and admonished that "of making many books there is no end; and much study is a weariness of the flesh" (Eccl 12:12). So why this book, and why now? And in particular, why a book for Christians especially, about the challenges vexing gender and identity in contemporary America?

My emphatic answer is that we *need* this book! Almost every moment of cultural and historical significance has had its contentions underscored more than its agreements, but the present moment has seen unprecedented contention, and comes at a moment in time where life is difficult for many on many fronts, with social changes increasing in both variety and complexity. If the writer of Ecclesiastes was right then, how much more so today, when our media are flooded with books and blogs, op-ed pieces, and the biting and sniping of what feels often enough like vapid opinionating on social media. The problem is that the much of it only reinforces what we already believe, in the process blinding us to any truths that may be articulated on the other side.

Over a hundred years ago, British philosopher John Stuart Mill pointed out that as long as opinion is rooted in feelings, it resists or discounts any inconvenient facts because the feelings appear to be based on some deeper truth that rational arguments do not reach (*The Subjection of Women*, 1). It's quite easy to suppose that deeply held feelings are the same as moral clarity.

This is where we are with the questions Dr. Vincent (Vince) Gil, my colleague and friend, discusses in this volume. The term "gender revolution" has become the shorthand for a consolidation of sentiments about gender and identity; a term that solidified for many a kind of culture war. Literature on gender and identity comes to us fast and furious, with the word *furious* sometimes taking the lead. Each side then becomes ever more convinced by their feelings on a level where "rational arguments do not reach." All too often, the entrenchments solidify into non-negotiable positions.

In this volume, Vince reminds us again and again that conversations about gender and identity need not be set in opposition; indeed, they can become cooperative projects in which we seek together a third path. To do that, he insists that we begin by listening to the personal stories of the people who are directly impacted by these issues—those who are biologically intersex, who are troubled by sexual dysphoria, or whose family lives are directly affected by these questions. To understand the issues, we first must encounter and genuinely try to understand the people concerned. This book is filled with stories, some of them deeply anguishing, many enmeshed in physical biology or the workings of the psyche, others involving issues of spirituality and the impact of these questions on the journey of faith. While it's entirely possible to parse the issues theoretically and abstractly, we mustn't stop there. As followers of Jesus, we're asked to listen directly and carefully to the *people* who are directly impacted.

It is this attention to the persons involved that makes this book so useful for Christians. Here, Vince provides us a way that we, as Christians, can bridge this particular divide. When we take real people as seriously as Jesus would, when we pause long enough, listen carefully enough, and think ethically enough, we can begin to ferret out the significant nuances that lead to better questions, and then to better informed and more hopeful answers. Importantly, taking human experience seriously requires that we listen carefully, even when that process and the learning is uncomfortable. Let's call this, "principled listening."

Vince's core message is that when we practice principled listening in a context of accurate science and careful theology we discover that there is in fact a third way, not a reluctant compromise but a more generous, more patient, and better informed approach to answering the questions. This is an approach that takes science, scripture, and actual human experience seriously.

Doing so also requires us to be open to new knowledge. To paraphrase Eric Hoffer from the masthead quote in this foreword, "In times of radical change, it is the learners who inherit the earth . . . ." I could not think of a better "learner" than Vince to help us gain appropriate understandings about this contested space. He's one of those professors who continue to be learners themselves. My testimony comes from decades of shared, collateral service as faculty of a Christian university in Southern California.

Vince's continued path to learning has made him a medical and psychological anthropologist, sexologist, researcher, compassionate caregiver and counselor, and licensed minister. He is a distinguished and awarded educator, and a well-recognized researcher with dozens of peer reviewed articles, papers, and book chapters. Earlier than his research years, he founded *Interlude Ministries,* a nonprofit counseling service for the sexually problemed Christian. It is this rich background, precisely, that enables him to address gender identity and intersexuality questions from the expertise of his exceptional multispecialty.

Those receiving his counsel on the journey toward psychological wholeness have also gained a deeper, more authentic faith. His ministry to students has been astounding, especially among those who are struggling to understand issues of their own sexuality, gender, and gender role expressions. I've watched as they've flocked to his classroom or slipped quietly into his office, hoping for help in sorting out the issues, not only for themselves, but also for their families and friends.

The issues they bring to him are never easy. What are they to do when they find themselves in the contested space between the simple binary of male or female, or trapped by discomfort with the role expectations that go with the binary? How are they to understand their gender and identity in the context of their own faith journeys? How can they help their family members, or friends who are struggling?

How should a parent understand a child or adolescent who is gender-nonconforming? For some, the issues are vocational: as they prepare for, or are now in, pastoral ministry, how are they to understand the experiences of the individuals who will come to them for care? This book addresses all these dimensions by tailoring chapters for parents, for clergy, and for those with their own gender-identity questions.

There's an old conviction among academics that both Vince and I teach our students: *Before you can say you disagree, first you must understand.* But precisely because the issues are complex, the effort to understand requires that we investigate from multiple perspectives, using a variety of tools. The physical aspects of our selves can be studied objectively, neutrally, through the tools of scientific research. These are the tangibles, replete with statistics and validations. Vince explains these things with admirable clarity, disentangling the various strands of the scientific evidence, then setting them into a framework in which their complexities become clear.

Other aspects of the questions are psychological and emotional. These are better understood through the lens of real-life histories, histories that give substance to the issues. In this book, Vince brings his professional expertise and long experience to unpack the stories, helping us to hear them more sympathetically, always probing for deeper and more general meanings.

Vince uses the tools of the social sciences to help us understand the ways the issues are also complicated by sociocultural factors, like gender ideology and social role expectations; they're made more difficult by opinions about what is or isn't *normal*; what is or isn't *normative*, what is or isn't *acceptable*. What Vince *doesn't do* is challenge the fact that there are norms. Many of these are upheld by science, not just society or theology. He calls our attention to the impact of our current cultural norms, their effects on people caught in the deeply personal spaces between family expectations for themselves, their beliefs, their faith, and their inner realities. He also calls us to explore the current movement to self-identify outside *any norms*; to consider its influence on how many now think of themselves, how we think of ourselves, and what our children are learning. In this way, what he *does* do is open up space for more informed conversations, and for genuinely helpful pastoral care.

The reason these questions are so important is that it's precisely here—in the centered space between the physical, the psychological, and the sociocultural—that we position our ideas about what it means to have a *self*. This is where we determine who we *are*. All of these combine to form those basic frameworks for understanding where we fit and what it means to live authentic, meaningful lives.

As we learn from the numerous case studies in this book, it's precisely here, in this centered space between the physical, psychological, and sociocultural dimensions, that some of us discover that we're woefully out of joint, alien, or deeply dissonant. Since what is at issue is the *self*, these dissonances can become profound and extensive; and when such happens, they inevitably raise questions of existential and religious significance.

Because the dissonances have religious significance, clearly what's needed is a redemptive response. To explore that, Vince brings in yet another set of tools, this set attuned to the interpretation of ancient texts and long-standing religious tradition. Unfortunately, here too, things are problematic, and the dissonances are even more deeply anguishing when normed expectations are couched in terms of "biblical authority." This is a matter of my own expertise: biblical scholarship. Biblical scholars know, but don't often share, that original biblical texts are often difficult to translate from the Hebrew or Greek into English. When there are multiple meanings or layers of nuance, translators must often choose one, then set aside the others. The resulting translation can appear to support a single, clear, unequivocal reading, where the original may be less clear, or contain other useful information.

Vince understands this. Importantly for us, he examines the relevant biblical texts to probe those additional nuances that are lost in translation. This is hard work, but it can provide deeper understandings and, in most instances, add clarity to how we read the Bible. In the case of creation, and our procreation, such nuanced exegesis helps us better align our understanding of scripture with what science is now telling us about ourselves. So Vince calls us to become better informed about what the Bible does indeed teach, and what it does not.

The issues are also theological: How do we understand our bodies "in God's image," when these seem so frightfully out of touch with our minds; and in combination, with what we may have been taught as Christians? How do we understand the body as a temple of God when what we're taught is that the feelings we may have are inherently immoral or godless?

For Christians, the issues finally come home in this: Who we are is more than a natural biological, psychological, or social construct. Who we *are* is a work of divine creativity; before anything else, the critical clues about who we *are* are found in the theological concepts of the image of God, and the transformed self as part of the body of Christ.

However rapidly our wider culture might be changing, Vince asks that we examine it carefully, and that in the care of individuals we take time to slow down the opinionating, find the facts, and pay careful attention to the issues of faithful and authentic personhood. He calls us to a more informed, generous, open-hearted approach to those who are dealing with these difficult questions, and in that way helps us map a pathway forward toward positions that are better informed, more compassionate, and ultimately more redemptive.

Indeed, to tweak John Stuart Mill here, Vince is asking the church of Jesus Christ to cultivate a social regard for the intersex and those with gender conflicts that is more thoughtfully narrated, seeded with up-to-date and accurate information, and a revisited theology. Above all, he is asking us to include *in our feelings* those which embrace empathy, compassion, and the hope Jesus offers everyone.

Jerry Camery-Hoggatt, PhD

Emeritus Professor of New Testament and Narrative Theology, Vanguard University of Southern California (Costa Mesa, CA). Jerry is a widely published scholar in biblical studies and a popular fiction writer.

Preface

HOW DID I GET HERE?

Little did anyone expect 2020 to bring on the turmoil and tumults that we are now experiencing. I write this as the COVID19 pandemic continues to sweep through the US, and the rest of the world deals with secondary outbreaks. At the center of this moment, in the US and around the world, calls to aright racial injustices have broken through the social fabric, a result—yet again—of lives being taken inconsequentially. Protests have taken on proportions heretofore not seen; people of every race and ethnicity banded together to remonstrate for a better world. It's a narrative of seeking harmony, but like an earthquake, the narrative instead lays bare the faults of our vicious cultural and racial global history.

What does this, if anything, have to do with *gender*? I've spent some time of late in isolation pondering this: why do I think the current "moment" is akin to the *"gender moment"*? Here's what's become clear: both are part of a larger human problematic, one that suggests *identity* and *otherness* should be examined closely to determine if some should be *excluded* or *embraced*.[1]

The fact is, I could not dismiss the anguish I was witnessing. It circled back to the gender conflicts I had been privy to, lives I became part of professionally and personally. I also couldn't dismiss the myriad students in my Human Sexuality courses over the past years of this gender "moment," who had told me stories:

---

1. We have Miroslav Volf to thank for diving deeply into a socio-theological exploration of identity, otherness, and reconciliation in his opus *Exclusion and Embrace* (1996).

- Of their dad "outing" as transgender and going through surgery. Then the exclusions that followed when telling others about it.
- Of a sister who thought she was gay, only to realize it was all about her body not being right with her head. Then the exclusions that followed when telling others about it.
- Of themselves being gender conflicted, and Christian. Then the exclusions that followed when telling others about it.
- And the real kicker, a friend and colleague who had just discovered her child to be *intersex*, and was dealing with how to understand what she now knew about her little girl . . . who wasn't really, *all girl*. Then how to deal with the exclusions that will probably follow *her*.

Theologian Miroslav Volf reminds us that our "moral" and "civilized" selves too often rest on *excluding* those we feel to be "immoral" or "barbarous."[2]

For a few years, I watched my compassion toward such labeled individuals, and anger toward misinformation, grow. For the last year, I could not resist the deep-hearted urge to try to put an understanding to the transgender moment for the Christian I knew so well didn't have good answers. Then there was the tug of the Holy Spirit—moving my heart more than I can share with words.

So how did I ultimately *get here*?

Truly, there's nothing more exciting, or perplexing, than teaching a Human Sexuality course to college undergraduates. The perplexity grows when the course is taught in a Christian university, where what you think students *don't* know, they *do*; and what you think they *do* know, they *don't*! My colleague and friend Dr. Jerry had the serendipitous habit of opening my classroom door—in the middle of a lecture—and yelling in, "Be affirmed, all of you! Learn something!" That "all of you" certainly included me.

One afternoon, while teaching this course, I waxed on about distinguishing between what is *gender non-conformity* and what is *gender dysphoria*. I was making certain to describe typical experiences and patterns in each of these different classifications, while answering student questions that kept popping up.

---

2. Volf, *Exclusion and Embrace*, 62.

Nothing does better than an illustration when trying to teach about *gender dysphoria*, so I proceeded with my usual, "Let me give you a real-life example"; a clinical history pieced together from many I had encountered or counseled. I made sure that the most common elements were included, anonymously framed, of course.

Concluding the class, a student walked up and asked for a sidebar. "I want you to know," he said, "that you are the first person who totally described *me,* up there" (pointing to the podium). Curiously, I asked, "What do you mean, *me?*" He said, "Your description of *my* life-course—you described all the elements that I've wrestled with; my body, my mind, my soul . . . and I didn't have a label until now: It's about my gender!"

Unbeknown to me, a lot had come together to put this student in the class that afternoon. None more important than a rejection from his father earlier that same week, when he finally told his father he was having problems *not feeling man enough*. Other elements included life-long feelings he wasn't at all the boy, later the young man, his genetics and his learning said he should be; trying desperately to excel in sports—having an avid athlete father—to "grow" into the man he was supposed to be; failed relationships with peer women, not knowing whether he was in some way "gay" or otherwise, having only distant feelings for them; turning it Freudian and blaming his over-doting mom, when he knew better; avoiding women, when he didn't know what else to do. He hated his own body. Maybe he should have been born a girl and should be different—he had thought of how liberating that would have been.

Desperate for answers, he had enrolled in Human Sexuality. Maybe the shame of his feeling worthless and the unimaginable sense of despair that he felt—that dreadful loneliness—would have a reason. He knew his "sex" had a lot to do with "it"; but he didn't have a *label* for what framed his life-experience.

Everything's in a name, we say. Dread or liberation, futility or consolation. It's all there, waiting to be sorted and weighed, sometimes judged, sometimes vindicated, by a *label.* As I'll note later, labels can also be deadly.

For this young man, the terms he learned that afternoon gave him handles to begin to see and understand for the first time what was a syndrome of emotions and physical negations. That such would be irreconcilable with self, identity, expectations, and role obligations, he'd have to now figure out (I recommended a therapist).

No youth pastor, friend, or schoolteacher had ever *picked up* on the self-body-identity issues. None had invested time *with him* to seek an understanding of what was going on. For certain he had been prayed for, encouraged, sometimes even blind-dated at the urging of friends to help him with his "shyness," or with him being an "awkward dude." Nobody had thought to investigate his conundrum with a dimension of identity that now we are all conscious of, *gender*.

I couldn't any longer put away the stories I had been privy to hear; lives I became part of as they shared in counseling, in class, in corners of buildings and hallways, illuminating my need to *do more, and more that is worthwhile*. And their stories—in and out of counseling—kept growing.

Over the last decade and a half, issues that surround gender have surfaced almost as with a vengeance for not having had a place, a voice, in our cacophonous society. And I became even more convinced that the church needed to attend to *these* lives, *their* questions, their *exclusions*, in earnest. After all, questions from gender-conflicted individuals weren't that dissimilar to mine, the sexology researcher, the counselor. I wanted answers—they did too. As believers, weren't they also worthy of being considered "in God's image," *imago Dei?*

The more I paid attention, the greater grew the conviction that we as the church of Jesus Christ needed to get over our fears of contagion, our fears of gendered differences unraveling our theology of male and females. We needed to get over our judgments, and reach a better understanding of our procreated selves.

Even more, I now find it imperative that the church restate again its commitment to modeling how God embraces us through Jesus' sacrifice. In so modeling, we should become donors of our time and emotions, engaging acts of accompaniment for those walking through this gender moment. Donors include parents, pastors, other clergy, and you and me as emulators of Christ.

This book is the result. I hope to help us all understand a way through the gender moment—the "gender revolution"—the one that has swept into our consciousness and is now flooding our church doors.

My hope is that this work will become a resource and a way to respond, understanding very well that there's still a whole lot more to unravel. Let's do it together, with Christian mercy, a Christian *embrace*, and hopes of reconciliation through Jesus Christ.

Acknowledgements

Acknowledging my life partner, love of my life, and mother of our children comes first, since from early on in our lives together, she has been my educational inspiration and—quite frankly—coach on everything academic. We've gone through BAs, MAs, PhDs, postdocs, myriad certifications, two live births and two careers, literally *together*—forging alliances, and debating life on and off the dinner table. To her I owe time, time stolen to write, edit, and proof this work; and bottomless thanks for her unending belief that what I do matters. I would be a lesser person, and none of this work would have been possible *without her*. Thank you God, and thank you Mikki, for loving me so.

As you'll soon read, this book began as an effort to give voice and understanding to all those who trusted me with their stories of sexual and gender conflicts, an accumulation of over thirty-eight years' worth of working in the field of sexology and teaching human sexuality. I've been privileged to hear, and attend to many Christians, especially my students, who've engaged me with their questions, their tears, their nightmares, but also their hopes. To all of you whom I've engaged, thank you for your cumulative inspiration to tackle gender and identity through a Christian lens of mercy and reconciliation. My debt to you is great.

No work rests on one author. Those that cheered me on were the folks in Social and Behavioral Sciences at Vanguard University: our trusted coordinator Cheryl Jensen; her colleague coordinator Kathleen Durel; my former colleague Ed Clarke, who heard me tell and moan early on in this work; and from the Religion and Theological Studies Department especially, now emeritus colleague Jerry Camery-Hoggatt, former Professor of New Testament and Narrative Theology.

Jerry, who also acceded to writing the foreword, has taught me well, directly through many conversations, and through his myriad tomes in exegesis and New Testament studies. I also owe greatly to my friend of many years and colleague, Robert Mullins, Chair and Professor, Department of Biblical and Religious Studies, Azusa Pacific University. Bob was incredibly generous with his time in reviewing much of what I've included here from the Old Testament, as well as polishing the Hebrew and giving me lessons on rabbinic Judaism. Any "oops" are mine, not his.

More distant, but needing thanks, are those who trained me in sexological sciences, those of the former Masters and Johnson Institute, St. Louis; all those engaged in the Society for the Scientific Study of Sexuality, The American Academy of Clinical Sexology, and the American Board of Sexology. None recoiled from my Christianity, and none discouraged me from reconciling science with faith. To all, I owe my academic debt. In this category, I also owe much to "Joanna," who volunteered for more than a decade visiting my sexuality class, teaching about gender dysphoria by embodying it. You taught me much as well.

I am particularly indebted to Erin Bongiorno Donovan, former founder/director of HopeSprings (Baltimore), and now of RootED Consulting. Erin is a special friend, former student-turned-colleague, who not only supported this work from the beginning, but read assiduously versions of the manuscript and offered commentary *on every page*. Erin, this work is so much better because of your generosity, insights, and sharing. I am so happy we have learned much from one another, and have prayed through much with one another!

Thank you, Michael Thomson, acquisitions editor, for believing in this work and pushing it through the Wipf & Stock reviews. You never gave up on me. Thank you, Robin Parry, for editing this work and providing insight and polish from across the Pond. To all those from Wipf & Stock who've worked behind the scenes, I am indebted. It's an honor to join the Cascade/Wipf & Stock community!

Finally, thank you to Amy Hoffman for taking on the work of formatting and proofing this document, all the while watching out for the significant sentence, and giving me added insights. Your meticulous work is so appreciated!

Acknowledgements

To the God who created humanity and still guides it along—if we let God—my gratitude, for giving me the courage to speak to the gender moment with your heart in my head. More importantly, for keeping me somewhat sane, certainly reconciled, and offering me and our entire humanity hope in Jesus' name.

Abbreviations and Acronyms

AASECT:	Acronym for *American Association of Sexuality Educators, Counselors, and Therapists*
AMH:	Anti Müllerian Hormone
APA:	Acronym for *American Psychological Association*
AIS:	Androgen Insensitivity Syndrome, an androgen receptor deficiency in the AR gene. See also pAIS.
BBC:	British Broadcasting Corporation
BCE:	Before the Common Era
BRCA:	Acronym for *Breast Cancer Gene*. Mutations in two expressions, *BRCA1* and *BRCA2*, can cause cancers
CAH:	Congenital Adrenal Hyperplasia
CCCU:	Acronym for *Coalition of Christian Colleges and Universities*
CE:	Common Era
DBT:	Dialectical Behavior Therapy
DNA:	Deoxyribonucleic Acid. DNA is the main constituent in chromosomes, and carrier of genetic information.
DADT:	"Don't Ask, Don't Tell" was the official policy in The Department of Defense 1993–2011.
DSD:	Disorders of Sexual Development. Often called Intersexuality. Formally called Swyer Syndrome, expressed as 46, XY Gonadal Dysgenesis.

Abbreviations and Acronyms

DSM-5: Acronym for the *Diagnostic and Statistical Manual of the American Psychiatric Association, Ver.* 5

FTM: Female-to-Male Transgender

FSH: Follicle Stimulating Hormone

GD: Gender Dysphoria

GnRH: Gonadotropic Releasing Hormone

GnRHas: Gonadotropin Releasing Hormone Analogues

HIV: Human Immunodeficiency Virus

HIV/AIDS: Human Immunodeficiency Virus/Acquired Immune Deficiency Syndrome

HRC: Acronym for *Human Rights Campaign*

IdicY: Isodicentric Y, often parsed as *idic*Y. Abnormally formed Y chromosome in sperm

ISNA: Acronym for *Intersex Society of North America*

KS: 47 XXY Karyotype, Chromosomal Trisomy, known as Klinefelter Syndrome (KS)

LGBTQI: Acronym for *Lesbian, Gay, Bisexual, Transgender, Queer/Questioning, Intersex*

LH: Luteinizing Hormone

LHRH: Luteinizing Hormone Resisting Hormone (see GnRHas)

MGD: Mixed Gonadal Dysgenesis. Abnormal organ development during embryonic differentiation

MTF: Male-to-Female Transgender

pAIS: Partial Androgen Insensitivity Syndrome. A less severe form of AIS. Formally, Reifenstein Syndrome

PFLAG: Acronym for *Parents and Friends of Lesbians and Gays*

PRRI: Acronym for *Public Religion Research Institute*

ROGD: Rapid Onset Gender Dysphoria

TS: Turner Syndrome, 45, XO Karyotype, Chromosomal Monosomy. See XO

TSER: Acronym for *Transgender Student Education Resources*

UCSD:	University of California at Sand Diego
WPATH:	World Professional Association for Transgender Health
XO:	45, XO Karyotype. X (Female), O (No Male Y) Chromosomal Monosomy. Formally, Turner Syndrome (TS)
XX:	46, XX Karyotype (Female) Sex Determination Chromosomal Pair
XXY:	47, XXY Karyotype, Chromosomal Trisomy. Formally, Klinefelter Syndrome (KS)
XY:	46, XY Karyotype (Male) Sex Determination Chromosomal Pair
XYY:	47, XYY Karyotype, Chromosomal Trisomy. Formally, Jacob's Syndrome (JS)
YO:	Y (Male), O (No Female X) Chromosomal Monosomy. Aneuplody of X (lack of a genetic pair missing an X chromosome), lethal to fetus.

1

The "Now" Of Gender

We've entered the twenty-first century with an assortment of perplexing sexual issues still confronting the Christian church. However, this is not about sexual *orientation*, who turns one on, or whether or not the Bible prohibits it.

It's about identity—*sexual identity*.

It's about *gender*, and what gender means.

It's about whether one's gender and identity, one's sexual, embodied self, is determined by *genitals* (the sex parts one has)—what was assigned at birth, based on biology. Or, whether one has the right to choose *gender* and *identity*, *labels* and *roles*.

There are different voices now coming to the foreground. Some are from people who were born *intersex*, medically called "disorders of sexual development," conditions that heretofore were never given much room in our naïve biological views of male and female. These are people who seem to have been ignored by the church as really existing, in fact: people who don't fit into boxes of "male" or "female."

And there's more. Voices are also coming from those that feel *they aren't who their bodies say they are*—those who feel, many times, trapped. We've called them *transgender*, but some call themselves by different labels, depending on what they've determined:

He's *gender-fluid*.

She's *gender nonconforming*.

Ze (a new sexless pronoun) is *non-binary*.

And Andrew is *agender*.

If a child, or teen, can't decipher their gender identity, doctors can offer a solution. Doctors can put them on *puberty blockers* until these children, or their parents, or all of them together can decide what gender means to them—the child's or teen's, that is. In other words, we can actually stop adolescence for a while, and the body's morphing into sexual maturity!

It's an emerging vocabulary as well: We have novel adjectives, like *genderqueer*, *heteronormative* (formerly heterosexual), *cisgender*; and *cisnormative*, *Femme*, *bigender*, *polygender*, *pangender*.[1] We have verbs like *queering* and *genderizing*, and personal pronouns for over seventy-one different self-labels now on Facebook.[2] Or, one can choose no labels whatsoever. (We'll sort all these terms out soon!)

Anthropologists tell us that language is a mirror of culture, and I believe that to be true. Indeed, *our emergent language of gender* displays novel terminology not existing a decade ago. All of it illustrates the dramatic "outing" and "trending" of gender issues now in our society and, concurrently, sweeping changes in perceptions, understandings, attitudes, and values.

Gender—now meaning much more than male and female or masculine and feminine roles but indicating one's *identity*—has entered the public imaginary with intention. It confronts the church with very different expressions than those it is accustomed to using when thinking about men and women.

It's important that those from religious persuasions like conservative Christianity sort through these new understandings, come to a resolve on how to respond and move though this "gender moment."

Rather than taking an informed back step to reason out the parameters of gender identity and gender expression—how these come to be in and through our biological sex, enculturation, experiences, and sense of self—society has pushed what often appear as *premature positions*, and certainly, *premature labeling*. Gender activists lend their voices to the cacophony that has formed, calling for *gender fluidity* from the cradle forward. This social push to identify and name gender

---

1. National Geographic Magazine, *Special Issue on Gender: Section: Explore*, 2017 (no pages enumerated).

2. Oremus, "Different Genders on Facebook," 1–2.

as *individuated, self-identified*, often defies traditional definitions of gender, even biological sex, and seeks a *label*.

In response, those accustomed to historical definitions repeat the standard labels, these too, often pushing back and reifying them. But labels can be deadly, and in fact all sides agree, labels are often more troublesome than helpful. Labels can also become self-fulfilling prophecies.[3]

Moreover, reports from foundations and organizations continue to underscore a growing number of people who define as *gender nonconforming*,[4] including a host of school-aged children, adolescents, who question whether the sex label they have now is the sex label they *should* have. There are also consistent reports of pervasive mistreatment, harassment, and at times violence done to individuals who question their gender, particularly while in school (primary through secondary). Adults report job losses, denied promotions, and mistreatments at the hands of work colleagues—many in the form of verbal harassments, or even physical and sometimes sexual assaults stemming from work relationships.[5]

How, then, should the Christian church, and individual families within it, understand this novel landscape of gender? More to the point, how are families whose children, adolescents, and adults express gender confusion, or gender identity nonconformity, to broach the situations that confront them? How do we engage those that openly "out" themselves as *gender dysphoric*, or *nonbinary, androgynous, genderqueer*; or who discovered they were born *intersex*?

As *Christians*, how does our theology of human creation and procreation hold up to these challenges? Is there a need to revisit *our theology* and *our labels*? And, are there a series of responsible, ethical, moral, loving responses to the gender revolution that the Christian church can muster?

I didn't write this book to reiterate positions you may have heard before about gender. I also didn't write this book to challenge biblical doctrine on the subject, but rather, to understand better our theology of being. The twenty-first century doesn't require a new Christian doctrine of human creation. It does demand a better Christian

---

3. Solomon, *Labeling in Childhood*, i.
4. Hoffman, Estimates of U.S. Transgender Population Doubles, 1.
5. James, *2015 Transgender Survey*, 4–5.

understanding of our theology on *procreation*, on men and women, identities and roles, as well as our continuing need for redemption.

I want to explore with you the *science* of sex and gender, the *theology* of sex and gender, and the *social and cultural conditions* that inform them; that surround our understanding of both—all in the hope of becoming better adept than our past generation when responding to this present "gender moment."

EMBODIMENTS ARE NECESSARY

The best means I know to move through the issues, and through the reality of gender in actual lives, is first to present you with the *lives of people:* stories—cases—of real individuals. Nearly all those reflected in early chapters here are Christians who have shared with me their struggles, perplexities, determinations, confusions, guilt, and absolutions in dealing with their gender identity, or dissonances between these and their sexual body.

I have been privileged as a Christian clergyperson, sexuality clinician, researcher, and university professor, to engage with "those whose stories you are about to hear."

I share their stories, histories, early on and anonymously to ensure that the many discussions that follow aren't just abstractly represented. The Spirit often works on our understanding through embodiments.

Thus, sex and gender issues are "embodied" here *on purpose,* to reflect historical realities in the lives of these subjects. Embodied, so that we move beyond arguments and positions, to the realization that the people we refer to with gender identity or intersex conditions are *real people.*

Jesus was foremost a *people*-person. He addressed their problematics, physical, emotional, and spiritual; but he prioritized the person: Not just healing the disease, but the individual suffering from it. Not just the role of tax collector or moneychanger, but the person embodying the role. Not the prostitute, but the woman bearing the stigma, and the necessities fueling it. He went for their hearts, so that they could go for his.

He told their stories, directly and through the many parables he shared. The human elements—feelings, thoughts, positions, predicaments of people—"embody" the human and spiritual conditions Jesus wanted to pose for listeners, up front and personal.

And, sometimes a parable doesn't conclude the way we would presume; or the story is left open-ended, on purpose. Why? Through them we can ponder the meaning, dig deeper than the surface. In doing so, we appreciate the whole of the person and the contexts involved.

As "we see the people," I hope our hearts open to the issues, the challenges, as well as the medical, psychological, social, and most centrally those theological elements we need to address. I hope we are also led to formulate and work through compassionate responses. A gospel-driven convictional kindness may not settle controversies, but will open us all to listen in stereo.

Early on and along the way we will learn about these novel terms and what they mean. When there are controversies or different voices, I will try to distinguish these are we move through the terms and the ideology these bring with them. I discuss separately each situation, condition, context, bring in the science—what we know and don't know—and point to probabilities. We will also dive deeply into the theology of being and becoming in chapters 4 and 7.

If you are a Christian parent hoping to find some answers to your questions, I hope they are here. Chapters 5 and 6 address the concerns of parents with *intersex* children, and children or adolescents who exhibit *gender dysphoria*. We will review situations where pre-teen and teen children "out" themselves as "trans"; or who question their *gender identity* in non-conforming ways. Each have independent variables needing individual attention, and I strive in chapters 5 and 6 to help Christian parents in such cases move through the many layers, without making generalizations. Chapter 6 also reviews contemporary treatments—and issues with these—in resolving gender dysphoria.

CLARIFYING OUR THEOLOGY

There are also theological sticking points, as is always the case when sexuality or anything related to sex is discussed.

Reviewing theological and traditional interpretations of gender is never easy, and chapter 7 was especially difficult to write. I attempt to reconcile *medical science* with *theology*. In so doing, I urge us to make space to relate creatively between our orthodox faith and biology. In this regard, I also suggest revisions to our negative Christian views of science. I quote Christians who are scientists and render their opinions of how the two can be compatible.

Also to be revisited are our theological traditions—*not doctrines:* about the body, about our roles, and about our self-conceptions. I review them because the days ahead will require an evangelicalism that is not defensive, but rather more missional and reconciliational; full of truth, yes; but also full of grace. Such sorting out, as a church, we must do; not in the sense of conforming to a new ethic of what it is to be male or female, but rather to the imperative of fully recognizing what it is to be human as a procreated being.

Why is this sorting important? First, because our "old answers" aren't sufficient for contemporary problems. Second, because parents need this information. Third, because the clergy especially need better handles on the subjects we cover here.

By formulating more accurate theological understandings and integrating nonpartisan science, we can move to discussing pastoral and church leadership responses to the gender moment, particularly in consideration of churchgoers who may need support and guidance with gender issues. Chapter 8 devotes itself to ferreting out how clergy and lay leaders ought to self-examine their own understandings, add what information they need to "get" the novel landscape of gender, and then respond to those gender-conflicted in their congregations or in society. (Every reader should, nevertheless, benefit from this chapter's suggestions.)

On that note, I believe strongly in companionship. Notions of what it means to *accompany another person* through the difficult questions are discussed, instead of my providing "arguments" for or against certain positions. I urge clergy and leadership to remember it is the role of the Holy Spirit to lead people to all truth (John 16:13).

Throughout chapter 8, I propose clergy also teach their congregations civility and forbearance, since, if we accomplish such, we can live in harmony with differences of opinion and bodies.

The "Now" Of Gender

NAVIGATING THE "GENDER MOMENT"

Finally, we segregate out all the diagnosable realities of sex and gender from what we'll come to know as the *social movement of self-representation*—a now rather institutionalized rebellion against binary and sometimes *all* gender labels. We are experiencing a current of embodied individualism. Understandably, expressive individualism of the sort that self-defines one's sex and gender would be historically problematic for societies like ours, with gendered roles and expectations. But now, that problematic is giving way to an unbridled accommodation.

How we as Christians respond to this, the social push for gender independence, depends on whether we see it as a social and religious challenge or an opportunity to understand and be understood.

In chapter 9 and the concluding chapter, I review gender activism. I focus on explaining it, then clarifying what may be biblically unacceptable about its propositions and what may be justifiably accommodated. I suggest how to respond so we lessen dissonances.

The sexual revolution came, but never went. We are all continuously learning about our bodies, our *selves*, our nature—fallen and redeemed. Gender and identity are elements of our humanity coming to the contemporary foreground and needing our deeper understanding and benevolence.

My hope is that you find here a resource to consult, to help guide your knowledge in this brave new world of gender identity. We need to seek godly wisdom, compassion, and understanding, and to facilitate for gender-questioning and transitioning individuals—be these friends, family, your own children, *or yourself*.

As you engage the issues and ponder the repercussions—at all levels of the spectrum involved—give ample opportunity for the Holy Spirit to guide your thinking, shore up your dedication to love unconditionally, and move your resolve to a place of solid comfort.

I ask that you find it in yourself to be *that person*, be *that parent*; be *that fortunate Christian* who can offer mercy and reconciliation along with insight, tenderness, and understanding (Col 3:12).

2

The Language of Gender

Stories of gender now surround us. An array of issues that revolve around gender, which center gender in our public and private lives, is inescapable: from our schools to our medical professionals, to officials and protesters, gender is in our everyday conversations. But "gender" is often couched in novel language terms that we need to understand—definitions, redefinitions, and ideologies.

This chapter delves into both the language of gender that is familiar and the more novel language of gender, which we not only have to learn and decipher but also come to terms with.

I start here by clarifying some of the *basic terms*—old and new. Others you will find in the Glossary that follows this chapter's commentary; terms used throughout this work.

WE ALL KNOW THE TERM "SEX"—OR DO WE?

The vernacular definition is, of course, "intercourse," denoting activity when used as a verb form. "Sex" can also mean a *physical, genital identification*—that is, the physiology of reproductive "parts." "Sex" is customarily *assigned* to a newborn by doctors and parents via the neonate's anatomy. (What makes a "boy" or "girl" has, of course, socially constructed meanings as well. We'll touch on that fact later.)

Whatever else "sex" means, here I use it to note those *biological indicators* of male and female (or in some cases, intersexed persons):

internal and external genitalia, sex chromosomes, sex glands (gonads), sex hormones, etc. When I refer to other elements of "sex" I will call them so, such as intercourse (meaning "doing sex"); or gender identity, masculinity, or femininity. These latter three are all expressions of *gender*, the next term we define. Such distinctions are meant to make our job of understanding easier, not to obscure the fact that these terms—all of them—are interrelated!

Sex as a biological fact has generally been thought of as strictly *male* or *female*, based on the notion that one either has "XX" (female) or "XY" (male) chromosomes and thus "equipment" to match them. The notion that sex is *binary*—taking two appositional but complementary forms, *male* or *female*—seems normatively correct, since we "assign *sex*" to a newborn based on their reproductive anatomy and genitalia.[1]

But sometimes genetics and hormones don't differentiate the fetus into strictly two chromosomal alternatives, and may result in an *intersex* person, or what was heretofore called a *hermaphroditic* anatomy (a term not much liked now). While uncommon (affecting 0.05–2 percent of the population),[2] chromosomally different combinations and hormonal conditions that result in intersex individuals *are a reality*—a reality that socially and religiously has often been sidestepped. They vary in their chromosomal make-up and/or their reproductive anatomy, which makes them *not fit into a binary model*.

We will explore the biology of sex and intersex in chapter 4. Here, I underscore the use of the term "sex" as the bio-physical, genital identification of the person. This use *includes* physical sex outcomes that are binary ("male"/"female") and those that are physically intersex, who do not fit a binary model. (Let's also remember that in all ways, "sex," as well as other terms unpacked below, always have a socio-cultural backdrop and meaning inhered into them.[3] Thus, while I refer to "sex" as the bio-physical component, let's remember that the *meaning* of sex also has a *social construction*.)

---

1. Fausto-Sterling, *Sex/Gender*, 6. (See also, Green, "Robert Stoller's Sex and Gender"; and Money & Ehrhardt, "Gender Dimorphic Behavior and Fetal Sex Hormones").
2. Blackless et al., "How Sexually Dimorphic Are We?" 151–66.
3. Fausto-Sterling, *Sex/Gender*, 7.

GENDER AND GENDER IDENTITY

In the mid-1960s John Money, MD, research psychiatrist and endocrinologist, solidified use of the term "gender" to clarify distinctions between *biological sex*, *sexual activity*, and that *something else* which "sex" can also refer to.[4] A decade later, "gender" had integrated well into our vocabulary on sexuality. Even later, there were reformulations of it.[5] The term *gender* has been used to describe the *socially prescribed roles* that a sexually identified body enacts, as well as the "social institution" of gender statuses.[6] And beyond that, the term *gender identity* has been used to further the notion of one's persistent and inner sense of how one relates to one's sexual body.

In the late 1990s Judith Lorber viewed gender as wholly a product of socialization, and as such, subject to social influence and interpretation. In her view, gender is a *social institution*, comparable to the economy, the family, and religion in its significance and prescriptives.[7] She does not "locate gender" in the individual or even in their social relationships, although she acknowledges it shows up in personal identity and in human social dynamics.

This is a sociological rendition of the term *gender*. It's rather inclusive, and contains a lot of truth, but is hard to concretize in individuals' lives without a lot of digging. I therefore resolved to use the term *gender* not "just" as a social prescriptive, *but to indicate how gender plays itself out in the individual's life*.

Thus, my use of *gender* acknowledges the social structures that form the backdrop of what distinguishes "men" from "women"—or better put, "person from person" in terms of their gendered scripts. Most importantly, I use the term *gender* to help us focus on how these statuses situate themselves in personal lives. Here, my emphasis is on how people engage those labels and prescriptions: accept, refuse, or modify them in their lives.

---

4. Money, and Tucker, *Sexual Signatures*, 201. Money's literal definition of *gender*: "One's personal, social status as a male or female; or mixed; on the basis of somatic and behavioral criteria more inclusive than [just] the genital criterion alone," ibid., 201 (brackets mine). See also Money, "Gender: History, Theory, and Usage," 71–79.

5. Fausto-Sterling, *Sexing the Body*, 6–7.

6. Lorber, *Paradoxes of Gender*.

7. Lorber, *Paradoxes of Gender*, 1–2.

A little more, now on *gender identity*. The term has been consistently used to identify the emotional (affective) identification one has with one's sexed and gendered body (which I underscore, also include learned social behaviors).[8] This internalized gender identity eventually concretizes for a person how they feel about their sexual self, and how they act out that sexual self socially.

Thus, the terms *gender* and *gender identity* are centrally important to all ensuing discussions in this book, for they embody two foundational notions:

First, that one is more than one's biological sex, since the prescriptions of one's culture about one's sex have a lot of influence on our self-feelings, identity, and behaviors.

Second, that the sexual identity that one develops internally—thus one's gender identification—is not solely derived from the body, but also from those role behaviors we are requested to enact because of our body type. The sexual body serves most everyone as the initiating template, but this is not the only influence. Gender and gender identity concretize our self-understanding as a male or as a female . . . or today, maybe fluidly in-between, both, or neither. All are influenced by our social experiences; and now, so goes the rubric, our predilection.

Let's also clear up one more item relating to sex and gender. Lately, the term *gender* has been used as a synonym for *biological sex*. And, I presume, perhaps, it's because it's easy to understand how the components of one influence the other, and how both interrelate. Clearing up that gender is *not* an outright synonym for biological sex is important, because—as we will discuss later—some claim that *gender assignment at birth* is the problem for *questioning people*. This is not correct.

People are customarily assigned a *sex* at birth—as I stated earlier. And, it is true that because of that, there is a corollary gender schema that we *presume* for individuals. However, as I'll try to demonstrate in ensuing chapters, gender notions and identity grow their roots from environment, culture, and how we are brought up and educated about *sexual roles* (male/masculine, female/feminine)—in a phrase, from *gender role socialization*, not just assigned sex.[9] Change one's *socialization* and you may well change several key aspects of one's *gender*

---

8. Lorber, *Paradoxes of Gender*, 1–2.
9. In this, Lorber is correct. See Lorber, *Paradoxes of Gender*, 1–2.

identity, without having to change the *sexed body*. A lot depends on the gender enculturation of individuals, and the cultural leeway given to these to conform, or not conform, to established gender scripts. So, forward, to these very terms:

GENDER ROLE: MASCULINE/FEMININE SOCIALIZATION

Societies encourage, sometimes require, their members to act out their gendered roles in prescribed ways. Historically, gender roles have been predominantly *binary*, those *masculine-* or *feminine-defined behaviors* that a society feels are necessary to distinguish men from women. They come from a culture's *ideology* of what men and/or women are "supposed to be like." Until recent history, gender roles in Western cultures have continued a binary assumption, and carried forward social definitions of what it means to be a *masculine man* or *feminine woman*.

But the margins of such behaviors aren't often configured equally for the genders: there may also be hazy contours allowed for one gender more than the other. Let me elaborate: in our American culture, girls who don't conform totally to the femininity prescribed for their gender role might be nicknamed a "Tomboy"; but such behaving can still be included in the *feminine* repertoire without them leaving a binary female role behind. Certainly, we've all heard of the "Tomboy" label used in *admiration* of a girl who can assert herself and do well in sports, or defend herself against the hazing of older brothers.[10]

We also know that a boy's socialization often doesn't allow for that much leeway in the contours: boys are quick to be ridiculed and labeled for any "feminine" behavior, mannerism, or attitude. There is no corollary consolation in being called "Fem." Certainly, boys have historically had greater difficulty engaging with clothing and artifacts that the culture identifies as belonging to the female gender. Not so for many girls. While the designation of "Tomboy" for a girl might allow

---

10. This is an old term but usually means a girl who acts sometimes like a boy, doing "boy things." She's normally pre-teen and/or early teen, who likes to play like a boy but doesn't like a *guy*—she's just not ready to be a "young lady." Usually, she finds the restraints placed on girls stifling. Girls can do all sorts of things without being labeled Tomboys, but it's an old-fashioned slang term that has persisted in our descriptors of active females. Tomboyish girls usually grow up to be strong heterosexual women, and not prone to any other disposition.

her some crossover clothing, accentuate her capacity for the rough and tumble, and even earn her some credits, any boy's designation as "feminine" implies all sorts of weaknesses, deficits, and demerits.

Men, sometimes more rigidly than women, must fit into the binary role category that defines them.[11] But, nobody is a winner when social roles constrict abilities, and create generalizations and stereotypes.

Gender role socialization thus provides both biologic males and females a *schema* by which to construct their lives *as men* and *as women*. Included in these schemas are ways of thinking about what constitutes *manliness* and *femininity;* what may be the boundaries of these traits; and which traits may be allowed to "cross over." Of course, all of this is grounded in a culture's larger ideology of personhood, becoming a significant part of the *construction of people*—meaning, how a particular culture engineers unfolding these schemas in individual and collective lives.

Many social institutions participate in that unfolding. First is *the family,* and how it has inherited and then negotiated social gender ideology. Following right along is *the educational system*, and what position it plays in furthering gender socialization—strictly binary in formats, I might add, until recently. A society's *economic organization*, its *politics*, its many *institutions,* all play their parts and have something to say in the construction of its men and its women.

Traditionally, most men and women *conform* to these gendered status quos, simply because that's what they have been taught and learned to believe, and because these are often *required* of them.

The Christian church, and specifically the evangelical Christian church, has well-formed *ideologies of gender*, coupling them foundationally on uniquely formed male and female bodies, with uniquely formed male and female reproductive organs and capacities. Such forms are considered *essential* and *complementary* in that they mirror *the other* in unique ways, and together are said to also complement the image of God (*imago Dei*) in the human. (We discuss all this in chapters 4, 6, and 7.)

The bottom line has always been a *binary schema* of what constitutes human creation and procreation. There is normally no mention

---

11. Thompson, "Gender Labels," 339–47. See also Herek, "Heterosexual Masculinity," 563–77.

of anything but polarities; certainly, no emphasis or mention of anything *intersexed*—biologically or otherwise.

It follows that the church has also co-developed a well-defined set of *gender roles*, which are ascribed to each, male and female, based on their sexual typology. Roles are also to be complementary—although hierarchical models have tended to predominate, and thus "complementarity vs. hierarchicality" is still debated in many circles.[12]

Much of what is contained in those traditional role schemas has come from patriarchal societies, from tribal pre-Israelite, Israelite, and New Testament cultures, which historically ascribed leading roles to men and subservient roles to women.[13] In Western, Judeo-Christian communities, role ascriptions have continued rather rigid distinctions between men and women, often limiting women in their religious service. Such distinctions have thus been the subject of much debate, discrimination, litigation, and social movements over the last century.

The *language of gender*, which has thus formed and informed our perceptions of gender in the church, reflect these *cultural constructions of gender* and the storylines of *role socialization* that have been historically handed down to us.

This is not to say that there isn't a biologic foundation to *some* core aspects of our differences, as reflected in Scripture and as we will explore later. It is not to say all that comes from culture is necessarily contrary. It is to underscore that the meanings we understand *about gender* and *gender roles* have come from historic cultural models that assign inherent and often fundamentally different "natures" to men and women.

These understandings are being reformulated by arguments from the sciences, the social sciences, and certainly from society itself. Not to be outdone, theologians too have entered this discussion, both from conservative and more liberal persuasions.[14]

---

12. See Jewett, *Man as Male and Female*, 1990. Hierarchical models often imply males as authorities, and women as subservient to men.

13. My Jewish Learning, "Ancient Israelites," par. 5.

14. In particular, see chapter 7.

THE CURRENT LANGUAGE OF GENDER

Our current language of gender reflects a reformulation of *gender ideology*, and reconstructions of the *meaning* of gender itself. At times, it even questions the meaning of biological sex itself, and whether biological differences ought to matter. Thus, the novel language asks *tough questions that the church needs to address.*

Since 2008, there's been growing visibility of individuals who defy standard gender definitions—who feel they are *transgender* (or *trans*)—in proportions heretofore not seen in the US.[15] Transgender persons, whose life history aligns with criteria established by the American Psychiatric Association for *gender dysphoria* (as we define in the Glossary that follows), have been historically discriminated against and seen as not normal. The same goes for intersex-born individuals with *disorders of sexual development* (DSD). These also have been considered alien and been candidates for surgical reassignments, sometimes as children.

No more. Their need for air and visibility has enabled voicings that reveal not only moves for sexual/gender "confirmation" (another term we define in the Glossary) and recognition of intersexuality, but also for the *non-binary* labels many prefer to use for themselves.

As a label, "trans" now becomes a *cover term* for those who opt out of a binary schema, not just an identifier for transgender individuals. Some, opting for *no labels of gender*, thus coining yet another label: *agender*—"without gender." I've visualized these gender categories in Table 1 at the end of this chapter. Please refer to it.

This novel language of gender brings an awareness of human distinctives to the surface, and underscores our need to understand more deeply how in this twenty-first century we have continuing challenges to human self-understandings. In chapter 3, we delve into life histories to illustrate how individuals with *gender dysphoria*, *intersexuality*, or who "gender-bend" or are *genderfluid*, commission and use novel identifiers.

---

15. James et al., *2015 U.S. Transgender Survey*, 4–5.

QUESTIONS COMING FROM THE LANGUAGE

Coming into focus in this landscape of gender are a series of central questions, the cover one being: *Is gender to be defined at least in part by one's biological sex, or mainly on how the person sees themselves?*

- *Are the biological determinants (sex) to imply that if the "boy" has male physiology that he should naturally identify as male? (What is "male/masculine" and what is "female/feminine" anyway?)*
- *Should there be acknowledgement of gender reformulation based on that individual's predilection, their internal sense of self—one's self-identification of who they are—beyond their biological sex? (How one defines gender identity is critically important here.)*
- *Should intersex individuals or those with gender dysphoria be encouraged to choose their own gender identity and biological sex, rather than having society or medicine or parents decide that for them?*

Science and society already agree that there are *more than binary outcomes* from sexual biology (male, female, *and intersex*); and beyond that, assert we recognize a *spectrum of gendered identities*, or what people feel they are, to complement these.[16] These assertions raise additional questions for the Christian church—not all of them new nor wrongly asked, mind you—but certainly in need of responses. We'll explore the questions fully in chapters 4, 7, and 8.

Gender Politics and Ideology in Linguistic Form

Aside these re-brandings of self, there is an emerging and politicized ideology of *expressive individualism*. Here, the idea is that one's gender role and identity should be *solely self-determined*. The position is a clearly distinguishable voice. I must add, quickly, that while it isn't everybody's voice in the "gender moment," those that endorse the ideology are certainly speaking loudly.[17]

---

16. Even as this shift occurs, there are some—including feminist theorists like Rebecca Reilly-Cooper—who insist gender is not a *spectrum*. See her article "Gender Is Not a Spectrum" (2016). She would opt for the use of "personality" as a self-descriptor, and get rid of the term *gender* altogether.

17. For example, see Rude, "It's Time for People to Stop Using the Biological Sex

Central to such an ideology is the notion that *gender identity*, once conceived as rather fixed when internalized by the person, can in fact be *fluid and changeable*; that for some, this fluidity can then enable the emergence of what is believed *by them* to be their *true gender*—not the one socialized into them because of their genitals.[18] The dialogue is one contemporary political conversation fueling a good portion of the gender movement. And I need to discuss it, if only briefly here, for it ties into novel language terms.

As I describe such an ideology, we should keep in mind its underlying tenet: that gender *should be* solely self-determined; that one has the right to live out one's identity, whatever one feels it is . . . "Your sexual organs or society shouldn't determine who you are," is often voiced by those arguing for gender self-determination.

Ryan Anderson, author of *When Harry Became Sally*, calls it an "ontological assertion": people should be whatever sex/gender *they prefer to be*.[19] Further, that others around should (as is now politically correct) *affirm* that chosen identity irrespective of the form it takes, or how others feel about it. Frequently, those that take this position suggest there is no required argument needed to back up their decision about their sex and/or gender, or a need to factually justify it. (We'll touch on these points later.)

Questioning Gender Essentialism

Let me underscore that this current in the conversation can often set aside notions of *gender essentialism*.[20] Let me explain. Traditionally,

---

Construct" (2014).

18. These are not altogether new conceptions of the sexual self. We know in early cultures that gender didn't always conform to biological sex, and that individuals often lived out "trans" experiences, albeit with different labels. Greek culture, especially, saw biological sex itself as a *variable,* and often "intersexed" (from where we get the fused term *hermaphrodite*—from Hermes, the Greek god of War, and Aphrodite, the Greek goddess of love). We have sufficient sculptures from those eras to provide evidence that Greek societies allowed for a variety of sexualities and gender identities to coexist. More recent cultures—from South Pacific to Native American to East Indian—have made accommodations for individuals who are "trans" in their gender and identity: Hijras, Berdaches, and others. (See chapter 6.)

19. Anderson, "Transgender Ideology," 1.

20. *Gender essentialism*: The notion that the core of gender schemas lies in the biological nature of human male and female constructions. As the argument goes, the biologically binary is *sex irreducible*—it is basic and essential to an understanding of male

any expression of gender has begun with an acknowledgement of a base sexual format (usually, two sexes) and placed emphasis on the capacity for human reproduction, which the binary brings. Here, novel gender ideology *questions the need to formulate gender based on the sexual body:* it isn't about who one is biologically, or reproductively, or even societally, as much as who one is identity-wise.

The current self-determination ideology evades grounding *any form* of gender expression in a core based solely, or primarily, on *biologic sex*. Rather, it is a discourse in which human sexual biology becomes *marginal* to the argument: biology may need to be binary *for reproduction,* and in such binary cases *irreducible,*[21] but its formulation into *gender* is more apt to produce a *spectrum* of outcomes in *identities*, rather than just dualities, if individuals are to identify with their "true self." Biology is *one* of the ingredients—so goes the argument—but not necessarily *decisive* for gender identity.

The individual has the right, then, to be true to the self they feel they are, not the identity they may have been "assigned" because they have certain "equipment." (We'll discuss all this further, with many references, in chapters 4 and 7).

DE-SEXING LANGUAGE AND ALTERING UNDERSTANDINGS

One more point here. Instrumentally, general identity definitions based on sex and/or any gender are now *also* questioned: *Why have gender and sexuality be the core definition of people, anyway?*

As an example, the University of California in San Diego (UCSD) recently complied with the use of *new terms* to refer to Latinos and Chicanos, a change which is witness to the profound way many now define their gender and sexuality—or refuse to do so. The terms are being replaced with *Latinx* and *Chicanx* to promote those within these ethnicities, but leaving out any evidence of what gender, or sex, an individual belongs to. Normally, the ending of Spanish

---

and female forms *for reproduction.* But let's also remember that *gender* is *sex adjunctive* and not derived from the irreducible *alone.* See Money, *Gay, Straight, and In-Between*; and Fausto-Sterling, *Sexing the Body.*

21. That is, down to its core biology—genetically and hormonally. See chapter 4 and Figure 1; and Anderson, "The Philosophical Contradictions of the Transgender Worldview."

personal pronouns and labels is *gendered* by either an ending of "a" for the feminine form or an "o" for the masculine. "The change is being promoted by students, social justice activists, and the LGBTQ community, which are trying to get people to look beyond conventional notions of gender, sex, and appearance."[22]

Outwardly, these changes may not seem to be much other than *new slang*, but the current language—its terminology—alters the groundwork of essentialist thinking with replacement terms that ideologically argue against established norms. Is that bad? Progressive?

Anthropologists will tell us, this is the seed of a great deal of culture change: alter the terms, and eventually matching alterations in meaning will happen—also behaviorally—if the terms *stick*.[23] The embodiment of the new philosophy in a *linguistic format that alters conventions by generating new terms and/or altering old ones*, ensures those modifications can take root.

And, this is not only true for de-sexing gendered words, such as in Spanish; it is most significantly seen in the new repertoire of gender labels that have come into existence. These *remove* biological terms from the contexts in which they have been used. In so doing, such usage lends new terms a kind of power that leads to recognizing them as "legit" *outside of conventions*.

The novel forms aren't passive. Terms used usher in definitions which turn them into possibles, a kind of skew that can then turn itself to *ideology*. Instead of looking at concrete applications of a term, we disengage them from what actually exists (e.g., *the body: hormones, chromosomes, genitalia, physical results*) and instill in them a greater reality. "We side with words even when they begin to contradict the reality."[24]

22. Robbins, "'Latino' Is Out," 1–2.

23. McWhorter, *The Story of Human Language, Part I*. I can give no better linguistic example than the word *mouse*: In 1967 Doug Engelbart, from Stanford, applied for a patent on a tool that would enable an experimental computer to be used beyond the keyboard. Since the tool had a wire that attached it to the computer, it resembled a mouse—and thus was called a "mouse." It got licensed to Apple, and the rest is history. But to note, the *mouse* moniker changed the status of the term from a rodent to a computer tool. *Mouse* entered the vocabulary and changed our perception—to the point where if one today says "my *mouse* died," most often people understand it probably isn't your pet! The linguistic form alters conventions and ultimately meanings. It follows that we also change behavior: *"Now I have to go and get a new mouse. Can't live without one!"*

24. Wittgenstein, *Tractus Logicus Philosophicus*, 3, 261. An example of this kind of

For those on the *outside* of the "gender moment," the terms are puzzling. This is not just because they are new and different, but because they *challenge* what is historically understood as factual, and what the terms might refer to "out there," in the world.

In the Introduction, I make a case for language as a mirror of culture, and I restate it here: The emergent language of gender promotes new visions of the person—some helpful and insightful; others inherently difficult to embrace by Christians, and thus contested.

This is the crux of the "gender revolution."

SIFTING THROUGH TO THE PERSON

Yet, within that immense frame there *are* distinct, and very personal narratives of intersexuality, gender identity, and body conflicts that are often confused with the louder social voices of those who fight for self-legislation, *no matter what.*

There are many intersex or gender dysphoric individuals—children, adolescents, adults—some of whose life histories we'll hear in the next chapter, that I feel need to be *segregated out of the cacophony*; individuated; to truly make sense of and appreciate the tenor of their conflicts.

Such voices are often confused with those of "revolutionaries"— but the majority of gender-conflicted or intersex-born individuals are *not revolutionaries;* they are individuals seeking wholeness, living quiet, often unseen lives. When they *are* "out," some in society show their scorn. Surely in God's kingdom, and consequently in our missional narrative, we ought to make room to understand and embrace them.

"reality skew" comes from May Rude, whose scathing article on the term "biological sex" makes it out to be solely a "social construct": "Since 'biological sex' is a social construct, those who say it is not often have to argue about what it entails." And, "Sex isn't something we are actually born with; it's something that doctors or our parents assign us at birth" (Rude, "It's Time for People to Stop Using the Social Construction of 'Biological Sex' to Defend their Transmysogyny," 1). Such ideas don't sit well with professor of biology and gender studies Anne Fausto-Sterling, known for her expertise on the biology of sex and gender, who understands that biological sex is a *reality*, albeit a layered and complex one. See Fausto-Sterling, *Sexing the Body*, chapter 2.

Overall, grasping novel understandings can't be accomplished without diving deeply into its core terminology, that which gives substance to the conversation. We've already introduced some terms in detail, even digressing to point out how the changes can affect our thinking. Following, is a list of *other main terms* we need to explore. Please peruse the list as you move forward in your readings. We take up these conversations again and in depth in later chapters.

Table 1. Charting Novel Gender Schemas				
Gender Schemas as "Categories" *				
Cisgender	*Questioning*	*Genderqueer*	*Transgender*	*Pangender*
Cisgenders remain binary in gender identity. Genital sex remains essential to self-understanding. Gender role is an important component of gender identity. Gender identity is fixed and not perceived as malleable in most cisgender ideologies. Cisgenders believe in two sexes, two identities, which form a binary and complementary system of male and female. Genital binarism and reproduction are seen as essential components of identity and role.	Questioning individuals have become uncomfortable with their gender identity and/or assigned sex. These feel they have the right to question assigned sex and/or also question their gender identity/gender role. Many who question see themselves as rightly exploring alternatives to the sexual and gender binary.	Genderqueer is now a broad label used for anyone who has already moved from questioning to self-defining alternatively from cisgender. These embrace one or more non-binary gender schemas, or exist in a continuum between genders (gender variant). Synonyms are *gender-non-conforming*; *non-binary*. Gender is malleable, subject to being questioned and changed. These also feel the right to self-define is a better alternative than any social assignations of sex, gender, role.	Transgender is now a broad label that can encompass any/all that are not cisgender. More specifically, the transgender label is used when individuals have *transitioned gender* in psychological or physical ways, the latter having had hormonal and/or surgical "confirmations" (gender reassignment). In such cases the individual has often transitioned to the cross-gender of birth, M2F or F2M. Transgender re-assigned people tend to conform to binary sex schemas and possibly corresponding identity.	Pangender is used to describe an individual who does not prefer any single gender schema, or who, alternatively embraces more than one, or all gender schemas and identities. Gender identity is fluid and thus malleable to the person's self-identity and choices. Gender choice is a right and gender is malleable and fluid. Synonym is *omnigender*.

continued on next page

Intersex		
Male-Related Gender Expression/Phenotype Congruent	*Female Related Gender Expression/Phenotype Congruent*	*Gender Expression Subject to Rearing or Self-identification*
Jacobs Syndrome (XYY) Klinefelter Syndrome (XXY)	Turner Syndrome (XO) Triple X Syndrome (XXX) Androgen Insensitivity Syndrome	Mixed Gonadal Dysgenesis True Hermaphroditism

*Such categories are not exhaustive, but rather illustrate in "semantic domains" those expressions of gender that are now most evident among non-binary persons. Aside from these domains, there are individuals who call themselves *agender*, "without gender," or *neutrois*, "neutral to gender," others preferring to choose no gender labels at all. See chapter 4 for full details of intersexuality.

GLOSSARY OF TERMS[25]

Novel Terminology: Gender-Related Terms

Agender is a recent term used to either self-identify, or identify another person who opts *out* of having a gender label (the "a" meaning "*without*"). This is synonymous to being *genderfree*, another corollary term, or *non-gender*.

Androgynous formerly meant an individual with mixed genitals or intersex. No more. Androgynous now means individuals who self-represent with both male and female characteristics, notwithstanding whatever sexual biology they have. Those with indeterminate gender identity, and who mix self-presentations and role-presentations are *androgynous*. *Androgynous* is different than *bigender*.

Bigender means an individual who expresses *two gender identities*, simultaneously or at different times. Sometimes the change is context-dependent: An individual "changes" gender identities depending on the social situation. (See *genderfluid*.)

Binary refers to individuals who conform to either male or female identity/behaviors. It relates, as well, to the *model* of *binarism*, which implies that there are two, complementary but different, sexes; and consequently two, complementary but appositional, identities. In this *binary model* there is no room for either physical sexual variants or a gender-identity spectrum. The term is the antonym of *nonbinary* or *genderqueer*.

Butch implies a masculine gender expression, not necessarily a *masculine lesbian*, which was the traditional definition.

Cisgender (often abbreviated "*cis*") is used by and for people whose gender identity is consonant with the sex they were born, i.e., the sex assigned them at birth. Thus, a *cisgender* individual has a gender identity and role that are socially normed for one's sex. It is the opposite (antonym) of the term *transgender*. We also hear the derivative term

---

25. I've combined and paraphrased information from several sources to make terms more understandable: Sources used are National Geographic's *Gender Revolution* issue (2017); American Psychiatric Association, *Diagnostic and Statistical Manual* (5th ed.); Money's *Gay, Straight, and In-Between*; Carter, *Agender to Ze*; and the *Urban Dictionary*. I am solely responsible for the way terminology is phrased and parsed here. None of these sources is quoted directly or verbatim.

cisnormative, or *cisnormativity*, as adjectival forms describing people or philosophies that fit a binary model of sex and gender.

Detransitioning (see also *desistance*). The active verb form here implies someone who was going through transition, but is no longer doing so; or is not wanting to transition further. *Detransitioning* implies a willful "stop" of any transitioning possibilities—either through social acts such as not proceeding with a change of name, all the way to stopping hormones, or even attempting reversion surgeries. People who are in this process—usually adults—are labeled "detransitioners."

Desistance is an oft-confused term. At its root, *desistance* means when someone who used to experience gender dysphoria no longer does—as happens in the case of some children, who at an early age are diagnosed dysphoric, but who by the time of their later childhood or adolescence no longer feel the identity-body disjunction they experienced before. At a later stage of life, desistance can mean an act, as when someone who used to identify as *trans* no longer does. In this case, *desistance is synonymous with "detransitioning."*

Fem, or Femme is a term that denotes the feminine in gender identity or gender-role expression. The term is sometimes a "put-down" used to mean "too feminine," and can thus be used toward gay males who are über-feminine, or toward lesbian females who are also too feminine.

Gender dysphoria (GD) is defined with significance by the American Psychiatric Association in its *Diagnostic and Statistical Manual* (DSM), now in Version 5 (2013). It replaces the term *gender identity disorder*, to prevent the stigma associated with the term "disorder." The new classification distinguishes between *childhood-*, *adolescent-*, and *adult-onset GD*. Overall, "GD involves a conflict between a person's physical sex or assigned gender, and the gender with which he/she/they identify. People with GD may experience significant distress and/or problem functions associated with this conflict, between the way they feel and think of themselves, and their physical sex or assigned gender."[26] Regarding diagnostics, there needs to be *strong, significant, persistent* desire to be of the other gender; to be treated *as the other gender*; and *to be rid of one's primary and/or secondary sex characteristics*.

---

26. American Psychiatric Association, "Gender Dysphoria," sect. 302.85 (F64.9).

In children, there needs to be a *strong, significant, persistent* preference for cross-gender roles, toys, activities, and *expressed desire to be the other gender* or an *insistence that one* is *the other sex*. In some children, there is also a *strong desire for the physical sex characteristics that match one's desired gender identity*.[27]

Genderfluid refers to a person who prefers flexibility in their gender identity, and consequently, can fluctuate between identities as male and female, masculine and feminine. Sometimes genderfluid individuals manifest both gender qualities (male/masculine and female/feminine), even none, in the same identity. Sometimes the terms *nonbinary*, *bigender*, or *polygender* are used as synonyms.

Genderqueer is often an "umbrella term" for gender identities that don't fit the masculine-feminine binary polarity. The "-queer" portion of the term is not to be interpreted via the customary "gay" meaning usually assigned to it (i.e., a homosexual male). It is now a cover term that identifies the *non-binary*, sometimes *pangender*, status of individuals.

Heteronormative became a popular term around the 1990s, used by LGBTQ populations to mean "binary people." Now it mainstreams to mean *norms, roles, and lifestyles that follow distinct and complementary gender formats* (i.e., man/male, woman/female in the "traditional" socio-cultural renditions). Heteronormative individuals base their "natural roles" on biological assumptions, and thus assume that heterosexual behavior is the norm for sexuality. Such can include negative ideas about marriage to the "same sex," i.e., as between a man and another man. The Christian worldview is thus heteronormative *and* heterosexual.

Intersectionality (noun). Used to describe how social inequality is experienced as an "intersection" of several forms of discrimination: For instance, a transsexual African-American woman experiences *intersectionality* because she experiences *transphobia as well as racism and sexism*. Intersectionality proposes that social issues are connected on a deeper level than individuals themselves can unravel, and thus deal with. Non-cisgender persons are said to often experience

---

27. American Psychiatric Association, "Gender Dysphoria," sect. 302.85 (F64.9). See added section on childhood gender dysphoria in the 2017 (formally unpublished, but e-documented) revisions.

intersectionality, especially if other inequalities are present in their lives.

Non-Binary (Nonbinary), similar in meaning to *genderqueer*, but often used to mean the individual who does not support *binarism*, or who is non-binary in their self-presentation and/or gender identity. This can include *gay, trans, transsexual, intersex, queer, questioning*, or other gender minorities.

Queer used to be used to designate homosexual men, often as a slur targeting their effeminacy. Today, *queer* is another umbrella term used to denote gender minorities that don't conform to heteronormative or heterosexual gender binary models. There is broad use of the term to mean different things by different audiences. This includes the more academic use as a particular reference to literature genres, such as "queer literature" (i.e., literature that doesn't concentrate on, or advocate, heteronormative viewpoints). To be *queer* today means one is included in the range of people who don't subscribe to, live out, or identify with *heteronormativity*. The term can also be used as a verb, as in "*queering* the argument."

Questioning. To be unsure of, or re-examining one's previously assumed sex, gender identity, or sexual orientation (who one is sexually and erotically attracted to). As in, "Taylor is questioning zir gender." (See *zir* below).

Rapid Onset Gender Dysphoria *(ROGD)*. The term is controversial and not a medical designation, but rather, reflects the sudden manifestation of gender dysphoria-like symptoms by adolescents, despite parents not having witnessed any gender confusion or otherwise earlier in these. Dr Lisa Littman (see Bibliography) studied this phenomenon and created the controversial label—for which she was derided, her research forced to make revisions and seek republication. Her results, however, remained unchanged. The term is included here due to it signaling aspects of a *culture-bound syndrome* (see chapters 7 and 8), which seems to coexist along with diagnosable cases of gender dysphoria in our present, gender-hypersensitive climate.

They/them. Pronouns typically used by persons who wish to self-identify as gender neutral. Yes, the *voice* is plural, but its *use* is singular. (Very confusing, I know.) Used as in, "*Jans thought they was* *exceptionally friendly to pets, especially cats."* Or, *"They is going to the movies tonight. Do we want to join them?"* (I think we've changed English *syntax* too . . . .)

Transgender is now a term used broadly, but often misinterpreted. Transgender has become the "umbrella term" for a variety of binary-non-conforming persons. The overall inference when the term is used is that the individual's gender identity is changing/has changed; or that the individual is physically transitioning sex/identity (see *transsexual*, below); or that the individual merely opts for another gender label than the binary. I define *transsexual* (below) to ensure that this older term, which designates a physical sex/gender transition, when used, is also understood. Is a transsexual a transgender? Under this umbrella, yes. Is a transgender a transsexual? They can be, if they have experienced sex/gender incongruity and begun/completed a physical sex transition. Some would even say "yes" if the person has changed their gender *self-presentation*. (I would opt here for *genderqueer*, but it's a preference!) Ultimately, some use the term transgender as their preferred moniker, and "trans" as the shorthand to indicate they are not binary. One more element to note here: being transgender does not imply a particular *sexual orientation* (to whom one is erotosexually attracted). One can be transgender *and* heterosexual, homosexual, bisexual, polysexual, or asexual.

Transgressive. A new adjective. Definition: *cool, hip, daring,* as when ze bends gender: "Wow, zir's outfit is so transgressive!" Or, in *describing* a person who *gender-bends*: "Ze is now so transgressive!" Can also be used as a verb modifier, such as in "What we need now is transgressive action."

Trans man. Means a biological female who now identifies as a male. The designation can remain at the gender-*identity* level without the person having hormonal or other physical/sexual transitions; or it can include these. The reference is to *a gender-identity shift,* not just to the sexual body per se.

Transsexual is a person, male or female, whose *gender identity* differs from their designated birth sex, and who is in sex/gender transition or has already completed it. The term is an earlier designation, which is not much admired by "trans" individuals (see above); however, it retains its medically correct description of such a transition. The transition itself is now referred to as a *"confirmation"* vs. a *"reassignment."* The transition can include hormonal and/or surgical procedures to bring about desired sex-body changes.

Trans woman. A biological male who now identifies as female. In a similar fashion as *trans men,* this is about gender identity and not the sexual body.

Ze/Zir are new *gender-neutral pronouns*. One refers to a person as "ze" when their gender is unknown, or to avoid assuming their gender. The term "zir" is the possessive form: "Ze writes novels. The last one ze wrote zirself, without editorial help." The assumption is that the name or pronoun(s) someone goes by shouldn't necessarily reveal anything about the person's gender or identity/ies.[28]

Redefined Terms Related to Sexuality

Bisexual persons are attracted to two genders or two biological sexes, not often at the same time nor equally. This is a *sexual orientation* label, not an *identity* label per se, although an individual can refer to themselves as "bi" (the preferred abbreviation). The label is one of *sexual attraction* preference(s) at its core.

Gay, traditionally meaning a *homosexual male*, now takes on a more colloquial meaning, not only for men who are sexually attracted to members of the same sex, but also to include all LGBTQ persons. In this sense, the novel meaning of *gay* is *anyone not subscribing to heteronormative and binary sexuality or identity*. It is now yet another "cover term."

Gender confirmation/gender-confirmation surgery is the newer moniker for the older term, *surgical reassignment*. It is now preferred, since the belief is that any genital-altering surgery only "confirms" who the person *really is*, rather than "reassigns" them. When the term is used without the "surgical" added, it means any steps an individual takes to solidify their *gender identity*. This can include elements like

---

28. Adapted from www.mypronouns.org/ze. Names and pronouns tend to be publicly shared, because they are part of the language commonly used to refer to people. However, identities tend to be private, i.e., many people don't proactively share their gender; just as many people don't proactively share their race, class, or sexuality with mere acquaintances.

a legal name change, use of other gender pronouns, change in gender attire, physical looks, etc.

Heterosexual. The term keeps its original meaning, that is, a person who is erotosexually attracted to the opposite sex, who usually gender-identifies in a heteronormative way. Men and women can be heterosexuals, preferring the opposite sex for both partnership and sexual acts. The label is one of *sexual preference* and *sexual orientation*, and not about gender identity. *Cisgender* individuals are customarily heterosexual in preference and orientation.

Homosexual stays with the traditional definition, to mean men who are erotosexually attracted to, or have sexual relations with, individuals of the same sex (i.e., other men). The label is one of *sexual preference* and *sexual orientation*, and not about *gender identity*.

Intersex means an individual's sexual anatomy at birth doesn't conform to typical physical formats for male or female organs. Medically, intersex individuals have a disorder of sexual development (DSD).[29] *Intersex* as the standard label for reproductive or sexual anatomy differences to the binary formats has included chromosomal, gonadal (glandular), or genital variations. Sometimes these variants are "blended" forms, and thus make it problematic to designate an infant at birth as "male" or "female," regardless of chromosomes. Today *intersex* is preferred over the term *hermaphroditic (hermaphrodite)*, which is considered offensive, inaccurate, and outdated. Intersex individuals often identify as male/masculine or female/feminine. Few use the label *transsexual* or *transgender*.

Lesbian derives from Lesbos, the Greek island's name where female poet Sappho lived and loved in the sixth century BCE. Her poetry portrayed "girl love" and alluded to female homosexuality. Thus, the term *lesbian*, popularized in the 1970s, became a mainstream word to identify women who had sexual and romantic attractions to other women. *Lesbian* as a term, and in its definition remains the same. It is often the cover term for the community of women who formed part of the sexual-political liberation movement called "The Gay and *Lesbian* Liberation Movement."

---

29. Intersex Society of North America, *Consortium on the Management of Disorders of Sex Development*. See esp. p. 4.

Sex, as a term, has been, and continues to be, problematic. This chapter has discussed issues with the different meanings given to "sex." I use the term *sex* to mean the biological (chromosomal, hormonal, gonadal, reproductive) features and organs that enable procreation and sexual fulfillment acts. In this context, "sex" refers to the biological; and only by extension to any acts that are enabled by these organs and human social behaviors. I distinguish *sex-biological* from *gender*, and from *gender identity*, only to clearly distinguish the body and/or individual sexual behaviors from the socially composed *gender* categories ("conventions") and how those categories are internalized as *gender identity* by the individual.[30]

Transvestite designates a cross-dresser, a person who has either a fetish for the other gender's clothing, or who chooses to self-represent as the other gender—on occasions or rather continually. It can also be a *disorder*, a *paraphilia*, as classified in the DSM-5 when the individual exhibits sexual arousal via the act of cross-dressing, but finds this behavior distressing (DSM-5 302.3 [F65.1]). Transvestitic behavior is often transient, that is, it is not engaged in all the time, unless the person chooses to self-represent as the other gender continuously. An important point to make here is that *transvestites* most often *do not* have a desire to change their sex, such as *transgender/transsexual* individuals do. They do not want to "be" the opposite sex, but mostly "act out" in that other sexual-/gender-role framework. *Transvestites* are predominantly men, and more *heterosexuals* are represented in transvestism than *homosexuals*.[31]

---

30. Fausto-Sterling, *Sex/Gender*, 6–7.

31. There are few current studies on transvestism, mainly because the focus has shifted to its more generic inclusion into *transsexualism*. In a 1997 study of cross-dressing behaviors by Docter and Prince, which also included a longitudinal comparison (1972 to 1997), it was found that 87 percent of transvestites were men, and self-described as heterosexual: 83 percent had been married, and 60 percent were currently married. "Today's transvestites strongly prefer both their masculine selves and feminine roles equally. [But] . . . although the present generation of transvestites describe themselves much as did similar subjects 20 years ago, the percentage (5 percent) migrating toward full-time living as a woman is greater." Docter and Prince, "Transvestism: A Survey," 589–605.

Understanding the New Language

For practice, *here is a fictitious paragraph* that attempts to integrate both the novel language of gender as well as its ideology, to give us a "flavor" of how the discussion of our times would be heard. This is for practice, so hold on if *genderspeak* is new to you!

> Loren's friend Mead made an argument today which sounded as if *ze* was *queering* the discussion! Mead implied that many whom *ze* knew would probably side with *non-binary* people for the sake of not reinforcing *heteronormativity*, and allowing *trans* and *queers* to have their say in who they want to be. Bruce, who is *cisgender* and yet understands *gay* people since his sister *outed* last year, chimed in with this to say: "I'm *cis*, but hey, I get it: I am not *genderqueer*, but I get that the individual with gender dysphoria may want to celebrate their *transition*. My own sister is going through *confirmation* as we speak. I don't think anything of it anymore since I've been living with a *trans 'brother'* now for over a year." Mead responded by saying, "That's awesome Bruce, I wish that more *cisgenders* would come to the place where the *non-binary* was believed to be as true as the *binary*."

Here's the Translation

> Loren's friend Mead made an argument today which sounded as if *she* was *favoring non-binary people!* Mead implied that many whom *she* knew would probably side with non-binary people for the sake of not reinforcing *male-/female-only roles and identities*, and allowing *individuals with different gender identities and positions* to have their say in who they want to be. Bruce, who is *male and masculine* and yet *understands gender-different* people since his sister *openly re-identified her gender* last year, chimed in with this to say: "I'm *male and masculine,* but hey, I get it: I am *not defining myself differently than the norm*, but I get that the individual with gender dysphoria may want to celebrate their *gender transition*. My own sister is going through *gender reassignment* as we speak. I don't think anything of it anymore since I've been living with a *gender reassigned* 'brother' now for over a year." Mead responded by saying, "That's awesome Bruce, I wish that more *normatively identified males and females* would come to the place where *the non-binary status of people* was believed to be as true as *the binary status of people*."

3

Portraits of Gender Today

In the following pages, you'll read *life histories* that embody a good portion of the "spectrum" of gender as it is rendered today.[1] All names are pseudonyms, and many of the contexts have been altered to insure anonymity. All cases are grounded in the reality of lives and events as these have come to my knowledge through counseling, or as a friend to some, colleague to others; and still others as a professor-mentor receiving their stories.

---

1. These are case narratives that reflect unique histories. All the case histories I draw on here are from individuals who have come and gone in relation to my work and personal relationships, and therefore are all historical. However, for the sake of anonymity, I have not only changed names but edited out facts that are not germane to the points being emphasized. As well, I have ensured that nothing is traceable to anyone whose particular history I've engaged (nor to their family members). None of the editing diminishes the accuracy of facts discussed in these cases, or their revealing significant insights into presentations of gender in our contemporary world. Such treatment follows the Code of Ethics of numerous professional societies of which I've been a part (Society for the Scientific Study of Sexuality; American Board of Sexology; American Academy of Clinical Sexology), all clearly stating we will protect the privacy rights of our subjects and ensure these are anonymous if reported. The practice of "unpacking" cases, as I do later in the chapter, follows analytic processes in the social and behavioral sciences and medicine, which rely on research, published clinical and diagnostic criteria—as in the *Diagnostic and Statistical Manual* of the APA, 2013, and other refereed sources. As well, narratives are presented in the long tradition of anthropological ethnography, which engages field and informant knowledge, and reviews, in formulating understandings of "the Other." When anyone is quoted, statements are as close to verbatim as possible.

Each is a "case study," a life history that after being introduced, provides us opportunities to "unpack" it later in the chapter: I ask and answer pertinent questions of how to understand gender today "beyond the binary." My purpose is, again, to ensure that those whom we refer to, whether with novel or old monikers and pronouns, remain clearly in our line of vision *as persons*. Persons who deserve our understanding, and more.

MEET LACEY/LUKE

Born a genetic female with no condition to suggest otherwise, and named Lacey to honor a loving aunt, she was reared in a warm conservative Christian family home in southwest Virginia, attending Christian pre-school and going on to a Christian K-6 school. She loved playing with nearly anything, her inventive mind creating and recreating "toys" from sundry artifacts she would find as she roamed around the house as a toddler, and then finally, as a kindergartner. She had her dolls, she had her trucks to resemble those in her farming community; and she had lots of love, a dog named Mutter, and a mom and dad who read her nightly Bible stories.

At age five Lacey came home from Pre-Kinder saying she was missing her "wee-wee." Baffled at the statement, her mother asked her how she thought that . . . and Lacey's answer began the floodgate of surprises to come: "Matthew peed in his pants! [chuckle]; and then pulled his pants [down]. I saw his wee-wee. But I don't have mine . . . . What happened to my wee-wee?"

From that moment to the time Lacey transitioned into Luke as a teen, Lacey never doubted that her body wasn't what it was supposed to be. Early on, when she was told that girls "didn't *have* or *need* a wee-wee," she exhibited all the trauma of someone being told—presumably as an adult—they were missing a part after surgery. She was never to feel complete.

Despite all the ensuing therapy—through her childhood and adolescence; despite all the attention from family, pastors, doctors, and eventually psychiatrists, Lacey increasingly identified with a male body and despised her own for missing the right equipment.

Parents went from resisting to eventually conceding that Lacey needed accommodations. They allowed gender-neutral clothing and tried desperately to keep a semblance of normalcy.

By age fourteen Lacey had pressed so often and fought so hard to be a boy, that her parents finally agreed—this on the advice of numerous therapists (some Christian) who responded again and again with, "If you ever want to see Lacey content and feeling complete, you must let Luke emerge." (By then Lacey had herself insisted on being called Luke by everyone who had either begrudgingly, or understandably, come to know the Luke in her.)

At fourteen she started hormonal therapy, and by sixteen Luke had emerged with male musculature, stature, and a deepening voice to match. Hormones had made her clitoris grow out and into a rudimentary penile-like structure, which elated Luke. Luke, at seventeen, was looking forward to his reassignment (now called "confirmation") surgeries, which were to follow soon at eighteen. These would erase all vestiges of her femaleness and reform her sexual architecture in the likes of a man. She would have a mastectomy, followed by a hysterectomy and closure of her vagina; a fusion of her labia to make a scrotal sac, where then testicular implants would be placed. Later, if Luke wanted, the urethra could be relocated through her now larger clitoral shaft so *he* could urinate standing.

MEET CHASE/CASSANDRA

Unlike Lacey, Cassandra was born genetically male. Like Lacey, Cassandra, then Chase, had no abnormalities biologically or physically that would warrant any perplexity about his biological sex or gender identity.

He grew up in a Chicago neighborhood that was gentrifying, and attended very integrated public schools. By the time he had reached junior high, Chase was already questioning the hard life of a boy in Chicago—the toughness necessary, the sixth sense needed to navigate the subways and not be groped, mugged, or pushed around. Bright and reflexive, he was attracted to dance, spent time in his summer days walking around the Lake's many parks, sketching tall buildings and collecting weedy flowers along the running tracks. His friends were limited. He had no attraction to girls, although he got along and danced with them splendidly.

As he entered high school, he began to change his attire, his winter clothing especially, wearing flowery scarves and tight jeans and calf-high boots. Now Chicago city schoolers either mock the nonconforming or make a space for them as a nod and accommodation to diversity. He began to articulate his emergent philosophy of gender: one can choose, one can select what one wants to be, and how one presents one's self to the world. Yes, he had made good use of libraries and the internet and was convincingly articulate when pressed by anyone—his single mother, the few friends he did have—about where all of this was eventually to land.

By his junior year Chase decided he wanted the life of a she-man (now called *genderqueer,* or *genderfluid*), not at all discontent with his body, but overwhelmingly discontent and thus disavowing of the gendered role as male he had been pushed into believing and performing. At eighteen and with his single mother's permission, Chase formally changed his name to Cassandra, the Trojan Prophetess that announced the fall of Troy. His life and mission seemed prophetic. *She* (now) would inhabit this interspace of external femininity while retaining internal masculinity—in check—under *her* purview and not that of society's. She liked the attention accorded to, and now demanded, by urban women; she felt women's wear enabled the body to dress in myriad emotions, thus liberating the self from the strictures of grays, plaids, and blues.

Her sexuality, you ask? Cassandra, now twenty-six, loves men, and not just their physicality, but because she isn't "one of them" any longer. "You could say I'm a gay person, but that would miss the mark." [How would that miss the mark?] "Because it's not about the sex of the person who you are attracted to . . ." she quips; "It's about who you are when in relationship with them." And, "When I'm with a guy [now], I feel my femininity, my core self, coming to the fore. That's what it's about." And then, the closer: "Maybe someday I'll be with a woman, when the man in me seeks consolation."

Cassandra is a study of gender fluidity and choice. Sexual orientation gets involved, but it isn't the primary motivator, as she explains it: it's how "her" *self* feels when expressing the feminine that made her determined to identify as a *woman-man* (*genderqueer*). The male in her isn't dead; it has just been freed from the constraints of masculinity.

Having done so, her female nature emerged as the stronger, more enduring identity. She's not been at war with her body: she's been at war with *gender ideology, binary systems*, and has "won the war" by liberating her feminine side. She embraces a fluid approach to gender.

MEET LYNETTE/KYLER

Kyler transitioned at twenty-six, after a brief marriage as the woman he was before, Lynette, failed miserably.

By then she had attempted suicide twice while an adolescent. She had been in and out of rehabs and finally got sober at twenty. Eventually trained by a Jobs Corps program to help engage her in income-producing activities, she was then stable. Invited by a friend, she started attending a Christian church and eventually made a profession of the faith, and within a few months got baptized. Life felt steady for the first time.

As it often happens, she met a man at church—and a relationship developed that rather quickly turned into engagement, then marriage. By twenty-three, Lynette was settling into married suburban life on the outskirts of a medium-sized Colorado city.

Then came the reality of all her backwaters. She kept breaking down into a puddle of tears every time she and her husband were intimate: she knew why. She knew!

This was not the truth! The truth was that her body was rejecting *penetration*; all of her winced at the idea that this should be her role—the female being penetrated—when in fact the *he* in her was screaming to be let out.

And so it was that all her secrets eventually came out like a floodgate, drowning the relationship and the marriage. It was the bad genie out of the bottle that couldn't be contained. After she broke out the truth of her life and her past, her husband took steps to do the legal filing, and in due time end the marriage in dissolution.

She had prayed, and prayed, and prayed. No-one in the church knew the struggles she'd had—struggles that had led her to be rejected by her family, then into drugs, alcohol, climbing her way back to sanity (she thought). Now, devastated, where was God? Now knowing, where was the church? Except for her pastor and one other church couple, once the word was out that Lynette "was out," she was abandoned like a leper. Avoidances were palpable.

She thought of suicide, and planned it. "God must be merciful to those that suffer so much," she thought. She had it all timed—and then the big question came: If she were to live (again), how would she live? Right then and there, she resolved that living was only worth living if she were to become the man she had inside. She went back to therapy, which confirmed her long-standing *gender dysphoria*.

At twenty-five, Lynette began the transition to Kyler. She chose the name Kyler because it seemed to command strength, a Germanic label for "small warrior." The small warrior would also stay in church and resolve to love God through it all.

Not surprisingly, her church had problems with the emerging Kyler. In a few months of injecting testosterone, Lynette began to fade and Kyler began to appear: He gained muscle weight, he transitioned clothes, he started to get a jowl and hair on his face. His voice went down an octave, just enough to make it within the range of men.

Then came a rigid divide between those that supported Kyler, and those that felt Kyler now embodied an abomination. Some made it known that one's identity should be in Christ, and transgender people have chosen gender identity above their Christian identity. Others continued to avoid the whole affair, and Kyler in person. The pastor tried to remain neutral by quoting scriptures' teachings on not judging others.

Responding later to the queries, Kyler stated, "*I want to share that from a trans Christian perspective, it is possible to have both: My identity in Christ comes first and foremost to my gender—and when I did transition I promised myself that gender would not get in the way of my serving God and his church.*"

Kyler eventually found a new church home in that nearby Colorado city. Nobody would know his past nor suspect he was a former she . . . the physical transition and surgeries were that good. Besides, he grew a beard to underscore his masculinity. By twenty-six, Lynette had "died" and a "resurrected" life as Kyler had begun in earnest.

MEET SAM[ANTHA]

Sam's mother's pregnancy had been normal throughout her term, and as delivery neared, both parents and family were excited to bring this couple's second child into the world. Their church friends anticipated offering them provisions of help and food, popular aids among young couples' groups in Christian churches. Her friends would baby-sit the older son when time came for her delivery. It would be a natural childbirth. They were told it would be another boy, and had sonograms to cement that statement.

Little did Sam's parents expect an "intersex" baby.

During a moment in delivery, after the baby's cries and a sigh of relief, their obstetrician neared the couple and stated, "Congratulations, your child is healthy, and we think it's a boy—but let's be sure—there is some ambiguity to the genitals. We need to check him out, and we'll proceed to do that stat. Don't worry, he's perfectly healthy . . . ."

"Ambiguity"—a medical term used to note that there's a problem identifying the infant's organs as belonging to one, or the other (binary) sex category. It was then confirmed: Sam had *ambiguous genitals*. (We will discuss this outcome in detail in chapter 4.)

Since the clitoris and penis are derived from the same structure in development, in intersex situations the chromosomal instructions may get mixed, or are absent, or partially coded. In some cases, there are chromosomal abnormalities. Any of these can result in a baby boy having an abnormally small penis, or a penis not entirely formed. He can also display undescended testicles; a scrotal sac that isn't "sewn up," but shows up as two folds of skin, much like female labia, and undescended testicles. There can be a "blind vagina"—an opening going nowhere. Internal organs of reproduction may be equally mixed, or not totally developed. Thus, it may be very difficult to determine the actual physiological sex of the baby despite it having XY chromosomes (as it turned out in this case).

Sam had a partially undifferentiated penis, undescended testes, and a "blind vagina." He also had a malformed urethral opening or *hypospadia*, which would need correction for him to urinate properly.

Genital ambiguity for Sam threw this family into a series of medical informationals about what they needed to know, followed by suggestions for decision-making, all of which overwhelmed them.

As devout, conservative Christians they first felt that *God doesn't make mistakes*, and consequently whatever genitals there were to deal with—Sam was a boy. That position didn't last long as physicians and therapists explained Sam's condition, and medical options were explained in full.

It was a result of miscoding in utero. Sam would be infertile; and even though chromosomally he was an XY, his genitals were neither male nor female, but a mix. His testicles were underdeveloped. He barely had a penile-like structure, and the opening resembled the likes of female genitals. Their pastor, consoling them, suggested all human harm comes from the Fall, and the earth's continued *groaning*: it was nobody's present mistake.

More to the point, what to do with this "boy," now that the genitals and glands wouldn't provide solid identifiers for his body; and of course, of what role he was to take on in later life.

Physicians were cautious not to push undue influence, but suggested two alternatives: surgeons are now capable of reconstructing, sometimes *constructing*, the genitalia of intersexed babies; even though these modifications or "corrections" don't change the genetic biology (that is the sex, XX or XY) of the baby. In theory doctors said, it can give the child a more "normal" life if altered to the sex/gender that seems *most likely to succeed* via such surgeries. The baby would then be brought up as the corresponding sex and, of course, within the corresponding gender schema to match it. Hormonal therapy at different stages of future development would ensure the body morphed to match the sex selection.

Alternatively, and this came with lots of cautions also, Sam's parents could keep from doing any physical modifications, growing the child as *one of the genders* as best as they could, and monitoring how that identification progress was internalized and corresponded to the developing role. In Sam's case, there would need to be some minor surgery regardless, to align the urethra so he could urinate without spraying. But any actual gender surgeries could wait till a tad later . . . or even when he was an adult.

After a lot of soul searching and prayer, Sam's parents decided to only do the corrective urethral surgery right after birth, and decide later if this child could indeed be surgically realigned with a "binary" sex. Sam would probably have to become *female*, given the limitations of what could be done with his malformed male organs. He would have to become *Sam[antha]*. How successful would that be?

MEET DAVID/MICHELLE

Introducing David/Michelle is especially poignant for me, given that as Michelle she became a trusted colleague and friend who visited my Human Sexuality class yearly, to share her story with my students. Her history is well known to me, also to the press under another name—so much more could be written—yet here are her essentials:

Born into a family of Michigan Lutherans who went to Church on Sundays, David's first recollection of his attraction to the female form came when, walking home from church and seeing a nun dressed in a habit walk past on the other side of the street, he stated to his mother: "Someday I want to be a nun." David was around six, he recalls. The mother, missing the sexual and gender contexts completely, responded, *"David, don't be silly! We're Lutherans, not Catholics."*

Even before that, David was talking and acting more like his sisters than his brother. And, while he knew he had male anatomy, he continued to feel "more like a girl than a boy."

By fifth grade, he was pegged as a *sissy* because he carried his books like girls did, and didn't have that *macho* stride. He was tormented through junior and high school; and although he tried to talk to his parents about his feelings, it didn't work. He was told to "Suck it up, you are a growing man!" They quickly enrolled him in the Naval Cadets in high school.

And *suck it up* he did. He buried his feelings of being in the wrong body, and decided that if there was any hope, it would be in formally joining the military after graduating: after all, they "make men, men." He joined the Navy, and within a few months took the great step to show everyone and himself that he was "normal" by dating a girl and eventually getting married. The marriage turned disastrous.

For one, he couldn't "satisfy" his wife's needs, a painful realization that his discomfort with his own body wasn't going away.

Nevertheless, he tried to persevere, and his wife eventually had a son. This complicated the marriage even more.

His response was to *try harder*, delving into his Navy career, serving in Vietnam at the tail end of the war, making himself physically strong enough to become a submarine warfare specialist and Navy Seal. After over a decade together, David and his wife divorced.

But he tried harder again, liking intensely another woman and thinking their commonalities would make it work out, he married a second time. And again, he couldn't "give" what she needed. The thought finally came, *"My God, I'm ruining this beautiful woman's life. My secret is the cause."* He broke down and told her of his feelings, his self-identification as a *transsexual*. To his surprise—she talked about what needed to happen then—and it wasn't divorce.

With her encouragement David went through counseling and evaluations, and was diagnosed as a *gender dysphoric* male. It took a few years, a dishonorable discharge when the Navy found out, then eventual hormonal and surgical reassignment for him to emerge as Michelle. She then fought the discharge, all the way to the Supreme Court, and returned to military service in the Army *as a woman*. At that point, the new Michelle and wife had an amicable divorce. Michelle was eventually honorably discharged with distinction.

Michelle's story doesn't end there: at its core, it could be typical of many transgender individuals, repressing the dysphoria, "trying harder," and crashing out. It is all similar, but for the fact that she eventually felt that ancient calling again, to be a nun.

She followed that sentiment to its full fruition.

In due course, Michelle was recommended to join an order, went through theological training, confirmation, and became the world's first transsexual Episcopal nun, taking on vows of poverty and chastity. She has lived her life as a pious Episcopal nun in a para-Episcopal ministry, later as part of the American Catholic Church, operating numerous outreaches from her home base, touching thousands of lives in the process until her retirement.

UNPACKING THE CASES

Each of these cases presents us with information we can assess to better understand each dimension of sex and gender being illustrated—unraveling elements, always conditions and situations; and of course, the contextual, which informs as well as forms perspectives. I shall add more information and research as we "unpack" these, below.

Lacey/Luke Again

Children represent special and sensitive cases when assessing gender problems. Lacey/Luke presents us with a case of *early onset gender dysphoria*, which *was* the eventual diagnosis given to Lacey through myriad stages of her and her parents' therapies. *Gender dysphoria* is a clinical designation supported by the DSM-5 criteria.[2] It is difficult to assess in children specifically, because nearly all children go through phases of gender-nonconformity, or are prone to crossing "gender lines," exploring the *other* gender role—even identity—as they initiate play and consume social identifiers.

The *persistence* of Lacey's rejection of her female body is a telltale sign here that there may be dysphoria going on, however rudimentary at this stage. At this age level, children with gender dysphoria can display a basic conflict between what their bodies say about their physically assigned sex and the gender identity with which they increasingly identify. The discomfort, in most cases of dysphoria, continues to grow and becomes especially acute when puberty sets in. This, of course, because puberty initiates those physical, secondary sex characteristics that would heighten any distress and disjunction between the body and the identity. Girls who think they are/should be boys start to grow breasts and menstruate; boys who think they are/should be girls see muscles, penile growth, and ejaculations.

A question frequently asked is *whether there could be some biological basis for a transgender identity*. Neurobiological and genetic research thus far has *not* concluded with evidence that there is a biological basis for transgenderism.[3] Research physicians Mayer and McHugh clearly state in their 2016 opus report on "Sexuality and Gender," which reviewed *thousands* of research findings:

---

2. American Psychiatric Association, *Diagnostic and Statistical Manual*, section 302.85 (F64.9). See also Steensma et al., "Factors," 582–90.

3. Mayer and McHugh, "Sexuality and Gender," 104.

In this context, it is important to note that there are no studies which demonstrate that any of the biological differences being examined have predictive power, and so all interpretations, usually in popular outlets, claiming or suggesting that a statistically significant difference between the brains of people who are transgender and those who are not is the cause of *being* transgender or not—that is to say, that the biological differences determine the differences in gender identity—are unwarranted.[4]

It is clear from their own research and the many others they reviewed, that the development of gender identity is itself *not innate*: there is at present no link between one (biological sex) causing the other (gender identity), or the dissonance.[5] And, "Unlike the [physiological] differences between the sexes . . . there are no biological features that can readily identify transgender (dysphoric) individuals as different from others."[6]

Dysphoric children, such as Lacey, may eventually express wishes to be the "opposite sex" and may show symptoms of depression. Some may demand that they be recognized (as did Lacey) using an opposite-gender name—the demand can also extend to clothes, hairstyles, and anything that would validate the identity they feel they are.

But let's be clear here: *Gender dysphoria is not the same as gender nonconformity*, which often and early on can get confused with it.

In *childhood gender nonconformity*, the child isn't necessarily rejecting their *body;* but they *are* refusing some/many of the expected *behaviors* that gender norms suggest. Such may be meaningless. Pursued as an adolescent, and later as an adult, these behaviors may signal gender dissonances with *role*, or with the suppositions imposed by a certain sexual identity; but again, this may not be dysphoria at all.

For the classification of dysphoria to be accurate in the case of a child, it must be *embodied*, somehow, "strongly and persistently"—usually as an eventual rejection of some part, or all, of their body. Yet even with this persistence, a clinician (or set of them) must be cautious. (The DSM-5 now include separate criteria for GID in children.)[7]

---

4. Mayer and McHugh, "Sexuality and Gender," 104.
5. Fausto-Sterling, *Sex/Gender*, 57.
6. Mayer and McHugh, "Sexuality and Gender," 105.
7. Zucker, "The DSM Diagnostic Criteria," 33–37.

Case history suggests Lacey was placed in therapy around age six, in particular because of the growing fixation on not having a penis as "all boys do." She was consistently monitored, without much change in the worsening—read *strong and persistent*—gender-identity conflict. Household and church life were a seesaw, given that the emerging "Luke" expressed his boyness several times in Sunday School. When he refused to wear dresses by age eight and asked to be called Luke, his family transitioned him to more "gender neutral" clothing, not knowing what else to do; including his Christian school uniforms. Out went any skirts and blouses and in came an array of possibles, mostly boyish-passing attire and all bottoms as pants.

What we don't know from the clinical record is how the family and peer dynamics could have influenced the development or persistence of gender-nonconforming and body-rejecting behaviors. This is *not to say* that Lacey's family or peers are responsible for either the onset or maintenance of a dysphoria. It is to underscore what some voices are bringing to this conversation, about the influences that *may* come to bear—within the family of rearing and the social environments—on cross-gender behaviors and feelings. And this is often not the voice that is included.

One such voice is psychologist Dr. Kenneth J. Zucker, who has decades of dealing with children experiencing gender incongruity, and has written extensively on it.[8]

He suggests "predisposing" and "perpetuating" factors, all social-contextual, among which are: *unwitting parental reinforcements of cross-gender behaviors, family dynamics;* even *parental psychopathologies*. He further suggests that as part of assessment diagnostics, a therapist should investigate *the child's peer relationships*, and *the child's own fantasy world* where he/she may see themselves as a member of the opposite sex.[9] To Dr. Zucker, knowing the broader contexts and the specific inner mental life of the child is imperative for an accurate diagnosis.

Again, this is *not* to suggest that dysphoria is caused by the factors Zucker isolates, but it is to suggest that social forces do come to bear on how a child maneuvers their feelings, and in turn, how

---

8. Zucker, "Children with Gender Identity Disorder," 362. See also Fausto-Sterling, *Sex/Gender*, 56–57.

9. Zucker, "Children with Gender Identity Disorder," 363.

the family tries to maintain function. I discuss these points further in chapter 5.

Lacey's history shows that the family was initially in an upheaval and on a spiritual roller-coaster. They were hearing different voices—pastoral, clinical, secular, religious—on what this all could mean and, most importantly, what to do about it. Courageously they started therapeutic interventions, to maintain their sanity and that of "Luke's." Pastoral guidance pushed restraints on all levels; while clinical ones suggested interventions short- and long-term. Lacey's family history shows resistance to the idea that gender could be changed, but a consistent opening up to his growing *masculinity*.

Would gender-exploration therapy have worked on Luke?[10] That is a question that cannot be answered by the clinical data made available; however, I can fairly surmise that gender-exploration, or *desisting therapies* were probably the *least* available or attempted. Why? Because as has been the case with *sexual orientation*, and any therapies aimed at "exploration" or "desistance," the American Psychiatric Association has gone on record refuting their effectiveness and denouncing them as harmful.[11] Christian therapists have been warned not to attempt them, with threats of losing their licensure if discovered.

In their Canadian homeland, Dr. Zucker and colleagues treated children with gender identity disorders with psychotherapies whose aim was to help the child come to terms with their biological sex. They reported astounding statistics: of those treated, only 8.33 percent "persisted" in their gender identity disorder, while 91.6 percent became gender concordant in identity.[12] These statistics have been hotly debated. Zucker and colleagues became surrounded by controversy, ultimately leaving the Center (for Addiction and Mental Health). Reported elsewhere were data reviews by Mayer and McHugh, who stated ". . . there is little evidence that gender identity issues have a high rate of persistence in children, overall."[13] These statements also

---

10. "Gender desisting therapies" refer to those that attempt to help the child/adolescent reconcile their body and their feelings, i.e., they "desist" from the push to reject their body sex and begin to embrace it, also their gender role. These therapies have been negated as invalid, improper, and therapists who practice it chastised by the American Psychiatric Association and sundry other professional licensing and certifying bodies.

11. American Psychiatric Association, "Position Statement on Therapies."

12.. Zucker et al., "A Developmental, Biopsychosocial Model," 369–397.

13. Mayer and McHugh, "Sexuality and Gender—Part Three," 106–07.

have been contested. All sides review data differently, but what is of essence here is to recognize that we need further evidentiary data and research on desistance in minors.

We explore these issues and reviews by Singal, his prolific search for answers, in chapters 5, 7, and again in chapter 9.

Luke's family came to terms with his persistence as an effort to avoid what has been very common in such cases: that the child-turned-adolescent would find the dissonances so acute that they may attempt to take their lives.[14] Given that probability, his parents finally consented to Lacey's wish, to be a "total boy" when he turned fourteen. They resolved their religious doubts as someone read them Matthew 5:30, and suggested it may offer the right (literal) course of action: "And if your right hand causes you to stumble, cut it off and throw it away. It is better for you to lose one part of your body than for your whole body to go into hell."

In chapter 7 we will return to such Scriptures and try to ascertain what this verse, and many others that are quoted in such situations, mean. (How these verses are interpreted need clarification.)

Luke's family still clings together, and are slowly reconciling themselves emotionally to their new "son." They are content that an even greater depression in later adolescence didn't take the life of their "boy." Luke is now finishing high school and has enjoyed a year of playing in the men's soccer team.

Cassandra Again

Cassandra's case is *especially important* to discuss because he/she represents, and embodies, one wave of the cultural tsunami of gender change now on everyone's shoreline. It's no exaggeration to state that in the most recent surveys that compare long-term data, developed countries like the US and Great Britain are experiencing the largest growth in identified transgender individuals ever.[15]

Alongside this "outing" in census-like reports, comes the growing openness of Millennial, Gen X, and Gen Y generations, who question binary formulas of *sex and gender* and who increasingly see both

---

14. Mayer and McHugh, "Sexuality and Gender—Introduction," 8. See also Johns, "Transgender Identity and Experiences of Violence," 67–71.

15. James, "Report of the 2015 U.S. Transgender Survey," 18–22.

as *fluid*—that "spectrum"—if you will. They also see gender identity as sometimes *transient;* meaning, people can go back and forth in gender categories or positions, giving gender not only fluidity but mobility in and through time.[16]

Cassandra's generation do not base their rejections of binary gender on science, on "evidence"; but may rely solely on an *ideology of individualism—expressive individualism*—as I mentioned earlier. One's personal testimony of how one sees one's self is *sufficient;* and the demand for the right to determine one's gender preference seen as a hard-won freedom. Cassandra is the postcard of the idea that one's gender identity *should be self-determined.* Thus, her case is important as a reflection of this type of gender-questioning, "gender-bending."

And this may be the greater wave of gender change at present in younger populations. For some in this cohort, if one takes another position than the right of self-determination, one is relegated to "transphobia,"[17] the idea that if you are not *for* trans, you are *phobically* against it.

Let's remember, Millennials and young adults have grown up with the technological means to communicate and express themselves through mediums that "feel" more authentic—*life online*—than those experienced in person. Not only do these generations get their information from online sources, but online outlets provide "safe spaces" in which to try on different personas, express differences, and mainly be rewarded by other posters doing the same.

YouTube, Instagram, Tumblr, and blogging sites all have "transition blogs" that can be used to express one's self and one's experiments with gender. Often the emphasis is that *being complicated is okay*, and that going beyond what you see is now essential to being.

It's not that these generations suddenly realize they are at war with cisgender norms and historical heteronormativity. But I do believe that as they navigate the world, and try to find their spaces within it, they are more prone to thinking about all those exposures they have been subjected to—all those alternatives that go into the

16. Simon, "Gender-Fluid Added to Oxford Dictionary," 1. See also, Human Rights Campaign, "Growing Up LGBTQ in America," 3–36.

17. *"Transphobia"*: an irrational negative response to transgender and intersex people, as well as other forms of gender-bending and gender non-conformity. *Urban Dictionary Online*, s.v., "Transphobia," https://www.urbandictionary.com/define.php?term=Transphobia.

decision-making process: this seems a movement of *increased identifications*—one that rejects what has traditionally been told them or educated into them about how they should represent themselves.

And they go forward to try on different aspects of gender representation—at first slowly, watching the reactions and committed to assessing how they feel in those moments. Sam Stiegler, a young doctorate student from the University of British Columbia, whose focus is on the everyday experiences of trans, queer, and genderqueer youth, wrote recently in an interview with *The Sound*,

> This generation is carefully navigating how they can move through the world. For example, I used to work with a young person who at first would only dress in gender-affirming clothes. And then one day they [changed their look,] took the elevator and stood in the lobby . . . and then walked down the sidewalk; . . . later they would walk to the Starbucks. I think that decision-making process and how they're coming to know what's safe and what's unsafe . . . is evidence of the complex, sophisticated thinking that goes into a young person's gender identity and expression.[18]

In Cassandra's case, the hard life the urban male Chase was encountering just wasn't the role he was comfortable with. In school, he met others who shared the dissonances of gender and were on a path to "gender-bending,"[19] a term that became vogue during his high school years. Chase wasn't a social butterfly and preferred alone activities, but he did find comfort in knowing that there were "others" out there that were not comfortable in the role definitions they had been given. In school, he encountered alternative narratives, and the internet and public libraries of Chicago provided him new terms to name his experiences.

---

18. Stiegler, "A Gender-Bending Look into GenEdge," 1–4. (Brackets mine for clarity.)

19. "Gender-bending" can be thought of as both (a) a form of social activism aimed to do away with rigid gender roles and (b) as a form of an individual's own gender-nonconforming—a person who finds gender roles oppressive and chooses to self-identify and act otherwise. In the latter case, the more personal adjective is "gender-bender." Again, gender-bending has been around a lot longer than recent generations: performers David Bowie and Boy George quickly come to mind. The difference here is that gender-bending is as much a philosophic rejection of gender as it is a personalized "choice" for the many who explore alternatives to the binary. It is not art- or performance-based, nor does it seek crowdsourcing for self-acceptance, as in the case of mentioned artists.

Many youth, like Chase, are trying to situate themselves outside the binary box, for reasons that are at once psychologically personal but also serve as coping mechanisms for non-binary feelings. Possibilities now available socially to *self-reconstruct* allow them to move beyond their "assigned" identity.

Such a search for new identifiers is typical of a subset of young people today who do not take at face value those socially crafted categories of gender that traditionally go along with binary sex. They feel that nature doesn't decide where the category of "male" begins and the category of "female" begins. *For them, it's human culture that decides:*[20] Blue is for boys; pink is for girls! Culture-making includes gender-making, and culturally specific expressions of masculinity and femininity are just that: it doesn't and shouldn't have anything to do with what adorns the thighs.

And this self-reconstruction can be felt as *mind-expanding*. Scott Beauchamp, writing for *The Public Discourse*, suggests:

> To become "gender-fluid" is a kind of contemporary "mind expansion," a subjective experience elevated to the achievement of a higher ontological state. What does it mean to experience the universe all at once? Is it similar to what it feels like to be "genderqueer"? Both seem to exist [now] in an ineffable space beyond communication and, conveniently, critical analysis.[21]

Cassandra is at the cusp of a post-sexual-revolution revolution, the "transgender moment," in which some participants look to deconstruct traditional understandings of how human beings embody that biological sexual dimorphism. How, by applying what the culture has already taught them about essentialist individualism, they can demonstrate an "alternative truth."

---

20. Let's be real and acknowledge that there is truth in this. While genetics do determine the *baselines* for males and females through the differentiation process, *what to do with those parameter differences* is a consequence of human action. That is, the meaning that is inhered into those categories (male, female), and the extent to which those categories become rigid boxes, is a cultural outcome. It's argued that much of this is necessary due to its "predictive value": humans can then tell how to act with one another, express what we know and feel, and maintain "order." But the order we maintain, the hierarchies we sustain, have led to discriminant roles, authority and power differentials for the genders. Youth's denial of socially constructed categories as "truth" has as much to do with this tired backdrop of inequalities and differences, as much as it does with donning on a new persona.

21. Beauchamp, "The Kids Aren't All Right," par. 7.

Thus, in such cases we may be experiencing a "culture-bound syndrome"[22] in this transgender moment, one that takes its energy, reactively, from those rigidities and inequalities brought forth with strict gendered roles. (We explore this fully in chapters 7–9.)

Cassandra, then Chase, felt suffocated under his experience of masculinity. He chose otherwise—because he could. And here is the distinctive in this case: there is no narrative in Cassandra's story of strong rejection of her *physicality* as a biological male, only the growing refusal of a role that she found she did not want to inhabit.

This is the crux of the difference between gender nonconformity and any form of dysphoria, in that, in the former, the dissonance and discontent comes from *role-related incongruities* with the self-*image*, not the self-*body*. Cassandra is *rejecting roles, not her body.*

Let's also note that Cassandra makes obvious her gender preference through self-presentation—the expression of one's appearance, physically. She dons items that have typically and until very recently belonged only to females. By so doing she cements her self-presentation as *gender fluid*, by mixing clothing genres to achieve as much femininity as she wants to illustrate. And this can vary, again, over time and space based on her predilections.

Now let's revisit her sexuality.

As genderqueer, Cassandra is now in relationships with men, which traditionally has meant a label of "gay," or homosexual. But she argues in her retort that this label would miss the fact that it isn't about the *sexual orientation*,[23] or to whom you are attracted. Rather, it's about *how one's self feels* when with that person. She is pointing us to the fact that sexual mate selection—in this narrative—is a dependent variable. Meaning, that her self-presentation as female warrants her being with a male (in an oddly binary manner, I might add!) If all of

---

22. A *culture-bound syndrome* is a broad rubric that encompasses certain behaviors, emotions, and ways of thinking seen *only* in specific cultures. These manifestations are out of the ordinary from the usual behavior of individuals in that culture, and thus are reasons for distress/discomfort. I explain this more fully in chapters 7–9. See also Guarnaccia and Rogler, "Research on Culture-Bound Syndrome," 1322–27.

23. *Sexual orientation* refers to one's erotic attraction to a particular sex; an erotic affect that arouses the person sexually. How this orientation forms is a result of many variables, and includes one's sexual and brain development; but also, the experiences, exposures, and emotions that forge a direction for one's erotic feelings. All this can happen unconsciously, semi-consciously, or consciously—and often results in a particular sexual preference . . . but not always. See Gil, "To Feel or Not to Feel," 1–32.

this makes heads spin, let me rephrase it: the position of *genderqueer* or *genderfluidity* proposes that our common assumptions about body and gender, and sexual attraction, are rational *only* because we deem them to be so; and consequently, must fall into this linear pattern of XY being male and thus liking XX *because* one is male.

The linearity—in this argument—is viewed as a *limitation* on *identity* and *role freedoms*; barriers to be transcended, instead of the cornerstones of maleness and femaleness. Cassandra has shed that rationality of *singular sexual orientation* in favor of what she feels comfortable with.

And so, it is to follow, if she is embodying the "woman," that *she should be attracted to* "the man." (Oddly, it seems to me, Cassandra *reinforces* male and female roles when she plays the woman and likes the man. The only distinction here being, *she* can choose when she desires either and is not bound by prior labels, but by labels of her own choosing.) Note, again, Cassandra isn't *wanting* the body of a woman; she isn't *rejecting* her sexual organs or claiming she should have been born a woman. Being *genderfluid* allows Cassandra to invoke a feminine/female form at will without rejecting anything of "himself," just his *role*. True enough, *two* gender identities have been formed, one from willpower—one, for the moment, taking precedence.

Later we'll address the implications of these lines of thought more thoroughly, and Christian theology's problems with it in chapters 7-9. This is not *her problematic*, however, since Cassandra is not religiously inclined.

It's enough for now to suggest that Cassandra feels she has "won" her *self* by recommissioning herself into role fluidity that frees her from the *linear* binary. This position of *genderqueer*-ness "delivers her" from the role strictures of a male polarity, which she found suffocating. Then again, "There may come a time" (in her words) when Cassandra's male will, "like the Phoenix, rise from the ashes" to move her otherwise.

Kyler Again

Kyler's case is another essential illustration of how different gender-identity issues can be. What is so central here is the historical repression and suppression of *gender dysphoria,* and its eventual wrecking-ball manifestation at a later stage in life, this time *when a Christian.*

Coming from a broken home, an alcoholic father, and a passive-aggressive mother who needed more emotional care than she gave, the then-Lynette found consolation in the rough-and-tumble play entertained with her two older brothers, one of whom would join the military at eighteen to flee from the home environment.

That departure at her twelfth birthday left her feeling alone and without a defender. Lynette had always played the part of Tomboy, not just because she had to learn early the art of self-defense against the "brotherhood," but because it just felt more natural to her. And her brothers believed she was, *really,* a boy—inside.

Her mother despised the seeming toughness and incessantly chose to re-indoctrinate Lynette into femininity. What nobody noticed until it happened was that Lynette was insecure, internally frail, depressive, and ultimately incapable of not cutting herself, not isolating herself (and here everyone thought she was protecting herself from the brothers). She tried to end it all by swallowing a handful of her mother's antidepressants at age fourteen. But she survived, and came back after rehab to an even more stifling environment.

She felt completely "wrong" as an adolescent girl. In her diary, she dared to write at fifteen, "I should have been a boy—maybe then I could win my life."

By the time she was sixteen she had found the alcohol at home and was drowning in its wake. She was put into rehab and lost a year of school. Sober, but spiraling into another depression shortly after release, Lynette found consolation in a girlfriend—her only real friend—a relationship that turned sexual, but with a twist.

Lynette discovered that she didn't like her body to act the feminine, and instinctively was repulsed at the thought of vaginal contact. She played the male, despite her menstruation serving as an otherwise constant reminder.

So disgusted by her body's "betrayal" (she wrote again in a would-be diary), that she spun out of control. She drank, and in a drunken stupor determined to cut her wrists and end her misery. But again, she survived.

This time rehab was long and arduous. But it seemed to stick. She had to also confront the lesbianism, and came to understand it as a reflection of the depression, and her unwillingness to accept her femininity. But as it sometimes happens, therapy focused more on the sexual *role* and *orientation* than the sexual *identity*. That was left, for the most part, unexplored. Entering a job training program and finishing a high school equivalency degree gave her a sense of normalcy. She was out of the house and in a sober living environment, and *working*.

The world changed when she was twenty-one and invited to an evangelical church, where she encountered "happy, sober people," who claimed forgiveness and cleansing, a helping God and brotherhood in Christ. It sounded fantastic. She would commit to trying it! Within a short while she was baptized and joined the congregation. The Lynette she couldn't reconcile seemed now reconcilable.

We know from Lynette's history that there were unresolved conflicts that, when compared to the myriad life histories of *gender dysphoric* individuals, read like parallels:[24]

- (For some:) Dysfunctions in the household of rearing.
- Gender nonconformity due to a variety of reasons, some sensical; some, obtusely related to body dysmorphia cum dysphoria.
- Depressions, use of drugs, alcohol as coping mechanisms or escapes.
- Experimentation with gender orientation—in this case a jump into lesbianism—only to find *orientation* isn't the basis of the issue.
- Repressions and suppressions of real feelings about body, image, identity.
- Attempts at suicide or self-harm.
- Possible immersion into the "appropriate role," only to find it eventually suffocating.
- Realization of the dysphoria's persistence and ultimate acknowledgement of it.

Her role conformity and marriage are not uncommon steps in a dysphoric's attempts to normalize what would *seem possible*. I've been

---

24. Parekh, "What Is Gender Dysphoria?" sects. "Diagnosis," and "Challenges/Complications."

colleague and friend to some who, only after similar scripts of body dysmorphias, depressions, drug use, trying on other sexual orientations, failed marriages, lots of therapies and children in-between, have come to the stark realization that their gender dysphoria isn't going away.

And, as it sometimes happens, the would-be *repressed dysphoria* is brought back again by events that may have deep emotional roots. In Lynette's case, it was the physical intimacy with her husband and those particular moments of sexual penetration that her mind-body needed to reject. It brought forward that historic root of dissonance with her body that became, once again, intolerable.

As her story reveals, and possibly most significant for us Christians to realize, is the dimensional social spaces within which dysphorics, once "out," must navigate. That her church family didn't provide a more sustaining environment—*even if just for the sake of loving a troubled individual through their crisis*—is both a statement and testament of how much work the church needs in embracing *this type* of mercy and *this type* of reconciliation.

After the divorce, and when Kyler started to appear, it became significantly dissonant for those in the congregation that had not taken time to inform themselves. Some did not want to understand. Oppositional sides formed. For Kyler, it was too much too handle, along with the body transitions.

Making it clear that his faith and service to Christ were *not* the issue, and with strong resolve now to live as a man, the emerging Kyler crafted a plan to disappear and then reappear in yet another physical community: this time as the man he needed to be to live, and live fully.

I repeat this story to drive home two points, early in this book: *First,* to frame what are, unfortunately, common historical travails in the lives of many who experience gender dysphoria. *And second,* to firmly underscore how much work we, as the church of Jesus, still need to accomplish to comprehend this phenomenon of gender—particularly *diagnosed dysphoria*—as it plays itself out in the lives of individuals in the church and in society at large. It is a monumental task that we are barely beginning to address; and no, the biblical-exegetical, and ontological work isn't complete on these issues, by any measure.

Sam[antha] Again

Any intersex birth is initially traumatic for parents. Most sonograms suggest a baby's early assignment to one of the two dimorphic sexes; but capturing the exact structure of genitals in womb sonography can sometimes be deceiving.[25]

There are also two scripts that we could follow here. One is that of the family; the other is that of the child—at least the way the child's script could be written. For parents, an intersex outcome is never a good outcome regardless of the courage or optimism mustered. And it's not because of the condition as much as society's historical problem in engaging the intersexed: both parents and child face significant challenges.

For Christian parents, there are added trials in attempting to understand why it happened, and how God's will enters into the picture. Then there are parental responsibilities, choices to be made; how to engage these in consonance with what is understood from the biblical text about human creation, about science, about the body, about so many other attendant elements. I delve into all of this in chapters 4–7.

Sam's parents were confronted with two propositions, which shape themselves more-or-less in ways described in the literature as "models" of treatment: the *concealment-centered* or the *patient-centered* models of care.[26]

Growing out of Johns Hopkins' *"optimum gender of rearing"* system,[27] *concealment-centered* views see intersex births as needing "normalization." That is, medically necessary interventions through surgeries and hormonal reassignments to afford the child a modicum of "normal adjustment" into an *assigned* (physical) identity and role.

In the past, such individuals might have been considered *hermaphrodites* (a term that, as previously mentioned, many in the intersex community now consider derogatory). After surgery, the child would be raised as the *assigned gender*, irrespective of their chromosomal (XX or XY) status. Often the child's record of such surgeries

---

25. Whitlow et al., "First Trimester Diagnosis of Gender," 301–4.

26. It should be noted some medical centers seem to still practice a concealment model. Sam's parents' center gave them options. See the Intersex Society of North America's website for additional information on both approaches, at http://isna.org.

27. Dreger, "Ambiguous Sex—or Ambivalent Medicine," 24–35.

and reassignments would be "sealed." Later as adults, these were denied information of their former intersex status and medical records.

Historically, many of these children when grown *do discover* their former intersex status and its concealment. Such discoveries have many outcomes, but one central common theme runs through them all: shock and disappointments galore. "*Why the lies and cover-ups?!*"

Georgiann Davis, in her recent book *Contesting Intersex: The Dubious Diagnosis*, writes,

> I was shocked and confused. Why had my medical providers and parents lied to me for so many years? I thought I had surgeries because of health risks. Was having an intersex set of traits that horrible? I remember thinking I must have been a real freak if even my parents hadn't been able to tell me the truth.[28]

In this concealment approach, intersex is a problem because it challenges the traditional order inhered into gender, and into the biology of sex (i.e., the binary model). The problem thus needs medical "fixing," and the child isn't in a position to decide—so the burden of decision-making is on those legally responsible, the parents.

In the *patient-centered model*, intersexed genitals are *not* a medical problem. While these conditions may be the result of genetic or hormone distinctives—and can therefore include metabolic conditions that *do* need to be monitored, often treated long term—the genitalia are not diseased.[29] Certainly, there may be the need to repair urethras or openings to sustain functions like urination, or even eventual menstruation if possible; but the notion of *correction* to make any child into a "real" boy or girl is to be avoided as false.

And this is exactly what Sam's parents determined they would initially do: minor *hypospadic* (urethral) repair, and then wait. Wait for what . . . ? Wait until the child is older. The Intersex Society of North America (ISNA) recommends two to three years.[30] Meanwhile, the Society does recommend that the child be *given a gender assignment*. This, after initial medical work-ups and psychological/

---

28. Davis, *Contesting Intersex*, 4.

29. See explanations in full for this position at https://rarediseases.info.nih.gov/diseases/8538/46-xy-disorders-of-sexual-development.

30. See Intersex Society of North America for their recommendations, at http://isna.org/faq/patient-centered.

psychiatric evaluations in the first years of life point to which gender the child is more likely to identify with as they grow up.

None of this is a move towards an eventual, specific surgery—quite the contrary. It is a move that sustains a likely gender identification as opposed to "no gender," or a "third gender." A no-gender or third-gender approach, in this view by ISNA, would be labeling the child with a category that "really doesn't exist in fact," despite what transgender advocates may suggest. (Intersex is not, and may never be, a discreet *biological* category, given the broad spectrum of outcomes it covers.) Thus, assigning an intersex, third-gender, or no-gender identity would, according to ISNA, be unnecessarily traumatizing to the child. ISNA recognizes children still grow up in a largely binary world order. I detail these positions further, in chapter 5.

Sam's malformed male genitalia and blind vagina "looked more female" and trended toward a *female* sex of rearing selection as the more plausible alternative. Sam's family opted to assign Sam as Sam[antha], regardless of chromosomal sex. She would be reared as a girl.

Sam[antha] would eventually be told the truth, which is that her genitalia may look different, but that they were just as OK as anyone else's. If later in life Sam[antha] wanted to live like a male Sam, and have Sam-concordant genitalia (a surgically constructed male anatomy), she would knowingly consent to having them. If she felt more natural as Samantha, an alternate surgical reconstruction could make her genitalia *even more* female-defined.

Above all, it was their hope that Sam[antha] would accept herself as unique and be helped to live out her life in healthy, self-accepting, and gender-of-rearing, *female*-concordant ways. This seemed to them to be the most likely option as well as the most genitally respectful. We continue this conversation in greater depth in chapter 5.

David/Michelle Again

Michelle's life history is typical of early-onset gender dysphoric children who *do not* resolve their gender incongruity as they move into pre-adolescence and adolescence, then later adulthood. Michelle recounts myriad moments in his growing up years as David where his identification with the feminine, with his body as an awkward repository of male sex, generated disjunctions of both esteem and identity:

> As much as I tried to "suck it up" it always oozed out in some way. I remember wanting to wear skirts but being incredibly afraid to try one (in secret), since I was supposed to be a "boy"— and these feelings only cemented the difference I felt between what I was *supposed to be* and who *I really felt I was*.[31]

These feelings only grew more intense as he entered higher grades, where David was taunted and often isolated from other boys' play and friendships.

For dysphoric children growing up in the 1950s, "trying harder" often became a mantra. This, at a time when our social understanding of gender identity itself was rudimentary, and strictures of role were unforgiving. It is no wonder that David married, joined the military, in earnest attempts to fulfill male role obligations. And he did that twice!

But here's the problematic: even fulfilling role obligations doesn't quell the *identity issues* inside the person. So many in those decades "tried harder" to become the men they were supposed to be; and while gaining physicality, talents, position promotions, such became even stronger voices of disconnect within the self.

David's story tells us of that common "breaking point," where adults diagnosed with gender dysphoria come to the realization that not only is the dysphoria *not going away*, but that unless it's addressed, their lives (and often the lives of others) will continue in distress and agony.

However, let's not generalize here. Not *all* gender dysphorics lead lives of distress and agony. Some come more gently to the realization that they are transgender, or that they can become who they should be *only* via gender reassignment ("confirmation").[32]

For David and his second wife, the only way forward was for him to re-emerge as the inner female person whom he had always been. And this brings another point to the surface: not all gender dysphorics in marriages end in terrible straits and immediate dissolutions. Many spouses attempt to "be there" for their mates, and in fact some

---

31. Quoted from personal communications.
32. There are many that express this sentiment: Jennifer Finley Boylan, as example. See footnote [*33*], following.

stay together—often for longer than anyone predicted. Some even have long-term successes *after* the transition, having or continuing to raise families as couples.[33]

Emerging as Michelle now gave her the courage to confront the military's dismissal and challenge the dishonorable discharge, at a time when the "Don't Ask, Don't Tell" official military policy wasn't yet in place.[34]

But perhaps the most challenging part of David/Michelle's story is that of her spirituality. Born Lutheran but not a practicing Christian, Michelle recounts,

> I can't say I was religious, but I was certainly spiritual. And oh, did I pray to God to somehow take this mantle of gender away! But it soon became clear that if He was listening, it wasn't going to happen to me. God was never at fault in my mind: And that's the honest truth. If I recall the "nun moment" when I was around five, I can honestly say I kept that sentiment in my heart, tucked away somewhere in there where it was safe . . . until it blossomed later.[35]

Michelle's realization that she was drawn to a life of service came a few years after she was a woman and working for transgender justice, and yes, asking the meaning of how life "now," "as a woman," should unfold.

She was invited to an Episcopal service to speak on behalf of her work, and was overtaken by the liturgy and the spirituality of the moment. She had attended Baptist churches and Anglican churches in her youth; but it was then, there, that she felt that ancient idea of service re-germinating: "*What if life were to be devoted to doing good?*" After all, she had been through hell and back, literally, at the tail-end of the Vietnam war. After all her struggles, and her re-emergence . . . "*What was this "second chance" all about?*"

She again found her calling: A life of service and devotion!

---

33. Boylan, *She's Not There*. See also the continuing story of "Electric Dade" on YouTube ("FTM Transition: One Year on Testosterone"), who transitioned while married to his wife, and remains married.

34. "Don't ask, don't tell" was the official United States policy on military service by gays, bisexuals, and lesbians, instituted by the Clinton Administration on February 28, 1994, when Department of Defense Directive 1304.26 issued on December 21, 1993, took effect, It was in place until September 20, 2011.

35. Quoted from personal conversations.

Some Christians did suggest she was dreaming of the impossible. First, she wasn't your typical woman! To be considered *a woman* by a Christian denomination with nuns would in many ways require that their *sex*, not the *person* or their *gender*, be acknowledged first—something we know is often problematic in such situations. Moreover, whichever bishop would recommend her would be risking his reputation and possibly his credentials—assuming her application were acceptable for a postulate in a nunnery.

And yet it happened. Suffice it to conclude here that the history of becoming Sister Michelle is a testament to a clerical bishop *seeing the person*, not just *the transition*, and *discerning the spiritual call as authentic:* a calling authentic enough to enable her clerical education, her eventual dedication to a life of service, taking oaths of celibacy, chastity, and prayer; and a public blessing by a bishop. Paraphrased here for the sake of anonymity, the bishop declared,

> For a time I was concerned about her being transgender, but after watching her concern and dedication to the needy, I was willing to go forward and support her regardless of the consequences. I saw her love and faith in action. My feeling is that when Christ came to minister to us and die for us, his second commandment was to love our neighbors as ourselves. There was no exclusionary list attached to that.[36]

Not without controversy, but certainly with profundity and dignity, the testimony of this process lends credence to the fact that God is no discriminator of persons or gender.[37]

Sister Michelle's life speaks to us clearly about *not judging*, not *predicting results* for people who transition gender to nullify the dysphoria.

Christians are often eager to cite statistics that state that a good proportion of those who radically transition via hormonal and surgical reassignments end up wishing they hadn't done it; or worse, living depressed lives thereafter because they couldn't adjust to their new identity and role.[38] And while some certainly do fall into these catego-

---

36. From a conversation the bishop had with news media circa 1998, and openly shared by Sister Michelle as part of her life-history interviews. The statement here is directly from Sister Michelle, paraphrasing the bishop from printed sources she had.

37. See Isa 56:3–5, 7–8. Relate these passages to Acts 10:34; 15:8–10; Rom 10:12.

38. Drescher, "Five Myths on Being Transgender," item 4.

ries, there are many whose transition opens them up to life well lived, and yes, even a calling from God to serve.

Finally, Sister Michelle's case is also a clear example of why we shouldn't mistake *gender identity dysphoria* with such as *homosexuality* or *transvestism* (see chapter 7).

It is very much the case here that David *was never attracted to men*, but instead *tried to be a man*. David remained *heterosexual* throughout his years as a male. When he transitioned, so did his sexual orientation, however short-lived; which gives credence to the malleability of orientation prompted by identity change. But let's underscore: *sexual orientation* isn't the motivating factor in gender dysphoria. As a new woman, and briefly, Michelle dated men; but this phase was short-lived: she found her calling at about the same time.

While paradoxical to some, becoming Michelle opened the door for her calling and significant ministry to emerge. Now, there were no emotional restrictions on *living fully*. No energies being consumed by a hidden self, tortured relationships, or self-loathing. Michelle had no problem vowing to a life of celibacy and chastity in the name of serving her new-found Lord, her emerging order, and her calling.

In chapter 7 we return to this—how a transition may open the door for some to become truly *decentered*, so that Christ can become the center. However paradoxical or controversial it may seem, Sister Michelle and others are living testimonies Christ is not absent in their lives.

WHAT MUST WE LEARN FROM THESE LIVES?

Gender identity and any consequent expression of how it is embodied can take on myriad formats. There are expressions grounded on genetic, hormonal, and biological results—the sex parts, those more normative genital formats; but there are other factors. Factors such as rearing, culture norms, one's experiences and learning, which are equally formative of the specific gender framework of an individual.[39]

---

39. I quote Fausto-Sterling: "Understanding sex and gender as a developmental dynamic in which the social, the cultural, and the body [genetics, hormones, physiology] are so intertwined that if we try to disentangle them we end up losing the forest amidst the trees." Fausto-Sterling, *Sex/Gender*, 111. (Brackets mine.)

Intersex results, while small in numbers, render sexual physiology variations unique to the person. Decisions about how to move forward in these cases, we have stated, are difficult and not totally predictive of future outcomes—in terms of sex- and gender-identity. But we do hear the recommendations from ISNA to rear such a child in the most *probable gender format* that aligns with their genital form.

For yet others, those with diagnosed *gender dysphoria*, we have discussed how complex and unanswered its origins still are. And, although there are myriad rationales proposed, none yet have been scientifically or totally validated. We hear that a child's *persistence* may be temporary and may resolve in adolescence. We also hear that for some it does not, but factually worsens. We should understand the importance of family dynamics on the processes and the critical need to not make decisions out of haste or pressures, nor delay them unnecessarily. *Gender dysphoria is real*, it is diagnosable, and often immutable.

As Christians, we need to work on our conciliations with intersex and dysphoric individuals. For those struggling with gender-identity issues in children, we must urge families not to act in haste. Time and capable therapists here are truly of the essence.

We have also heard how patently wrong it is to assume that one who gender transitions loses their connection with God, or with God's calling. Emerging as the other self at times frees the person to be authentically a follower of Christ—as astounding as it may sound to those of us not of these experiences. Again, we return to some of these points in greater detail in chapter 7.

For those *gender nonconforming*, we have discussed how for some, their present manifestations are grounded in contemporary sociocultural trends of expressive individualism. These positions permit the individual to reject traditional binary formulations and provide themselves the needed autonomy to reason their own gender renditions sans any justifications except their own will. Huge questions remain for the church regarding how it will address the nonconforming.

Fausto-Sterling may have captured best our present predicaments, when she wrote the following,

> What are we to think about the future of gender? Is it disappearing (I doubt it); should there be more than two legal gender categories (possibly); do we know enough about sex and gender

to deal intelligently with a genderless future (no)? Don't societies all think (more or less) the same way about sex and gender (no)? Perhaps there are things about sex and gender that we can never know.[40]

Summing up preliminary understandings by way of this chapter, I hope it has become clear that an individual's gender-identity issues can be unique, consequently our drawing patent generalizations only hurts our ability to know in depth.

I have attempted to make those differences stand out here via parsed case histories, an effort to sort through genuine medical and psychiatrically diagnosable conditions and contrast these from ones grounded on the current cultural revolution *about* gender.

In the chapters following we dive deeper, understanding more and ferreting out how to respond to such differing outcomes. Throughout, I urge you to embrace Christian compassion and grace while we work through the tough terrain of change.

---

40. Fausto-Sterling, *Sex/Gender*, 2.

4

"Fearfully and Wonderfully Made"
Essentials of Sexual and Gender Development

> For you created my inmost being;
>   you knit me together in my mother's womb.
> I praise you because I am *fearfully* (נוֹרָאוֹת)
> and *wonderfully* (נִפְלֵיתִי) made;
>   your works are wonderful,
>   I know that full well.
>
>   Psalm 139:13–14

David, in Psalm 139:13–14, uses the Hebrew נוֹרָאוֹת *(nôrā'ōt)*, literally, *to be dreadfully afraid and awed*. The participle is a feminine plural—as to be dreadfully afraid and awed *as a woman would be afraid and awed*. Hmm ... What does it mean to be afraid and awed at the same time—as a woman would? Add to that his Hebrew נִפְלֵיתִי *(niplêtî)*, a perfect first person singular, which literally means *to be distinct, distinguished, marked out or separated* (as in unique), and we get: David, marveling in awe and fear, *so unlike* his own manly awe and fear he's pulled to revere and be astonished; but *so like* his own distinction and separation as king of the Israelites.

David's "having a moment"!

This is a combination of emotion and language idioms that can only suggest David is totally taken aback in realizing his own awesome, unique, wondrous creation by God. A set of sentiments so inexplicable as to cause shock and marvel to this manly king. He senses it with his entire being.

David also exclaimed, "My frame was not hidden from you when I was made in secret" (Ps 139:15); and "Your eyes saw my unformed body . . . when I was woven together" (v. 16). The privilege of the Creator to know our hidden knitting, our constitution, from our very beginnings.

Good deeds done in secret don't remain hidden forever (1 Tim 5:25; Mark 4:22). What was incomprehensible to David, we now have genetics and hormone chemistry to explain: *We now know a great deal about the wonders of our making!* Genetics and hormones can also help us understand when there are physical differences in outcomes, and how these come to be.

THE BIOLOGY OF OUR SEX

Most of us claim to know how fetuses become males or females: We say, "Fathers contribute an X or Y chromosome, and mothers always contribute an X." In this simple algorithm, a combination of an X and a Y chromosome produces a *male,* the Y chromosome dominating. Likewise, the combination XX produces a *female,* two XXs without a dominant Y.

Factually, *the genetic contribution of parents isn't the whole story, and certainly, these aren't the only predictors of physical (phenotypic) outcomes.*

Sexual outcomes from genetic contributions have correct results in about 98 percent of all human embryos. That is, the genetic combination inherited and recombined ultimately results in male or female organs. But, there's more to differentiating males from females than X or Y genes! So, let's continue.

The Sequence

If we assume normative genetics, our inherited genes direct the developing glandular system to produce *specific hormones.* Genes give instructions as to when to produce them, and in what quantities, so that the evolving fetus can *differentiate* male or female body parts: internal reproductive organs, and external genitals.

Initially, we all develop a sex "bud" and sex glands (officially called "gonads") both of which are *undifferentiated:* the glands and that "bud" can go "either way," becoming *testicles* or becoming *ovaries; penises* or *clitorises,* etc. There is also a "genital groove" that forms; and it will either stay open, or close up.

The developing fetus also produces internal connecting structures—two sets, actually—one of which will either develop or atrophy, depending on which way the hormones tell these to go: "Become male" or "Become female."

It is the case, then, that we are all created with dual potential, "dual plumbing"; and it is the action of hormones on these structures that will determine the outcomes, glands and organs.[1]

Take a minute to ponder the depth of this: the idea that all of us as procreated human beings start as undifferentiated; we then develop dual potential and plumbing—*in effect an androgynous fetal framework*—before we become one or the other! See Figure 1 at the end of the chapter.

This is a far cry from the assumption that we are male or female from the beginning. We are literally, potentially, "male *and* female" before we become male *or* female.[2] To get the possible implications, we ought to read Genesis 1:27 and 5:2, in the context of Biblical Hebrew!

Let's first quote the Genesis 5:2 verse from the NIV: "He created them male and female and blessed them. And he named them 'Mankind' [*ādām*, "the human being"] when they were created." This is a near-verbatim repeat of Genesis 1:27 in the phrasing of "male and female he created them." For Christians who don't relate to biblical Hebrew, it's unknown that these verses, despite all their brevity, are complex to translate—the original Hebrew escaping any easy

---

1. This is sometimes an unfamiliar fact. Every embryo forms with "dual plumbing," and sex glands, developing genitals that embody the potential for becoming *either* male or female organs. "In the beginning, male *and* female (not *or!*) . . ." takes on a new meaning! This initial "duality" is present regardless of chromosomal type (XX or XY). Hormone action differentiates the sex of the fetus by "cancelling out" one system and "encouraging" the other. But "in the beginning," we are all *both* male *and* female in potential before we become one or the other!

2. Arnold, "A General Theory of Sexual Differentiation," 291–300. For hermeneutical clues in the biblical texts referenced, see Trible, *God and the Rhetoric of Sexuality,* 1–17; 60–72.

understanding. Thus, we often bypass these accounts of human creation and concentrate on the more known account, in which woman is created from man in Genesis 2:21–23. We miss the deeper meaning of the conjunctive *"and."*[3]

Part of the issue is the lack of punctuation in biblical Hebrew, fluctuations between singular and plural, and use of conjunctions, all of which can change the understanding of a statement when we try to translate it. Not to get too detailed here—but it *is* necessary to provide some detail: while the conjunction *"and"* (as translated) can be rendered "male *and* female" to mean the joining of two nouns, it can also mean *"and"* as in the blending of *two qualities*.

As example, Genesis 2:17, where the verse literally reads (in Hebrew) "But-from-tree-of-the-knowledge-of good and-evil not you shall-eat-from-it." The English translation treats the conjunction as simply joining two words and phrases. But in Genesis 2:17, the conjunction joins the two knowledges that eating from the tree of life could give—"knowledge-of good *and*-evil." Both are joined as a *conjunctive conjunction*—which in simple English means they join here two similar essences, a *connective* relationship, not just a *contrastive* one (highlighting differences). Good and evil can certainly be viewed as contrasts, but they run along a *spectrum*, and thus represent end-points of the essence being highlighted—knowledge. The same conjunctive conjunction is in Genesis 1:27 and 5:2. The translation can never be "male *or* [אוֹ] female," since that is an *alternative conjunction*, which only highlights differences that are highly distinct and "separate."

Genesis 1–2 certainly play on both unity and differentiation, similarities and differences, but the most important element to note here is that "and" conjunction. In conservative Judaism, the question is asked: *What is the creation of the first human male and female all about?* Can the text(s) be read to reflect, and at the same time help us to understand what science is telling us about our early beginnings?

One rabbinical tradition holds that the first human was a *golem* [גלם]—an undifferentiated, perhaps ungendered being. This "*undifferentiated* Adam"[4] is created in God's image, who is *sexless* and

---

3. See conjunction reference information at https://uhg.readthedocs.io/en/latest/conjunction.html.

4. In Genesis 1, *'ādām* means "humankind" and refers to the collective human

genderless, because *God has no sex and no gender*. It is when Adam is separated into *'ish* (man) and *'ishshah* (woman) in 2:21–25 that two sexes are created. The interpretation illustrates how, in the rabbinic period, certain ideals about sexual and gender differences were understood. Whether this interpretation is what the author had in mind, or not, we'll have to wait to ask God in person "on that day."

Important to note, none the less, is that although the above rendition doesn't imagine a world where people identify as *both* male and female, the creation story is more about our initial *"and"* duality; our potentiality to become *either*. It's about our similarities, complementarities, "bone of my bone and flesh of my flesh" (Gen 2:23). All of this, science seems to have validated brilliantly in the last decade of the genome project.

The Outcomes

With *androgen* from the adrenals and eventual *testosterone* production from testicles, males will grow an outward penis and foreskin, and genital grooves will close and fuse together, making a scrotal sac possible. The descending sex glands, once in the body cavity, now morphed into testicles to be housed in that scrotum, drop into it.

Internally one set of "plumbing" (the female-coded one) will disintegrate via an added gonadal hormone (AMII), and the male plumbing will fully develop.[5] Along with it, men differentiate several male-specific internal organs, such as seminal vesicles (to house sperm), and a precious prostate (to pump them out).

With *estrogen*, females stay "open" and will "groove further inward," in-growing a vaginal canal. It will connect with the forming uterus. The genital folds will become labia, and that little "bud" will become a clitoris and hood, instead of a penis and foreskin. The

---

race gendered as male and female. In Genesis 2–3, *'ādām* appears with the definite article, and means "the human" *(hā-'ādām)*. There is no particular gender implied until "woman" is created in Genesis 2:22–23. Here, "the human" is made distinct as "man/husband" *('ish)* and "woman/wife" *('ishah)*. Beginning in Genesis 2:25 and depending on the translation, the first couple is called "the human and his wife," or "the woman and her husband." Of course, the Hebrew is clearer than most English translations as to what is meant.

5. Males need the Anti-Müllerian-Hormone (AMH) to cancel out female internal organ development. It is produced in special (Sertoli) cells of the developing testicles.

gonads become ovaries and stay in the body proper, eventually linking with that formed uterus via newly developed fallopian tubes.

What was "male plumbing" will atrophy without testosterone and AMH, and female internal structures will grow into place on their own, *without adding a thing.*

After birth, when the time is right for puberty, the now distinct sex glands are prompted to produce more of the correct hormones in the right quantities by the pituitary gland. Pubescent men will start to show *male secondary sex characteristics*—they grow their genitals, musculature, and later beards, body hair; even maybe start balding. Adolescent women will begin their *hormonal cycling*, thus beginning first menstruation (called *menarche).* They grow breasts, and their body contours also change accordingly—wider hips, a tad more fatty tissue (for future baby-padding), and greater pain tolerance, readying them for possible childbirth.

ARE RESULTS ALWAYS MALE OR FEMALE?

In some way or another, we've all heard portions of this development sequence: we nod and affirm that the products of biology—genetics and hormones—are *always male or always female.* We assume and often get stuck with the either/or, "black/white" dichotomy.

However, there are many chromosomal and hormonal results that tie into what *body sex* one eventually develops, meaning both internal and external reproductive organs, both of which may not fit the binary chromosomal XX, XY schema at all.

The results are not always "male" or "female"! Even if results fit a chromosome scheme, there may still be sexual ambiguities, mainly due to hormone action.

And this is where it gets difficult: what counts as *intersex* can have *broad variation,* some with so noticeably atypical internal and external genitalia that specialists may be called in to figure out, exactly, what the child's sex "is." Other newborns can have very subtle forms of anatomical variants, some of these not showing up until as late as puberty. But the idea that intersexed bodies are "aberrations" or "defects" comes from our ignorance of what is a truth: *that in* procreation *there are more outcomes than two complementary, binary forms.* There are also many *androgyne* formats that can result.[6]

Resulting Alternate Formats

I'll review the more common ones here, to underscore that in *procreation*[7] sex differentiation doesn't always result in conformingly male or female sexual bodies.[8] Please consult Figure 2 as well, at the conclusion of this chapter.

In *Turner Syndrome,* the female often receives only one sex gene, an X, or as it is biologically parsed most often, "XO." The female can also receive extra genetic material from an abnormally formed Y chromosome (an "isodicentric Y," or "*idic*Y"). That *idic*Y does not contribute to the female's differentiation as male, but does create infertility.[9] Turner's is rare, about 1:2500 females have this occurrence. But when it happens, females are sterile, usually due to not developing ovaries or a uterus, sometimes both; sometimes only rudimentary internal organs.

---

6. *Androgyne* is the noun form of *androgynous,* a term used to denote a person with intersex genitalia. It is also used in contemporary speech to denote a person who is non-binary in gender identity. Here, I am using the term as defining the resulting forms that reproductive organs and the body proper may take, *beyond* the binary "male" or "female" outcomes commonly expected.

7. I distinguish *creation* from *procreation* on purpose, since creation as a descriptor term should refer only to God forming Adam and Eve and giving them life. *Procreation is the human form of reproduction,* and is not a "creation" in the same sense as that of Adam and Eve. In *procreation* we move the first creation forward through the sharing of genetic material which engages, then, a succession of human life. See chapter 7 for a full discussion of the importance of this difference.

8. The information that follows comes from a variety of sources: medical, endocrinological, psychological/psychiatric, as well as from my teaching on the subject for decades. Although most of this information is now readily available via medical online sources, I have especially consulted the following: for Turner and Klinefelter syndromes, see Rachna, "Differences between Turner and Klinefelter Syndromes"; for AIS, see US National Library of Medicine, "Androgen Insensitivity Syndrome"; for Mixed Gonadal Dysgenesis, see Cincinnati Children's Hospital, "Mixed Gonadal Dysgenesis Symptoms and Causes." The most recent review of sexual dimorphism comes from Blackless et al., "How Sexually Dimorphic Are We?" 51–166. (Here, researchers reviewed numeric estimates in studies from 1955–98 to estimate frequencies of sex variations.) Finally, Callahan, *Between XX and XY,* offers a comprehensive review of the biology and history of sex differences.

9. The combination of an X and an Isodicentric Y is parsed as "46, X *idic*Y." The fetus remains otherwise normal aside from the disruptions caused by Turner's.

As these females develop after birth, one can note several differences, including under-development (short stature), a "webbed neck" in some; and during puberty, undeveloped/ underdeveloped breasts, and often, no menstruation. Congenital conditions, cardiovascular and other issues may also be present, but not always. The female born with Turner's looks normal in external genitalia, but her internal organ structures may be different.

A condition that is often confused with Turner Syndrome is *Mixed Gonadal Dysgenesis* (MGD), which can result from either XO (Turner female) or XY (male) chromosomal pairing. *Dysgenesis* means abnormal organ development during embryonic growth and differentiation, and such can produce female-trending or male-trending genitals; or even a combination of the two. In MGD, chromosome and hormone instructions most often form two different sex glands: an undescended testicle on one side and an improperly developed gonad (should have been an ovary) on the opposite. This pairing of glands can't produce the right hormones for normal sexual differentiation in the womb; so frequently, the result is malformed sex organs.

MGD is one of the more common nonbinary sexual outcomes, and the second most common reason for *ambiguous genitals* (1:20,000 births).[10] When the results are a "blend" of genital forms, it is obvious from the moment of birth that this child is *intersex*, making it difficult to classify them as "boys" or "girls." (Intersex can also result from other chromosomal or hormonal coding instructions.)

Children with MGD will be normal in other body forms, *except* that they—like in Turner's—may not mature sexually without treatment. For those born with intersex genitalia, we discuss parental options for either maintenance or surgeries in chapter 5.

In *Klinefelter Syndrome*, instead of having XY chromosomes, males inherit XXY, or a *trisomy* of sex chromosomes (1:500–1000 births).[11] The "extra X" does push the differentiation to a more feminine appearance, although male genitals may be present and complete. Noticeably smaller testes at birth may be an indication of this condition. Internally, most Klinefelter males have under- or undeveloped organs, like absent seminal vesicles (the storage vessels for sperm) or

---

10. Cincinnati Children's Hospital, "Mixed Gonadal Dysgenesis," par. 1.

11. Intersex Society of North America (ISNA), "How Common is Intersex?" par. 4.

vas deferens (connecting ducts that move sperm from the testicles up to the vesicles). Thus, these males are often sterile.

As they enter puberty, such boys will grow lankier and taller than most, some with decidedly feminine characteristics—larger hip-to-shoulder ratios, longer limbs; some will have enlarged breast tissue, all due to lower production of testosterone from smaller testes. The overall physical appearance will be male, even though in some, voice pitch may be higher and an absence of eventual body and facial hair may give the male a more feminine appearance. Additional testosterone support may be needed.

Three more alternate outcomes are worthy of note: the first two are related to *androgen insensitivity syndrome* (AIS); and the third to *congenital adrenal hyperplasia* (CAH).

Infants born with *complete* AIS (cAIS) are genetically male (XY), but their bodies—at the cellular level—cannot respond to androgens/ testosterone *at all*. Thus, the forming body isn't capable of using whatever adrenal androgens are being produced to differentiate into male. Later, testicular testosterone (if these are present, however rudimentary or hidden) is also not responded to. Thus, both *before* and *after* birth, this XY male forms and looks like a female.

Complete AIS is a rare condition (2–5:100,000), but there are many who have *mild forms* of *AIS*, partial androgen insensitivity syndrome, or pAIS (formally, Reifenstein Syndrome, 1:13,000 births).[12] These can have genitals that look typically female, or genitals that have both male and female characteristics. These can even be born with typical male genitals, and the condition may not reveal itself fully until puberty, when the body refuses to complete its full differentiation. In chapter 5, I detail some of the challenges in assigning a gender of rearing specifically to pAIS infants.

Congenital Adrenal Hyperplasia (CAH) limits the enzymes needed to produce steroid hormones.[13] While forms of CAH can vary, the

---

12. Intersex Society of North America, "How Common is Intersex?" par. 4. In partial androgen insensitivity (pAIS) there is a change in the gene that recognizes and uses male hormones. This syndrome is passed down (inherited) from the mother's X chromosome that carries the mutation. To note, every female child has a 50 percent chance of carrying the defective gene—consequently family history is important in determining the risk for pAIS.

13. CAH is an inherited condition caused by mutations in genes that code for enzymes involved in making steroid hormones in the adrenal glands. Both parents can

one affecting sexual development is the "classic" CAH, which results in excess production of male sex hormones in women (from adrenal androgens and ovarian testosterone—1:13,000 births).[14]

While in the womb, CAH can cause masculinization of the genitals in XX females: an enlarged clitoris, fused labia that look like a scrotum, and malformed internal structures. Keep in mind that in normal female development *in utero,* there is little exposure to androgens or testosterone.[15]

With *classic CAH,* added exposure of male hormones from the adrenal glands is sufficient to disturb the effects of estrogen, the female hormone, consequently disrupting differentiation of female sexual organs. In other cases, CAH causes ambiguous genitalia, or intersex conditions in XX females.

CAH can also be the cause of significant illnesses related to the lack of other steroids not produced. Possible illnesses include *adrenal crises*; *blood pressure regulation issues*; *blood sugar, potassium and sodium level issues.* Children with CAH thus need *stat* initial diagnoses, treatment, and subsequent monitoring to preserve health and quality of life.

A WORD ON HORMONES, ENVIRONMENTAL INFLUENCES, AND BEHAVIOR

Understanding the effects of hormones on the developing brain is a continuing investigation. However, we do know that fetal hormones program the brain differently in males and females with respect to *the timing* of hormone production (a cycle in females, and no cycle *per se* in males); in the ability of tissue to later react to hormonal stimulation (as in puberty, where females are more precocious and thus mature earlier than males); in pain thresholds; and in some functions.[16]

None of these "knowns" should make us believe that the differences are so large as to insinuate one is *superior* or *more capable* than

---

carry the mutation, and both parents with a mutation are necessary for the condition to show up in their children. Such children have one in four chances of CAH.

14. Intersex Society of North America, "How Common is Intersex?" par. 4.

15. Kallak et al., "Maternal and Fetal Testosterone," 1–2.

16. Lippa, *Gender, Nature, and Nurture,* 11–22. See also, Berenbaum and Beltz, "Sexual Differentiation," 183–200; and Fausto-Sterling, *Sex/Gender,* 27–42.

the other. None should also make us infer that there is some sort of "gender coding" going on prenatally, since it has been demonstrated that what happens *postnatally*—variations in socialization, infant care, and social contacts—have much more influence on gender outcomes.[17] Biology's influence on gender is still hotly debated.

Thus, more to our interest is the well-established fact that *environmental influences* (that is, learning behaviors, social interactions, and experiences) impact most directly the template people eventually use to self-identify and behave as men or as women.[18] Even the effects of chromosome or hormone irregularities in the womb have *not* been established to "cause" or "influence" gender identity.

Gender identity depends largely on social-cultural influences after birth and the social experiences of the developing child, not biology alone.[19]

Fetal hormones don't directly affect *sexual orientation* (whom one is erotically attracted to) either, given the results of many studies on the subject—some since the 1970s when John Money and Anke Ehrhardt first took up the question.[20] More recently, a Penn State study by Sheri Berenbaum and colleagues revealed that *even* girls that had been exposed in the womb to androgen (male hormone) because of Congenital Adrenal Hyperplasia—recall, a genetic condition—didn't develop male gender identities. Neither did they "play more with boys," nor "like girls" (as in a sexual orientation).[21] We'll touch more on this in chapters 5 and 6.

To recap here: innate influences on how gender identity is formed are still hotly debated, but not at all established outright by scientists. Researchers like Paul McHugh, M.D., Professor of Psychiatry at Johns Hopkins School of Medicine, have consistently doubted there is a

---

17. Hines, *Brain Gender*, 145–54. Ultimately, Hines concludes that there simply isn't enough evidence to suggest that gender differences are grounded in innate biological or genetic factors. Those who do argue for such evidence tend to generalize finding from *quasi-experiments*, which only produce presumptive results.

18. Rosenblum, *The Study of Masculinity/Femininity*, 150–56. See also Money and Ehrhardt, *Man, Woman, Boy and Girl*.

19. Ehrhardt and Meyer-Bahlburg, "Effects of Prenatal Sex Hormones," 1312–18. See also Deaux, "Psychological Constructions," 289–303.

20. Money and Ehrhardt, "Gender Dimorphic Behavior," 367–91. See also Money and Ehrhardt, *Man & Woman, Boy & Girl*.

21. Berenbaum et al., "Gendered Peer Involvement in Girls with CAH," 1112–14.

biological "cause" for gender orientation or identity. "If it were obvious," he said to *Reuters* in a recent interview, "they [the scientists studying it] would have found it long ago."[22]

In sum, any of the variations discussed here can influence outcomes of our chromosomal inheritance; alter hormonal instructions; and consequently, produce a variegation of genital and internal organ results. Recognizing that there is *more* to what nature produces *in procreation* than strictly *male* or *female* formats is important in understanding how some of the differences interact with the development of *gender identity* in our world of social constructions.

THE BODY AND GENDER IDENTITY DEVELOPMENT

For most of us, genital and body forms initially link us to one of the two most common biological outcomes (male/female); outcomes that then trigger how we are *socialized* and *enculturated* into gender-appropriate scripts. This is the learning most of us initially get from our culture, through our parents and significant others, as to how we ought to understand ourselves as men or women. We learn to behave accordingly, within the learned boundaries of feelings, behaviors, and identifiers culturally specified for our sex.

Early on, most of us will also identify ourselves as either male or female based on the descriptions of anatomy we get from these scripts, how we view our genitals, and how we internalize their meanings.

The "formation" of gender as a socialized construction of one's identity, then, does not often occur independent from the maturing body; quite the opposite: most cultures emphasize that a child's sex should be concordant with the learning that *enables* that sex to function *within prescriptions the culture has established for it.*

And as the body matures, this consonance both reinforces gender identity and gender-role behaviors. There isn't a direct effect from chromosomes and hormones; but there is an *indirect effect* through how the culture "sees" that body and, eventually, how the person also learns to see it.

---

22. Trotta, "Born This Way?" para. 32. (Brackets mine.)

In simple terms, once you have been assigned a "sex of birth," most, if not all your learning in life will be embedded within the cultural script that fits your genitals.

As this happens, and as the body matures, the person—remember for the 98 percent of us with normed genitals—begins to identify their self as the sex that they are *assigned*—male or female—and learns to *act* like it: *masculine* or *feminine*.[23] Gender identity, in this view, is the unfolding and internalization of that self-perception.

Normatively, self-identification as male comes as a byproduct of the developing body "telling you" you are male, and as society underscores that view via its *scripts* for males. Plus, society often "demands" that you *act like one,* whatever that means in the culture.

Similarly, self-identification as a woman comes as the body changes, and society teaches you what script to follow *as a woman.* Society will also "demand" that you *act like a woman,* whatever that means in the culture.

This push to *biological* polarization also produces a *cultural* polarization of roles, and consequently, promotes gendered identities that foster concordance (agreement) between body and mind. As we've intimated earlier, most cultures generally require this concordance of its members.

OTHERS THAN "BINARY OTHER"

Recorded history *also* tells us that there are individuals who do not seem to "fit" into that required concordance.

We know, for example, that established cultures of long ago have left records of individuals who crossed these anatomical

---

23. Becoming *cisgender* (meaning, heteronormative) as a process of gender self-identification seems seamless enough for much of the human population. We identify with the assigned sex, start to recognize the specific body form that corresponds to it, accept it tacitly and then explicitly; and go on to internalize the conception with great concordances. What we often *do not realize* is that the socialization process is all the while *scripting this out for us* in ways subtle and direct—both ways, enough for most of us to get the points and adhere to them. Willingly. The *cisgender model*, once internalized, makes it difficult for individuals to see the world otherwise; to recognize that there are *men* who, for instance, don't see themselves as men; or who question their masculinity in ways that aren't just non-conforming deficits, but rather, as unnatural for them.

©Creative Commons Attribution 3.0 Unported License. Illustration from Connexions, http://cnx.org/content/col11496/1.6/ 2013.

boundaries—either because of physical differences (not known then as genetic or hormonal); or because they just didn't, indeed couldn't, agree that they were the sex they were born into. *In these cases, gender identity did not correspond to the sexual body, and many times to the roles these demanded.*

As a great example, in ancient rabbinical Judaism, persons who were identified in the Talmud as *tûmtûm* (טומטום) were neither male nor female or were both male *and* female (intersex); and those *'andrôgînôs* (אנדרוגינוס) were hermaphrodites. Both are also mentioned in the Tosefta (a compilation of Jewish laws from the second century).[24] Sages also recognized a *sārîs* (סָרִיס), a feminine man, often a *eunuch*; and an *'aylônît* (איילונית), a masculine woman.

Such persons were not ostracized from the community, but in fact were encouraged to participate in communal life, even though there were some restrictions placed on Torah readings, inheritance, the priesthood, and whom they could marry (Tosefta Megillah 2.7).[25]

It is in the Mishnah proper that "An *androgynos* is in some respects legally equivalent to men, and in some respects, legally equivalent to women; in some respect legally equivalent to [both] men and women . . ." (Mishnah Bikkurim 4.1, 5).[26] Judaic legal standings for intersex individuals were protected, with a death penalty for those who hurt, slandered, or in other ways harmed them.

Even more poignantly, if a child was born as a *tûmtûm* or an *'andrôgînôs*, the father could claim them as a male or as a female or as who they were—*tûmtûm or 'andrôgînôs*—and not lose any opportunity to be regarded as a pious man, a Nazir(ite), or ascetic Jew (Mishnah Nazir 2.7).[27] There was no stigma attached to parents of intersex children, nor were there efforts to "conform" the child to a binary gender via *any* Judaic law.

24. Cohen, "Tumtum and Androgynous," 1–11. The *Torah* is the Ten Commandments and Laws of the Jewish faith. It is the sacred inscribing of the words of YHWH. The *Mishnah* is considered the rabbinical interpretations of the Torah. The *Talmud* aggregates historical rabbinical conversations about the laws of the Mishnah. The *Tosefta* was a supplement, an addition to the Mishnah. All are regarded as canonical and included in the list of sacred books, officially accepted as authoritative in Judaism. See Israel, *Jewish Sacred Texts*, 1–4.

25. Cohen, "Tumtum and Androgynous," 1–11. See also Shoshana, *Tosefta Megillah*.

26. Cohen, "Tumtum and Androgynous," 1–11.

27. Cohen, "Tumtum and Androgynous," 1–11.

Societies made "room," and some still make "room," for such individuals. Some cultures even highly regard intersex and transgender, bestowing on them magical powers or honors because of their "particular natures."[28] The gendered roles these individuals either carved out for themselves, or were allowed, show a great range of physical bodies, identities, and behaviors.

Whatever the case, we should know that the challenges to "biology as destiny" and equally to "gender identity as prescribed" have been around as long as polar bodies and polar identities have.[29]

None of this justifies either "biology as destiny" or "identity as choice"; but it does underscore that the dilemma we now face socially with gender—how to understand biological variety and, most important, the social constructions of this variety—*is not a totally new issue*. The new problematic centers around what to do when people start to acknowledge the impacts of both and seek reconciliations, recognition of alternatives, and equality.

Maria Patiño's and Caster Semenya's Dubiousness

Let me illustrate with two contemporary cases, each well documented globally: María Patiño, once Spain's top female hurdler and Olympic contender in 1988;[30] and the current case of track and field Olympian contender Caster Semenya (2009, ongoing).[31] I'll start with María Patiño.

---

28. We have records of intersex persons, and others not fitting a binary male or female form, in Old Babylonian texts and terracotta plaques (c.1894 BC–c.1595 BC). Some plaques graphically display sex-ambiguous or intersexed individuals. Ancient Near Eastern cuneiform texts of that period also mention individual's roles, titles, and the terms that defined their sexual and/or gender ambiguity. Many worked in palace administration and other governmental roles. Descriptions testify these individuals were not necessarily of low status. For an intriguing read, see Peled, "Masculinities and Third Gender." We also have ancient Greek hermaphrodites, well represented in statuary and vases, from the seventh to the fifth century BC. We have Roman hermaphroditic statuary galore; and we have modern-day *hijras* in India, *berdaches* in Native American cultures, the Tongan *fakaleiti*, the Tahitian *mahu*, and the Samoan *fa'fafine*. For these, see Bader, "Third Genders," par. 3.

29. See for instance, Lee Bader's historical review, "Third Genders," in *The Evolution of Human Sexuality*.

30. Martínez-Patiño, "Personal Account," 538.

31. Longman, "Understanding the Controversy over Caster Semenya."

María had given twelve years to competitive sports and had risen to make Spain's Olympic team—she was that good. On her way to the World Games in Kobe, María forgot to bring her medical certificate, one that validated what would seem obvious: that she was a woman.

Having no certificate available wasn't a problem: María could (and did) report to the Femininity Control Head Office of the testing station at the Games, have her cheek swabbed for DNA, and that would be it. (She did just that.)

Then came the call a few hours later that there were incorrect results from the test. A second test ensued, also a pelvic exam with X-rays; and then the news: María's karyotype included a Y chromosome, and behind her labia were small, hidden testes. She had no ovaries and was absent a uterus.

Even though María looked like a woman, was brought up as a woman, identified as a woman, had a woman's strength, body shape, and all the morphological features of a woman, to the Games Committee she was not a woman. Frankly, in 1988, they didn't know exactly *what to call her*. Thus, she was barred from competing and representing Spain in the country's team.

María was then twenty-four. She had never had a period, but credited twelve years of sports for suspending her hormonal cycling; a condition (*athletic amenorrhea*) that happens often to elite female athletes. Her prior vaginal exams (she *had* a vagina!) always turned out normal. Now, she was spending thousands consulting physicians about her condition.

She discovered she had been born with *androgen insensitivity*, which, as I've explained, does not allow the body of an XY, at the cellular level, to use testosterone produced by any testicles. She was *intersex*—having both male and female formats, despite the XY karyotype. "When I was conceived, my tissue never heard the hormonal messages to become a male."[32]

In utero, the inability of testosterone absorption generated female sexual forms for María but didn't cancel out gonads turning into testicles. As a pubescent child, she had been producing testosterone, but her body's inability to absorb and use it never cancelled out the estrogen that testes also produce, thus morphing María with female

32. Martínez-Patiño. "Personal Account," 538.

secondary sexual characteristics that blossomed then: breasts, wider hips, female body contours, etc.

And so, despite her Y chromosome and "hidden" testes, Maria developed physically and grew up as a woman, a female who had always identified as being *her*. "Growing up, neither my family nor I had any idea that I was anything other than female. I went to the best doctors, I attended all appointments."[33] And, up to the point of karyotype testing, all her doctors confirmed *she was a woman*.

The news cost her dearly. Alison Carlson, summing up athletic issues with chromosomal testing, summed up Patiño's odyssey:

> After her diagnosis of complete androgen insensitivity and an XY chromosome complement was leaked to the press, Patiño's sports career as a hurdler was over; she was thrown off the national team and out of the athletes' residence. People pointed at her on the street, friends disappeared. She lost her fiancée. She went into hiding, trying to cope with the knowledge that she would never have children. "If I hadn't been an athlete, my femininity would never have been questioned," she said. "What happened to me was like being raped. It must be the same sense of violation and shame. Only in my case, the whole world watched."[34]

We can argue, like the Games Committee did, that chromosomal inheritance determines all about the person—but that argument doesn't stick when you are confronted with an *intersex* individual. They can be *both* male and female physically. *But are they both otherwise?*

In María's case, she is *female* in abundance in her physical form; and she is *female* in her rearing *as a woman*, her experiences *as a woman*, and her *gender identity* as a woman. She has always thought of herself *as a woman*, and sexually she is a *heterosexual woman* who had fallen in love with a heterosexual man.

Caster Semenya is a South African runner who has always identified as a woman. Once on the global scene at eighteen, now over a decade ago, Semenya was increasingly subjected to more physical scrutiny than probably any other current female athlete. Her agility in track and field, her consistent wins, quickly surpassed all female runners in modern history. Thus, speculations began—about her

---

33. Martínez-Patiño. "Personal Account," 538.
34. Carlson, "Essay: Suspect Sex," 539–42.

anatomy ("She doesn't *look* like a woman"), her gender ("Is she *really* female?"); some calling her a man, while other doubting her being a woman: "Maybe she's a woman, but not 100 percent," stated Pierre Weis, general secretary of the International Association of Athletics Federation's (IAAF) track and field governance.[35]

All this scrutiny led to a battery of tests imposed by the IAAF, designed to determine whether Semenya should be allowed to race *as a woman*. While the results of Semenya's tests have not been officially made public, information was leaked out. Tests showed Semenya had higher levels of testosterone than normal for women, a condition called *hyperandrogenism*.[36] (This is one condition of the many I've discussed under the label, *disorders of sexual development*, or DSD.) Semenya's body was then relentlessly analyzed by the media and armchair gender experts globally, some claiming she was a "hermaphrodite" (a term I've already mentioned is stigmatizing and misleading). Others, calling Semenya "a man trying to compete with women."[37]

The IAAF eventually ruled that female runners with testosterone above a certain level would have to take medications to lower it, to compete against other women in track and field events. The International Olympics Committee quickly followed with their own similar policy.[38]

Semenya's story isn't just about issues with female athletes and fairness; it's about when athletes—and their bodies—don't conform to normative ideas about what women are all about. "Certain bodies are never allowed to be female, are never allowed to be women, are never allowed to just *be*," stated Pidgeon Pagonis, co-founder of the Intersex Justice Project.[39]

Semenya's higher testosterone isn't necessarily nor always an advantage, as the arbitration panel duly noted in its conclusion. Other conditions in women (and men) may provide greater advantage

---

35. Longman, "Understanding the Controversy over Caster Semenya," 1.

36. Xavier and McGill, "Hyperandrogenism and Intersex Controversies in Women's Olympics," 3902. See also USA Today, "Hyperandrogenism Explained and What It Means for Athletics."

37. North, "I Am a Woman and I Am Fast," 2.

38. International Association of Athletics Federation, "2011 IAAF Regulations," 2011; International Olympics Committee, "2012 IOC Regulations on Female Hyperandrogenism," 2012.

39. Pagonis, "I Am a Woman and I Am Fast," 1.

than elevated testosterone, such as those that increase hemoglobin levels 50 percent higher than normal. Or, like Kenyan and Ethiopian athletes, that train and live at altitudes that naturally enhance their oxygen-carrying capacity.[40] Many physical characteristics give people an advantage in sports, but none have ever been demanded to change those characteristics or take medications to suppress them. Swimmer Michael Phelps has exceptionally long arms, which gives him an advantage in his sport, "but nobody's suggesting that his arms should be shortened."[41]

Caster Semenya's story is evidence of the discrimination people face when they seem to defy sex and gender norms. She has never identified as intersex; she was raised as a woman, identifies as a woman, has always lived as a woman; and devoted her life, like María Patiño, to excellence in sports. In Semenya's own words, "God made me the way I am, and I accept myself. I am who I am, and I'm proud of myself."[42] It would seem unjust and cruel to prohibit her from future Olympics because of her natural constitution.

It would seem humane and correct, then, to accord both María and Caster their *right to be a woman*. It seems correct to also reinforce enduring statements in rabbinical traditions, YHWH's words, and Jesus' own behavior, that all persons must be treated with dignity and respect; all being *b'tzelem 'Elohîm*, "in God's image" and destined to receive God's blessings (Isa 56:1–8).

SUMMING UP

We've unpacked the embryology of reproduction and noted that aside from complementary male and female forms, in procreation genetics and hormones also give rise to *alternative formats*, formats that we've argued are equally expressive of imago Dei and equally deserving of our love and inclusion.

We've detailed them here. We've seen how genetic contributions and the effects of genetics and hormones can yield body morphologies that at times *don't conform to a binary model—at all*. I've tried

---

40. Longman, "Understanding the Controversy over Caster Semenya," 1.
41. Pagonis, "I Am a Woman and I Am Fast," 3.
42. Longman, "Understanding the Controversy over Caster Semenya," 3.

to simply explain the different conditions that have been medically named in order to give labels to such, *not* to make them stand out as aberrations. We have *all* been "fearfully and wonderfully made."

I've noted that tie-ins to *gender identity* aren't the result of genetics or hormones *per se;* and even though these set up a template for the sexual body proper, it is *social learning* and a person's *experiences* that help *develop and internalize a self-conception sexually, bodily, of who we are* . . . or are supposed to be.

Gender as a social construction is explained here so we can in subsequent chapters turn to the scriptures and correct some misconceptions concerning *roles* as divinely constructed. I've argued for liberating our ideas of what constitutes *roles* and *identity* from imagined ideals, which are supposed to be in the Bible proper. I've focused our attention on how our culture, our socialization, in fact produces *gendered selves*. Chapter 7 will expand these points more.

Such understandings do not disparage a biblical theology of the body, which argues for the essentiality of the body in self-identification. However, they do correct the idea that it is *only the body* that is involved in gender-identity formation. I have outlined how, in *procreation*, the binary product can be *further differentiated* by the very nature of reproduction.

Thus, possibilities for variations and for *intersex* individuals are real. These, as with the binary, must work to reconcile body with identity—and this is not done, in either case, outside the context of culture and social experiences.

A biblical theology of the body that embraces only body essentialism in its binary formats isn't complete. It defaults on other formats resulting from reproduction, and offers no acknowledgement of the social elements involved in their identification. It leaves out *other* essentialisms—those of biological variability, and the significant role culture has in shaping identity.

It's a fact that there are *many other bodies* formatted along the lines of God's allowances in human procreation. And it is also a fact that there are many influences that come to bear on how that body—*any body*—is internalized into an identity.

Such may be new thinking for many Christians, and for some it may seem heretical. But the facts of our *procreation* are clear: not everyone winds up being strictly "male" or "female."

As we'll see in chapter 7, some in Christianity would rather catapult these outcomes into the box of "aberrations" resulting from the fall into sin; but I have a liberating alternative in that chapter . . . one that does not denigrate procreated differences!

We started this chapter with psalmist David extolling his creation by God in Psalm 139. We are now able to understand through biology and the sciences what was once "made in secret"—now revealed to exclaim human variability. *"And God saw all that He had made, and it was very good"* (Gen 1:31).

Figure 1. Differentiation of Reproductive System into Male and Female Structures

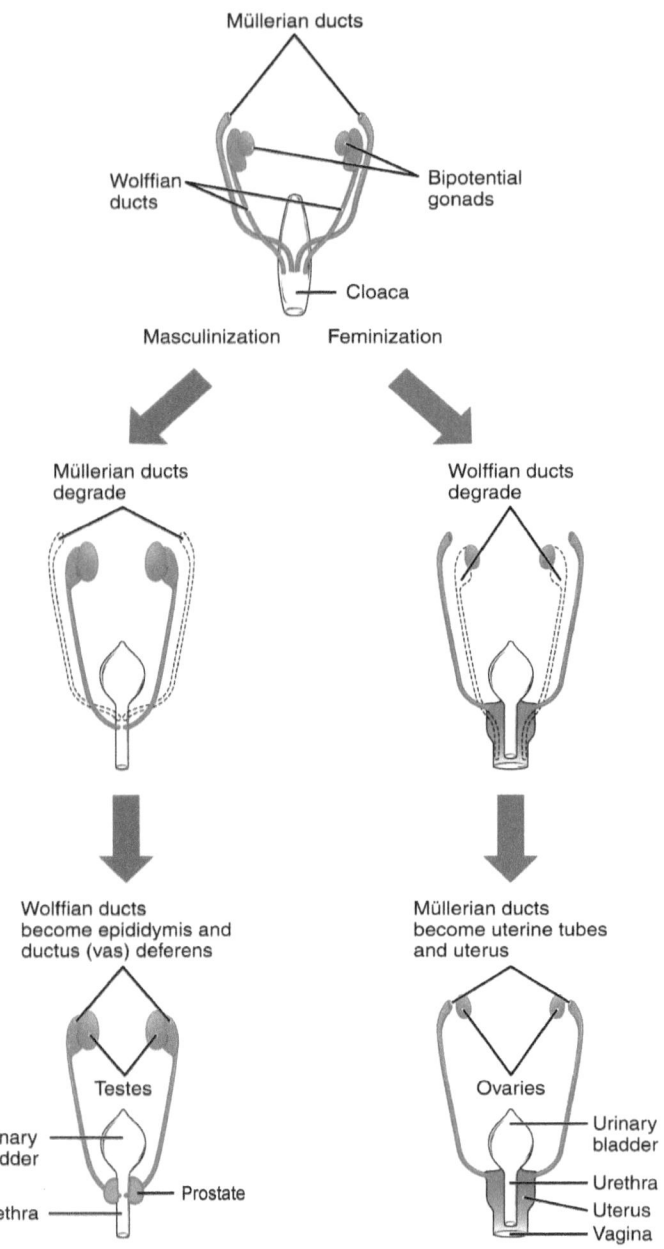

Figure 2. Chromosome Contributions, Normal and Syndromes

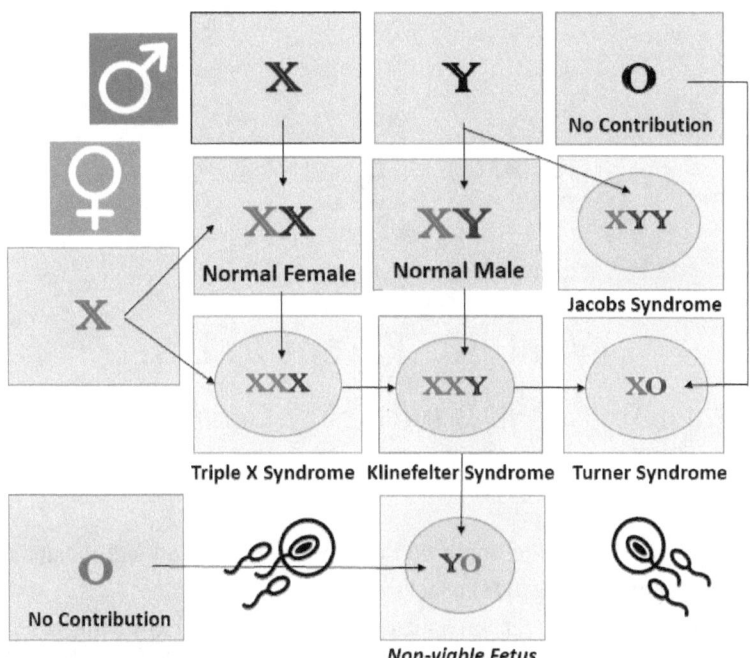

Chromosome contribution from parents are normally a combination of an X from the mother and an Y or X from the father. The combination of XX readies the developing gamete to differentiate into female. Similarly, the combination of XY readies the gamete to differentiate male. However, on occasion one of the parents may contribute one more, or no chromosome. Usually this happens in the parental sex cells: in the case of Y chromosomes, most often the cell division is in the sperm prior to conception. In the case of an extra or absent X, the contribution or absence can come from *either* the mother or the father. Interestingly, having only one X (stated as XO) *doesn't render the fetus non-viable*. It does cause *Turner Syndrome*, which creates infertility in females and possible secondary medical issues; but the fetus remains otherwise normal. However, an absence of an X in the presence of a Y chromosome (stated as YO) *does render the fetus non-viable*.

The necessity for a stable and complete X chromosome is due to it carrying more than 153 million *base pairs* (the building material of DNA). It represents about 800 protein-coding genes, compared to the Y chromosome which contains about seventy genes, out of 20,000–25,000 total genes in the human genome.

In *Klinefelter Syndrome* (XXY), the "extra X" produces a male body that can have some feminine attributes, but these can be slight. In *Jacobs Syndrome* (XYY), the "extra Y" does not create a superman, but does add height to the male offspring, and possibly some cognitive delays. The *Triple X Syndrome* (XXX) in females results in increased learning disabilities and extra height, but females remain fertile and otherwise normal.

5

What Is a Parent to Do?

When Your Child Is Intersex or Gender Conflicted

We now dive into some of the most pressing and significant elements of the gender crucible.

Parenting is never without its challenges, but parenting when a child is born with intersex genitals or conditions; or has gender identity conflicts that show up; or it seems as if the adolescent is embodying conflictual self-attitudes and pressing for changes to gender, then parenting can become overwhelming.

I divide the chapter into sections, which address each of these situations separately, although some elements are by design interrelated.

FOR STARTERS...

When gender issues arise, many parents first try to "go at it alone," or only with the advice of close friends or family. *None of these* are trained to provide the counsel that is needed to help parents sort out very difficult—often very technical, medical, or psychological information—as with our case examples in chapter 3. Reading articles and fishing the Web for information may prove useful, but parents sooner than later will need professional help.

My advice is always to get it early rather than later! And regarding this needed input, "do your homework" to find the best that is available: the best therapists, counselors, group support, or coaching. (More on these points below.)

Even if the following sound obvious, an early word or two here:

- *It takes both parents' involvement in getting knowledgeable and garnering the assistance needed.* It also takes both parents to deal with presenting issues. You will need each other (and I assume here a couple; if not, read on) to lean on and support the collaboration required.

- *If you are a single parent*, my initial advice is to get a trusted *accompagnateur* (a term from chapter 8) to "walk alongside you." It could be a significant family member whom you feel is open-minded and helpful; or it could be a friend you trust. It can also be a knowing pastor or someone from your congregation whom you feel has absolute confidence in you, and can keep your family's privacy. If you do engage an *accompagnateur*, be certain your child in question (if old enough) can relate to this person well. At the very least, that they do not see this individual as on your side only and not theirs. This is an important emotional point to underscore, particularly in sensitive pre-teen or teen cases of gender conflicts. Likeability and trust are key in selection here. In most cases, "It takes a village" to move through the many facets and layers of gender issues.

TO THE PARENT/S OF AN INTERSEX CHILD

Getting and Staying Informed

As we saw in the case illustration in chapter 3, the birth of a child with genital "ambiguity," "intersex," or any "malformation," is always a shock and a conundrum. I'd like to immediately bring to your recall that many such neonates are otherwise *perfectly normal*, and many times have functionality in their genitals, most importantly if their glands and urinary tracts aren't compromised.[1] Even then, and as

---

1. See and compare Diamond and Sigmundson, "Management of Intersexuality"; Dreger, "Ambiguous Sex—or Ambivalent Medicine?"; and Kessler, "Lessons From the Intersexed."

we've seen, there are medical interventions to correct or assist the functions and appearances later, if such is decided on.

Recall, as we've discussed, that in procreation there is the random chance that some coding may result in differences from the binary. This is not a consequence of any sin, historical or otherwise; nor is it that "God is testing you," in the sense of how this is often articulated by some in Christianity. It is certain that you should understand your child as a life born of you and imbued with the spirit and breath of life by our living God. For that is what they are. Value that gift, love and honor it by caring for it with all your heart and strength.[2]

With such births, becoming informed is the most significant and critical first step that parents can take. That means ensuring the medical information being given to you is clear, direct, and as much in lay language as is possible. If not, ask for it! Physicians should also explain to parents any medical interventions available to correct *functional* elements that may have been compromised.

Each case is different, so my effort here to assist you is based on what meets the baseline information needs of parents facing these situations. Given this baseline, you should, at minimum:

- *Obtain copies of all medical records for your infant child*, including any genetic tests, pathology, blood, or other laboratory and imaging investigations, and a designated diagnosis with an ICD Code (International Classification of Diseases). Even though your child isn't *diseased*, the ICD classification provides the *diagnostic category[ies]* under which the physician is classifying the condition. This will all be in your child's medical record; but unless you request *full copies*, you may only get the determined diagnosis and none of the background information from the onset. Included in these records should be any medical notations/comments made by the attending physician on the condition. If not,

- *Request and obtain information on the condition.* Most hospitals with neonatal wards have such information accessible if the condition is noted at birth; and most physicians can also obtain,

---

2. Read Cox's great volume, *Intersex in Christ*, for substantive integration of intersexuality and the gospel.

download, and provide you with specific information pertinent to your child's case if the condition is discovered later.

- *Ensure that you also receive supportive resources*, such as foundations, organizations, support groups for families with *intersex or DSD neonates* (another commonly used medical term). You should certainly consider contacting supportive resources, and obtaining assistance as required. Again, "It takes a village." Pick up a copy of the book *Raising Rosie*, by parents Eric and Susan Lohman. It is an intimate and caring portrayal of how the Lohmans are raising their intersex (CAH) child.
- *In some cases, it may be useful to obtain a second opinion or referral to a consulting physician*, to ensure that conclusions are medically consonant.
- *Often, you will need a referral to an* endocrinologist *(a hormone specialist) if not for early treatment, certainly for ongoing therapy*. If it's not readily offered, ask for names of endocrinologists, and particularly those that have treated cases like your child's.
- *You can also self-inform via the internet, with caution to use only medically credible sites*. One such is https://www.nationwidechildrens.org/. Follow their link to articles for parents of children with ambiguous or intersex genitalia. Another is www.isna.org, the Intersex Society of North America (ISNA), which has incredibly valuable resources and supportive information for parents. Also, look at https://rarediseases.org, which is the website for the National Organization for Rare Diseases (NORD). This organization has a link to the Ambiguous Genitalia Support Network (AGSN), which again, is a trove of help and support with local chapters, education, and materials.

Who to Tell, What to Tell, When to Tell

Parents of intersex babies are also immediately confronted with decisions of how this information is to be shared, and with whom. Websites mentioned above have great information available, and sundry recommendations for parents. But to be helpful here, I am suggesting that information given to others be as medically sound and as neutral as possible. With whom you share this information should be guided by your assessment of *their ability to receive it* and, with assistance, *process it.*

Certainly, immediate family members should not be kept in the dark—and I mean by that parental sisters or brothers, grandparents of the child, or any adult blood relative close to the child you feel should know. These should be informed early and as age-appropriate; but *only* when you as parents are comfortable in explaining *factually* what the child's condition is, and what may be the suggested protocols forthcoming.

I am encouraging you not to allow your child's condition to become a secret, nor be unnecessarily delayed in its being shared. Why?

Because "secrets" evolve a life of their own, which most often result in dissonances and problems. Eventually, secrets compound the child's or adult's feelings of confusion and shame. Your child's condition is nothing to hide. It is no different in fact than any other medical issue. (Some cultures unconsciously hide physical differences, since these are seen to reflect negatively on the family. Be aware if your culture or ethnic heritage does, and try not to perpetuate that aspect, if possible.)

As well, help individuals you tell "get over" the fact that the condition involves the sexual, especially if they seem to be squeamish about it. Anything "sexual" is often interpreted to be an issue for whispered conversation, even in today's open society—particularly among Christian groups, and in some ethnic cultures. Especially, "sex" having anything to do with intersex! Drive home the reality that intersex is more of a *social* than a *medical* problem!

I do think parents in such situations need wisdom as to when, and to whom, such information is given—largely because parents at this juncture don't need opinions, judgments, or more worries. What they need is understanding, support, and prayer. It would do well to share within these guidelines especially.

Remember above all, that it may feel like a tragedy or event with disastrous future consequences; but I am here to remind you, it is neither.

Yes, there will be struggles, even grief; and yes, there will be many difficult decisions—but recalling this event is *not tragic* is essential to your telling it correctly. Even more reason, then, for both parents to get informed and become knowledgeable, receiving energy and spiritual support from these efforts and each other (read Psalm 46 often!).

Be prepared to face different reactions. Well-meaning family, friends, and close associates may react with commiseration and pity (you don't need either!). Some may have never heard of intersex births, and may thus react with shock and disbelief. Pastoral help may offer prayer (which is good) and support (which is also good); but many in the clergy have not dealt with intersex births and are not schooled in the problematic or how to assist. Some may eventually react negatively to your decisions, such as to engage a particular gender of rearing for your child, one that doesn't match chromosomal sex. Be ready to be your own guides in this journey, since no-one else is, or can be, the parent!

Some may react out of ignorance and conservatism. I am assured most who are told will react with positive comments, and maybe even compliment you on how well you are "handling all of this." Do remember some people may be well-meaning but lack tact: take every response as neutrally as you can.

Tough Decisions Forthcoming

There will be many decisions, some gut-wrenching, because as parents you will not only feel responsible to do the "right thing," but know that such decisions have long-term effects. Out of all decisions you will need to make in the first few months, or first years of your child's life, one will loom as paramount: whether or not to engage surgeries to reformulate the genitalia if these have been affected; and later, use of hormones to alter the body of your child, if this is possible/or/necessary.

No-one can—or should—tell you what to do here. God's guidance is of paramount and central importance. Information from credible sources also help immensely.

Striking the right balance

It is easy for parents to overreact in any direction, making hasty decisions or delaying critical ones. Whether the child is an infant, a toddler, or a four or five year old makes all the difference in the world in how you approach what to do. And again, I assume that if there are medical issues that need *stat* attention, that these would of course be attended to with haste.

For the remainder, an effective *therapy plan* that includes both medical and psychological components, seems the wisest to recommend.

As in any plan, there is a timeline worked out for treatments. You do this with your child's physicians and your therapy counselors. All of it needs to be *tailored to the child*—taking into consideration their condition status, their age, their level of development, and, of course, how developed is their ability to understand and analyze (sometimes called "cognitive sophistication"). But don't forget, *you* also need therapeutic and social support as part of the plan!

Working out a therapeutic plan

Such provides parents and professionals the needed road map; and for parents especially, a pathway that reassures them that whatever is needed for the child's welfare is being addressed. Without a therapeutic plan, parents are often left to discern "the next fork" in the road, and may in fact feel less prepared to navigate the road ahead. In every sense, it makes good sense to construct that road map!

Surgical and/or Hormonal "Assignment"?

In some difficult cases, where intersex outcomes result in undifferentiated genitals, or further, may have produced incomplete or inhibited sex glands (testicles or ovaries), parents are left to make the decision whether to *surgically assign their child a sex*. Here again, significant prayer and investigation is necessary to produce best possible outcomes. The Hippocratic oath comes to mind, not as a prohibition for sex assignment, but as a reminder of the great caution needed to "*do no harm.*"

Doctors recommend such surgeries and hormonal supplementation in cases when doing so will assist the child's morphology, and eventual development in the most beneficial sexual direction. There is nothing foreboding or "wrong" in doing so—and Christian parents need to hear this, being their child's custodian. You are not "playing God," but you are making decisions on your child's behalf.

At the same time, parents need to consider whether genital surgeries can or should be delayed; and if so, whether they want their child to make those decisions later, as mature young adults, if this is possible. Nothing here is a facile set of decisions.[3]

What was medically routine a decade and a half ago is now questioned. Back then, the "answer" was seemingly simple: re-sculpt any malformed genitalia to the most binary-conforming model (i.e., as male or as female, being guided by what was most possible with the child's genitals); remove any sex glands (ovaries or testes); and then administer the appropriate hormones for the body to complete its assignment when needed (usually in pre-adolescence or adolescence, and thereafter for life). In some cases, this has led to tragic later results in the person's adult life.[4]

Surgical venues during childhood are now increasingly questioned by many in the intersex advocacy arena as unnecessary.[5] The pressure to alter the body, these feel, stems from the need to conform the body to one of the two polarities; the unnecessary "medicalization of conditions," "body politics," and the wrong assumption that surgery and hormones "fixes the problem." Dr. Anne Fausto-Sterling, a leading expert in biology and gender development states,

> [Doctors] faced with uncertainty about a child's sex, use different criteria. They focus primarily on reproductive abilities (in the case of a potential girl) or penis size (in the case of a prospective boy). If a child is born with two X chromosomes, oviducts, ovaries, and a uterus on the inside, but a penis a scrotum on the outside, for instance, is the child a boy or a girl? More doctors

---

3. Gardner and Sandberg, "Navigating Surgical Decision-Making," 1–9.
4. Fausto-Sterling, *Sex/Gender*, 44.
5. See for instance, Karzakis, *Fixing Sex*. Intersex advocates are not *activists*; they are individuals who have either undergone early life sex assignments or have been brought up *genitally intact*, but with little medical history or information to guide them. These form a substantive voice advocating for self-determination as one grows up, not just as an adult. They promote their intersex status as another normative (albeit fractional) expression of human sexual anatomy, and not one to abhor or even change. Such positions may work for some individuals. Certainly, those with more complications *may require surgeries* to correct not just genitals, but other conditions, and parents are the only ones capable of making those decisions in a timely manner.

declare the child a girl, despite the penis, because of her potential to give birth, and intervene using surgery and hormones to carry out the decision. [But] choosing which criteria to use in determining sex, and choosing to make determinations at all, are social decisions for which scientists can offer no absolute guidelines.[6]

There *is* growing evidence that intersex adults who have undergone what they themselves call "needless surgeries" in their infancy, childhood, or adolescence, often feel betrayed and lied to if not told the truth about their birth genitals or chromosomal make-up.[7] There are also studies that conclude that many with intersex genitals who have not been surgically altered *live perfectly normal lives* when reared well, and adjust well to their individuated genital forms.[8]

To guard against unnecessary surgical decisions on infants with atypical genitals, some state legislatures have introduced bills that would ban "cosmetic surgeries" on such children until they're old enough to consent.[9] Such a bill recently failed to pass legislative approval in California: SB 201 would have been the first legislation nationally to ban cosmetic genital surgeries on intersex babies. Surgical interventions on infants with atypical genitals has been condemned by the United Nations,[10] and the international non-profit Human Rights Watch has ruled it a human rights violation.

Explain to Your Child

If parents are to reassign their child sexually and/or hormonally, for whatever ultimate reason they conclude, then it must be clear here that the parents owe the child the truth. *How* that truth is communicated is, to me, a secondary matter; but not *when*.

As Christians, we should abide in truth, seek truth, and live out truth (Zech 8:16; 1 John 1:6; Eph 4:15; John 16:13). And the truth is that parents owe their child an understanding of their body, and an

---

6. Fausto-Sterling, *Sexing the Body*, 4.
7. Davis, *Contesting Intersex*, 4.
8. Davis, *Contesting Intersex*, 5.
9. Gutierrez, "Bill Stirs Intersex Rights Debate."
10. United Nations General Assembly (Human Rights Council), "Report of the Special Rapporteur (Juan E. Mendez)."

explanation for how their child may ultimately wind up feeling in that body. When of age, *start explaining*, and give them a reasoned line of thinking that supports your decisions. They, and you, will be grateful in the long run.

When your child is old enough to understand terminology, *use the right terms* to explain their condition. Parents often think the child won't understand the jargon; but if explained simply, they will. Just don't make the mistake that many do, to create a *label* out of the term for their condition, and use it regularly.

Labelling theory tells us that children are prone to repeating the terms, and these can quickly become *self-labels* if that is the term they hear repeated often. Moreover, labeling theory tells us that children will start to see themselves *through the label*, even extend the influence of that label to their self-identity and behavior.[11] *Take care, then, not to turn the condition of your child into a label by overusing the term. Explain, use the term, and then move on.*

Gender Rearing

Any decision on gender rearing should be based on the best accommodation of the child's intact genitalia, as well as possible effects of hormones forthcoming at puberty. In many cases, pubertal hormones—if they work—will eventually be a strong "determining factor" for gender identity, provided the body morphs into its chromosomal phenotype.

In chapter 3, I mentioned the strong suggestion by the Intersex Society of North America (ISNA) to rear an intersex child as one of the two binary forms of gender (i.e., "gender-based rearing").[12] What ISNA *isn't recommending* is rearing a child within a framework that, to them, "doesn't exist in fact" (i.e., no-gender). There are certainly many who disagree with ISNA, and we cover that alternative below, as well.

---

11. Taylor et al., "Labeling and Self-Esteem," 191–202.

12. *Gender-based rearing* simply means identifying the child *with one sexual format (male or female)*, and exposing them to gender-concordant behaviors, attitudes, and people. We would hope these are not *stereotypic* but rather reflective of contemporary understandings, such as the fact that men need to be tender and caring, and okay with failures as growth-motivators. And, that women are strong, capable, intelligent, can do what most men can, and don't need children to validate their femininity.

ISNA strongly documents its support of *gender-based rearing*, as opposed to *no-gender* (*gender-neutral*) *rearing*, or a third-gender (*transgender*) label.[13] In doing so, ISNA is encouraging a binary model and discouraging a non-binary one. On their FAQ page, they ask and answer the question of how to best rear an intersex child:

> *Does ISNA think children with intersex should be raised without a gender (agender), or in a "third gender"?* No, and for the record, we've never advocated this. We certainly would like to see people become less freaked-out by people who don't fit sex and gender cultural norms. But there are at least two problems with trying to raise kids without a gender, or in a "third gender." First, how would we decide who would count in the options? How would we decide where to cut off the category of male and begin the category of intersex, or, on the other side of the spectrum, where to cut off the category of intersex to begin the category of female? Second, and much more importantly, we are trying to make the world a safe place for intersex kids, and we don't think labeling them with gender categories that *in essence don't exist* would help them.[14]

A child's gender identity will most likely develop and be congruent with gender of rearing, *provided such gender of rearing is also compatible with what is possible in their body.*[15]

For example, if a child is born XY male, and has functional male testes but ambiguous genitals, or in some way compromised male anatomy (called *incomplete masculinization* in medical jargon), but is not AIS, the body will nevertheless "morph" into masculine development with the onset of hormonal puberty, without anything else being done. That will not fix the ambiguous genitalia, but it will differentiate

---

13. Intersex Society of North America, "What Does ISNA Recommend?"
14. Intersex Society of North America, "FAQ . . . Third Gender?"
15. This is a heavy statement, so please let me elaborate. Most everyone has been reared *within* the socially constructed parameters of a particular sex. This is called *gender of rearing* (see chapter 1, footnote 4, again). If, however, this rearing pattern doesn't seem to correlate (or in medical terms "*conform*") to how the body develops and "looks," the child might experience sexual/gender identity conflicts. To avoid this, helping the child become *gender congruent* means helping that child's body—in the present and in its eventual development into adult form—correlate to how he/she is being gender-reared. Advocates of *gender fluidity* and *agenderism* strongly condemn this "forced" gender rearing, and opt for the child to identify as *genderfluid*. As mentioned, ISNA is against such approaches. (See Parents and Friends of Lesbians and Gays (PFLAG) website, which advocates genderfluid identities, at www.pflag.org/tags/genderfluid.)

the body into masculine form, often adding male contours, muscle, hair, voice, etc. Per ISNA, it is best, then, to rear that child as a *male* and provide male gender identifying possibilities, than to rear that child as a female because they have a very small phallus, which could be surgically morphed.

I assume with these sentences that parents have opted for no corrective surgeries that would flip, truncate, or otherwise alter what could become a male individual. Parents could have opted for necessary surgeries to make the child's genitals more *functional*, as with urination issues; correcting undescended testicles; or to get rid of a "blind vagina" (an opening going nowhere), if the child had any of these conditions. Later, they could engage surgeries to "loosen" the phallus from its internal ligaments and provide greater length.

If an XY boy has *complete androgen insensitivity syndrome* (cAIS), the formed genitals at birth will resemble a female, but he has *no chance* of differentiating into a male at puberty (that is, his body transforming into a male body due to hormone action), because—remember—at the cell level, there is no response to testosterone.

Rearing this boy as a female is congruent with the genital form at birth *and with what the body will do later*, which is to morph into female via the effects of estrogen produced by the hypothalamus in the brain, and testicles.[16] He will be "female" in morphology by the time he finishes puberty. When cAIS infants are assigned a female gender of rearing, over 90 percent continue to feel like women, act as women, and accept themselves as women when adults.[17]

If, however, the XY boy is *partially androgen insensitive* (pAIS), a gender-of-rearing decision may become more difficult. The "predictive value" of how the body "may go," or—if "the brain goes along with it," isn't more than 50 percent. This, given the fact that half of those with pAIS assigned a gender at birth do not accept that gender when older.[18] Estimates are just that, but there are no hard numbers

---

16. University of Wisconsin-Madison, "Estrogen: Not Just Produced by Ovaries." It doesn't take much estrogen to move body structures to the "feminine form," given that this format is biologically the *baseline*—meaning the body continues to differentiate in the female format if male differentiation can't happen.

17. Karkazis, *Fixing Intersex*, 89.

18. Donaldson-James, "Intersex Babies: Boy or Girl and Who Decides?" 4. See also Karkazis, *Fixing Intersex*.

from research. Longer-term studies on how adolescents or adults have fared after gender assignment and/or infant surgeries are scarce.[19]

ISNA's logic of gender-based rearing is based on the notion that gender congruity often means *identity* congruity with *the whole body, not just the genitals*. If one focuses on the genitalia alone, and *not* how that body will ultimately form and take shape through the role of hormones over the course of development, one becomes myopic.

By allowing/helping the body to "become" what it may be able to become, and providing congruent gender rearing, parents are in fact assisting the child to embrace their uniqueness while finding a place in the normative gender schema. At the same time, they are helping their child to identify with others that look—and even act—like themselves.

The opposite view from ISNA's *gender-based rearing* is one where intersex children are left to determine who they want to identify as—eventually. What to do instead as parents?

In this view, parents should not only avoid "reassignment surgeries"—which ISNA is also against—but also adopt a *genderfluid* (or "gender-neutral") rearing style. In this regard, such rearing would theoretically enable the child to eventually determine which gender—if any—fits them best; or whether they would opt to keep a *genderqueer*, or *genderfluid* identification.[20] The genderfluid or gender-neutral approach requires that by age three or four the child undergo psychological evaluation to have "some kind of an idea" of where the child is heading regarding gender.

This all sounds possible, except for the fact that physicians don't recommend waiting to engage a gender, since "[gender rearing] aims at putting gender identity and role in sync with each other as the child grows older."[21]

Moreover, intersex children aren't old enough to voice a *gender preference* as a neonate, infant, or toddler. Every year that passes the child will identify with those whom they feel most alike, and thus the American Academy of Pediatrics' *Consensus of Care* was established in 2006 to address intersex children and their treatment.[22] There is

19. Klein, "Gender X: The Battle over Boy or Girl," 3.
20. Lucas-Stannard, *Gender Neutral Parenting*.
21. Baratz, "Intersex Babies: Boy or Girl and Who Decides," 2.
22. Lee et al., "Consensus Statement on Management of Intersex Disorders."

agreement that there must be gender rearing, but not unnecessary surgery. "The practice of deciding the better sex of assignment for the DSD child should be based on which gender that child best fits, and consider functionality, pubertal and adult development, and possible fertility."[23]

This not only makes medical sense—but moral and ethical sense as well: when the child is older, and if desired by them, any transition or surgery can follow.

Encouraging Body/Gender Concordance When There Isn't One

This section particularly applies to older children, further along the development spectrum, who *do* have sufficient cognitive sophistication to understand their body, and their gender identification. Parents may be medically encouraged to surgically transition the child's gender *before* the sexual body moves any further toward the other sex (i.e., an XY boy reared earlier as an XY boy, but now facing female body development via the effects of hormones). Such a transition will require special counseling and grace.

Any decision to transition a child after being reared in one gender schema, needs to weigh how identified that child is with his sexed/gendered body before considering radical/surgical transition. As discussed earlier, gender assignment via socialization of the child is often inhered early into the psyche of children. While malleable *in some* and *to some extent*, the development of gender and the child's social experiences have a major influence on gender-identity outcomes.[24] It is therefore an arduous process to help that child transition into a new body format and a new gender identity schema.

As parents, you need to ask the hard questions here: *Is the physical transition totally necessary? How can the child be helped, if there isn't a surgery, to accept the possibility that their body will change in discordant ways?* Or, if they are completely identified with a gender but their anatomy doesn't reflect that gender sufficiently, *should the anatomy then be changed?* If there *is* surgery: *How can the emergent new body be reconciled with the established gender identity? Are there*

---

23. Mieszczak et al., "Assignment of the Sex of Rearing," 10.
24. Meyer-Bahlburg, "Gender Identity Outcome," 432.

minimal surgeries that would accommodate the best sexual and gender outcomes?

Perhaps working briefly through some research findings may assist here.

Psychiatrist and endocrinologist Meyer-Bahlburg and colleagues from Columbia University examined and tested middle-childhood girls (age range, five to twelve years) who were diagnosed with *Congenital Adrenal Hyperplasia* (XX newborns, but with full genital masculinization). The question was whether these should be surgically reassigned as male, before the full onset of puberty.

Fifteen girls were in the study, and thirty as controls for comparison. None were surgically reassigned at birth—meaning their genitals resembled male genitalia more than a female's. All were reared *as girls*.

Results confirmed what they expected: CAH girls exhibited more "masculine behavior" (i.e., tomboyishness) than control girls across the board. But, reared as girls, no differences were significantly found between these girls, and the control group, on gender identity.

While the girls showed "marked masculinization" of their genitals,[25] there were no significant effects on gender identity, no increase in gender-identity confusion, or dysphoria. These identified *as female* and saw themselves *as female*. There was no significant evidence that their behavior made them *less female*. Meyer-Bahlburg and colleagues concluded: "Prenatal androgens do not indicate a direct determination of gender identity, and do not therefore support a male gender reassignment for these most markedly masculinized girls."[26]

The study strongly underscores that a gender identity resulting from gender of rearing isn't influenced by chromosomal or body conditions, despite the behavior not totally conforming to gender-role norms. Simply put: it isn't enough for these girls, as examples, that they were tomboyish and had masculinized genitals, to move them into a male gender identity *by changing their body to male*—particularly when they self-identified as girls (as females), even though they often crossed gender-role behaviors.

---

25. In these cases, girls were born with fused labia, a closed vagina, and a clitoris that grew phallus-like. Their urethra was open and these could urinate "sitting," but there was no outer opening to suggest a vaginal canal.

26. Meyer-Bahlburg et al., "Prenatal Androgenization," 97–104.

If surgical reassignment happened, it would include, for example, shortening the phallus-like clitoris, creating labia from fused tissue that resembles a scrotum; possibly opening the blocked vaginal channel, etc. In the end, such modifications may backfire: "Simone" (a pseudonym) stated the following in a conversation reflecting on her surgeries as a child:

> Nobody thought that I might grow up female and enjoy my body as it was. That having a larger clitoris may just have added to my pleasure. And if I didn't have a fully opened vagina, would I have really cared? I could also have fun with my phallic organ! I had to be conformed. I couldn't be different.[27]

I cite Mayer-Bahlburg's work and this commentary not to confuse parents, but to underscore the importance of critically thinking through all potential outcomes before making decisions to alter genitals. *Such decisions are irreversible.*

Thus, the guiding principle for parents with children who display an already-formed gender identity, is to be guided by that gender identity, and not solely by the anatomical body or chromosomes.

TO PARENTS WITH A CHILD DIAGNOSED WITH GENDER DYSPHORIA

We have already acknowledged that getting to a definitive diagnosis of gender dysphoria is itself a daunting challenge for families, especially if the dysphoria manifests early in the child's life. Once again, *there can be no generalizations here*, since every case is different and each merits individual attention.

We *can* say with certainty that the diagnostic process and treatment of gender dysphoric children and adolescents are complex, energy- and time-consuming for everyone involved. As well, we also know that the risks of children and adolescents with dysphoria developing co-occurrences of emotional and psychiatric problems is high.[28]

---

27. "Simone" was an informant who wished to remain anonymous. She is a CAH individual who was reared as a woman, identifies and lives as an adult woman. She was not told of her surgeries and did not find out until there was no menstruation at sixteen. Even at sixteen, she thought her anatomy was normal.

28. In studies from the Netherlands, 43 percent of children and adolescents seen in gender-identity clinics (and there are quite a few in the Netherlands) suffer from

Parents of diagnosed dysphoric children and adolescents should therefore be watchful of signs of depression, major or minor mood disorders, acting out, rebellions, all of which can naturally occur with an *identity in question*, but can often aggravate the issues, and thus need additional attention.

That said, what can I recommend across the board to parents of such children?

- *Foremost, a child's self-diagnosis of dysphoria or wanting to change their gender is not enough.* Parents and their child need to go through a process of investigation, assessment, psychiatric diagnoses of the issues, to ensure that the child's situation is fully understood.[29]

- *Listen to your child or adolescent.* At first, parents are likely to try and correct the child's statements, feelings, or perceptions; but this often only pushes the child away. How your child feels—beginning to end—is of ultimate importance to them, and should be foremost to you. Listen attentively to your child or adolescent. And, even though everything in you may disagree, expressing genuine interest in how your child feels, communicating care and warmth regardless of their age, makes the child feel safe. *Attentive listening* (see chapter 8) may also provide critical information for you, and for you to share with any other professional. Yes, you can ask the child questions about his/her feelings, but ensure that these are not phrased in ways that suggest you are questioning their feelings. Feelings are just that and "suggesting otherwise" most likely won't change a thing. Later we will talk about why they may have these feelings—the critical factor.

- *Depending on your child's age, express support for them, but don't shy away from calmly expressing your concerns.* This sounds contradictory, but in fact it's not. Supporting and loving your child, communicating that you understand their feelings and care deeply about how they are feeling, doesn't translate to you having to accept outright the beliefs that underlie them. But no child should be shamed or made to feel rejected, or even interpret a parent's words as punishment for expressing a conflict in gender

---

"major psychopathologies." Meyenburg, "Gender Dysphoria in Adolescents," 510–22.

29. Yarhouse, *Understanding Gender Dysphoria*, 2015.

identity. Lisa Marchiano, writing in *The Jung Soul*, provides a keen example here:

> If the child is particularly young, if the child seems to have begun experimenting with the idea of being transgender only very recently [and they wouldn't be using the term]; or if you see that gender identity exploration is an unconscious attempt to avoid a developmental challenge or otherwise manage stress or anxiety, it may be right to calmly and compassionately refuse to engage the possibility that the child is trans, for the time being. I have seen it happen where parents' responses early on in a child's gender exploration, communicating that they were the other gender, were ignored or simply not indulged. In quite a few of these cases, the child dropped the fascination with gender readily, and moved on to other interests. Obviously, deciding not to engage a child's gender exploration is not right in every case. These are decisions that only parents, who know the child best, can intuit.[30]

- *When a diagnosis is carefully concluded and factual, accept the diagnosis, but do not presume it is necessarily intractable, or non-responsive to therapeutic intervention.* Recall our quotes of studies in chapter 3, which suggest that a percentage of early childhood gender identity conflicts seem to self-resolve (desist) by puberty. While this position is often rejected by contemporary advocates of the transgender, the underscore here is to be cautiously optimistic, and certainly, to make no hasty decisions as parents.

  The treatment of young children with dysphoria—medically and psychiatrically—is still controversial. Puberty-suppression drugs ("hormone blockers") during the critical period of puberty come with significant challenges and issues, including health concerns. They only postpone the inevitable decision-making. (See chapter 6, following, to review details of hormone blockers during puberty.)

- *If your child is a pre-teen, or adolescent, try to ascertain early if this gender conflict or exploration is linked to other issues.* Tolerance and openness is one response, for certain; but so is the parental need to know, understand, and even *set limits* if it is deemed

---

30. Marchiano, "Guidance for Parents," 1–2. (Brackets mine.) Marchiano is a licensed psychotherapist and Jungian psychoanalyst.

necessary. The more you can unravel the better: whether gender conflicts are body-related (e.g., body dysmorphia); identity related (esteem issues); or related to the angst of growing up; or to teen "social contagion" or other issues, the better equipped you will be to assist your child through the difficult periods ahead. Again, Marchiano comes through with excellent commentary:

> I am aware of numerous families who cautiously embraced a child's self-diagnosis as an effort to be as supportive as possible. They responded to the announcement with openness, allowing eventual changes of names or hairstyle, for example, without fully committing either to transition or to demanding that the child wait. Several of these parents regretted that they met the initial announcement with such tolerance and openness, as partial acceptance of the child's [*read* also adolescent's] self-diagnosis put them on a slippery slope, wherein parents felt held hostage to the child's continued demands.[31]

I would also argue that the Christian parent is commissioned to have primary responsibility for their children and adolescents. They are not ours, but are gifts to care for and guide (Ps 137:3–5; Prov 22:6). Quickly giving up parental authority to the self-authority of a child, a pre-teen, or teen, when a lot of scientific literature tells us these aren't essentially ready or often capable of making self-decisions with long-term consequences is, I feel, irresponsible and derelict.

Ryan Anderson, writing in *When Harry Became Sally*, states, "Simply accepting the self-declaration of a gender-questioning child and encouraging persistence in transgender identity does not constitute sound, science-based medicine. But politics now rule the debate." And again, "A three-year-old child is just beginning to learn the difference between boys and girls, so how could that child have any sense of being really a boy when everyone says she's a girl?"[32]

The idea that children and adolescents are, generally, cognitively capable for such transitions to be successful ought to be weighed with care. Children can certainly teach us adults a lot of things, and gender dysphoria can manifest itself very early. But when it comes to the *persistent* and *consistent* manifestation of gender conflicts (recall the

---

31. Marchiano, "Guidance for Parents," 1.
32. Anderson, *When Harry Became Sally*, 35–36.

DSM diagnosis), a parent does good duty to investigate, assess, and not just relegate.

Therapy, Therapists, and More

Be aware that the therapeutic community guides itself by established criteria that are themselves influenced by politics and media, not just science.[33] There are many, myself included, who believe the psychotherapeutic community hasn't done well in providing treatment alternatives for children and adolescents with gender dysphoria.

I mean by this, the willingness of *most* therapists to outright *accept* and *never question* whether the gender-conflicted feelings ought to be examined closely to rule out possible precipitating issues.

Gender-exploration therapies are often disparaged, and *gender-desisting therapies* that provide alternative treatments for gender dysphoria are also discredited. This, despite such therapies having significantly good results in assisting children and adolescents to come to terms with and accept their bodies and the corresponding gender identity. (Again, see chapters 2 and 3.) As parents "be wise as serpents" in selecting therapists and therapeutic approaches, if these are warranted, for your child and/or adolescent.

A big caveat here, sadly. It has been my experience that the Christian therapeutic community has not kept up sufficiently with issues of gender conflicts, and modalities to deal with these, as they should. To put that right, Warren Throckmorton and Mark Yarhouse, both Christian psychotherapists, have proposed guidelines for managing sexual-identity conflicts.[34] The Christian therapeutic community, however, still needs to explore these, and develop a *network of trained clinicians* that can assist the intersex, or those with gender dysphoria. We need therapists that neither make dysphoria, especially, a "spiritual mental battle" and not give in to a facile diagnosis without historical and timeline factors, as outlined in the DSM-5.

Christian therapists *do need to know the science*, plus *specific therapy modalities* that work in such cases. Spiritual elements—often so personal and emotional—need to be factored in, of course. But

---

33. Parkhurst, *The Politics of Evidence*.
34. Throckmorton and Yarhouse, "Sexual Identity Therapy Practice Framework."

here, we can't repeat old mistakes, like fashioning an adolescent's feelings into a "phase" to outgrow *only*, ignoring clinical aspects of what may be really going on. Specific modalities and viewpoints need to coexist with elements of our faith; and both need to refresh our attitudes, our theologies of gender, so we *see clearly*, and not "through a glass darkly." (See chapter 7.)

Thus, the moniker of a "Christian therapist" is in no way a guarantee that the individual (a) has the appropriate training; (b) is capable of assessing accurately causes and conflicts; (c) can provide appropriate therapeutic modalities; (d) won't just "Christianize" the situation,[35] and (e) is willing to provide necessary referrals when needed. A cogent therapist capable of handling sexual- and gender-identity issues has the education and training specifically needed to treat sexual- and gender-identity issues.

Such cautions should not be taken as a general critique of Christian therapists. These are, however, my "insider insights" for parents in already difficult situations:

- *Choose wisely, prayerfully, and consider a therapist's specialized training.* Ask if they've treated any similar conditions, and get testimonials of parents who've employed them. See a list of questions at the end of this chapter you can utilize when screening a therapist.

- *If they are Christian, all the better,* since they can relate to the spiritual side of the variables; but try to avoid making "Christian" the sole criterion for a therapist's choice.

---

35. *Undestand me correctly here*: I've been witness to a few instances where licensed Christian psychologists have relegated everything to "prayer and vigilance"; or have provided premature diagnoses based on minimal sessions with patient and family. There have been some who suggest that gender dysphoria in children and adolescents is the work of the devil, and that some type of prayer-induced psychological *exorcism* is appropriate, denying any validity to feelings, to attendant and possible other issues, etc. I find these types of therapy practices an insult to both good science and Christianity. Good science and Christianity can and should co-exist in situations dealing with dysphoria. We need prayer; a Christian therapist certainly needs spiritual discernment; but children and adolescents *do have* emotional and identity issues, which *are not* the product of the devil, but rather of life circumstances and, in many, yet-to-be-understood causes. Thus, my advice: Be prudent, investigate, ask questions, and do not be blinded by labels.

- *A good therapist will respect religious boundaries*, and concern themselves with getting to the issues, not being side-tracked with positions.

Approaches to Exploration Therapies

As a final point, I review therapeutic approaches that help in clarifying issues related to symptoms of gender dysphoria. I'll briefly list three, again reminding the reader that *every case is different*. Any therapies engaged depend in large part on what the presenting issues are, and the child/adolescent's emotional condition.

Somatic therapies are forms of body-centered therapy that look at the connection of mind and body and use both psychotherapy and physical therapies for holistic healing.[36] These can be especially useful with pre-teen and adolescent children going through gender/body disjunctions. They can lessen one's discomforts with the body.

Dialectical behavior therapies (DBT) can provide new skills to manage painful emotions and decrease conflict in relationships. DBT specifically focuses on four key areas:

- *Developing mindfulness*, improving an individual's ability to accept and be present in the current moment.
- *Distress tolerance*, increasing tolerance of negative emotions, rather than trying to escape them.
- *Regulation of emotion*, teaching strategies to manage and change intense emotions that are causing problems.
- *Interpersonal effectiveness*, developing techniques that allow a person to communicate with others in a way that is genuine, that maintains self-respect, and strengthens relationships.

All therapies mentioned above teach *affect-regulation skills*, or how to effectively cope with feelings and emotions. Again, these therapies are most applicable to children and teens who have the cognitive capacity to understand themselves, their feelings, and the emotions of others. Such therapies are also useful with parents of children

---

36. Psychology Today Online, www.psychologytoday.com/. Source is used to abbreviate explanations for all therapy modalities subsequently mentioned.

undergoing gender conflicts, and help these develop coping strategies and skills. There's one more to mention:

Psychodynamic psychotherapy is used to explore the more unconscious dynamics that can be present, and underlying feelings about one's gender. It is an in-depth form of *talk therapy* based on theories and principles of psychoanalysis. Its focus is on the patient's relationship with his or her external world; but it can also be used to explore the "internal world" of the person—and in the case of gender conflicts, effective at drawing out elements of feelings and rationales. A form of psychodynamic psychotherapy is often achievable for children, since the talk therapy portion uses dialogue; and children, when comfortable, will talk.

This review should end by my making clear to you that if there is an accurate and eventual diagnosis of gender dysphoria in a child or adolescent, studies often state these therapies *don't work to change the dysphoria itself*.[37] They can, however, work to help the child, the adolescent, the adult, learn to live more comfortably in their body, lessen the dissonance, and even improve their psychosocial identity. Most current psychological sources conclude that gender dysphoria, once accurately diagnosed, is essentially intractable. I take that with a grain of salt, given the substantive research that concludes some children *do desist* by the time they are adolescents.[38] Researcher Anderson gives us this to think about:

> Normally a child is not encouraged to *persist* in a belief that is discordant with reality. A traditional form of treatment for gender dysphoria would work *with* and not *against* the facts of science and predictable rhythms of children's psycho-sexual development. A prudent and natural course of treatment would [first] enable children to reconcile their subjective gender identity with their objective biological sex, avoiding harmful or irreversible interventions.[39]

If these courses of therapy do *not* bring the child/adolescent to a point of *sexual identity synthesis*,[40] parents are then faced with consid-

---

37. Yarhouse, *Understanding Gender Dysphoria,* chapter 5.

38. Brooks, "The Controversial Research on 'Desistance.'" See also Brooks, "Is Three Too Young for Children to Know?"

39. Anderson, *When Harry Became Sally,* 117–44.

40. Yarhouse and Tan, *Sexual Identity Synthesis.*

ering age-appropriate transitioning; *or* allowing that child to decide for themselves later, if there is clear possibility that such will bring the individual a reconciliation with the self-body.

In chapter 6 following, I address two of the most pertinent issues of gender transitions for parents to decide—suppressing or not suppressing puberty; and whether surgical reassignment ("confirmation surgeries") can work long-term when done in minors.

There is much that parents can and should do when confronted with intersex births or gender-conflict issues in their children. *What is always at stake and central is the child's welfare.* We need to protect the rights of children, but also the rights of parents to determine what is age-appropriate and not harmful—and not rely on the child alone.

As we've seen with earlier case studies, children, adolescents, families, and ultimately adults with gender conflicts undergo significant travails and decision-making moments. Early in this book, personal narratives helped illustrate for us a truth that often gets lost in all the position-taking: that sex and identity are never just a subjective, personal matter, regardless of choice. We are webbed socially and emotionally, and any/all decisions will have impacts beyond the person involved.

Parents must thus make difficult choices between enduring some/much psychological and social pain, risk potentially serious side effects of medical interventions and lifelong dependence on hormone substitution, or relegate the decisions to their later adult child.

For those with diagnosed intersex conditions, parents face key and early decisions as to how to understand, rear, and encourage their child's anatomy as unique and singular, helping them to accept themselves fully. Or, in some rarer cases, *redirect* that anatomy in the best way possible for their child's future.

For those facing gender-identity incongruences or diagnosed dysphoria, parents have significant decisions to make, including issues of how to navigate their responsibilities as parents, and the child's best welfare and long-term outcomes.

None of these are easy choices to make. Each family must make their own decisions.

Here is the good news: God is forever with us in these hard times (Pss 46:1; 9:9). Remembering that His guidance is available, and key to our sanity, is central. *God does help* and can help us chart the best way for us.

Nothing in a believer's life is impossible. Moreover, the kingdom of heaven belongs to our children; Jesus welcomed and protected them. We should then do everything possible for them, their welfare, within that knowledge frame.

Table 2. Questions to Ask Therapists Who Treat Gender Conflicts (Christian- or Otherwise Self-Defined)		
General Questions	Specific on Ethical Accommodations	Specific on Therapy Modalities
What is your specific training for dealing with gender conflicts in children and/or adolescents?	Please explain your position in dealing with child clients/parents who hold a faith position?	Please explain your approach to formulating a therapeutic plan.
How many cases approximate in age to that of my child/adolescent have you treated? Can you review your training specific to treating sexual disorders? Sexual identity issues? Can you review your training specific to intersex patients? What is your training on the science of intersexuality? Disorders of sex development?	Are you comfortable with religious ideals of parents? Those that may lean toward a particular sexual and gender framework? Is there any position on religion you may have we should know about? If you are a religious therapist, what should we know about your faith? Will it inform your perspective in this case? If so, how so?	What specific modalities have you used that may seem helpful to (a) body reconciliation, (b) self-esteem (c) gender transition if it is deemed necessary? What specific modalities would you avoid using with (a) children, (b) adolescents?
Can you explain/share your views on gender, gender identity, and how these relate to the body in childhood and adolescence?	Are you [ ] comfortable [ ] neutral [ ] uncomfortable with positions that do not reinforce a gender-binary model? Are you open to gender therapies that initially do not take a position on affirming or desisting identity?	Please explain your position on the DSM criteria for diagnosing: Childhood GD Adolescent GD Are their points of agreement or disagreement with the DSM 5.1 that you have? That we should be informed about?

continued on next page

Table 2. Questions to Ask Therapists Who Treat Gender Conflicts (Christian- or Otherwise Self-Defined)		
General Questions	Specific on Ethical Accommodations	Specific on Therapy Modalities
How would you explain to us (a) gender nonconformity, (b) gender dysphoria, (c) crossdressing, and their differences?	How will you handle the wishes of parents if these seem to conflict with the wishes of the child/adolescent patient regarding (a) therapy (b) goals and outcomes?	On what set(s) of evidence would you render a gender dysphoria diagnosis in (a) children, (b) adolescents? A diagnosis of gender nonconformity? What are some age-appropriate therapy modalities for gender dysphoric children? Adolescents?
How often after initial sessions do you normally see clients and parents with similar presentations as ours? What can we expect?	Do you believe most children, adolescents can reach "sexual-identity synthesis" (concordance) as some of the literature claims? If so, why so? If not, why not	Do you hold a position on hormone blockers and their use in pre-pubertal or pubertal children with diagnosed gender dysphoria?

6

Manipulating Biology in Children and Teens with Diagnosed Gender Dysphoria

We are at a novel point in endocrine medicine, one that allows parents to stop the progression of puberty in children or adolescents with gender-identity dysphoria. Then, *if* and *when* sexual transition is desirable, sex hormone(s) and eventual surgical treatments can commence.

HORMONE SUPPRESSION THERAPY

The questions go something like this: If a child is diagnosed as gender dysphoric, can anything be done to stop the body from morphing into what these may consider the "wrong" anatomical sex to house their identity? Can a "neutral space" be constructed to give the child, and the parents, *time* to declare the identity *in fact*, before biology does the final declaring for them? In this view, buying some time seems the best option when other ones seem too conflictual or premature.

Puberty Suppression/Puberty Blockers

Science has had *some* of the answers for a while, in the form of "puberty blockers" or "puberty inhibitors." Essentially, these hormone blockers prevent the release of LH (luteinizing hormone) and FSH (follicle stimulating hormone), both of which are responsible for the progression of pubertal changes in older children and adolescents.[1] Often these blockers consist of gonadotropin-releasing (hormone) analogues (GnRHas). Histrelin acetate is the most common synthetic analogue, delivered by a subcutaneous implant, a small thin pouch inserted surgically in the upper under-arm.[2]

The combination of LH and FSH in both males and females activate their main hormones—testosterone or estrogen—and thus further the body's morphing progression into fully male or fully female body development. Originally, puberty blockers were used *only in cases of precocious puberty*—too fast an onset of puberty before the appropriate age; or when there were hormone-sensitive cancers in children, and natural hormone levels needed to be suppressed to not feed the cancers.

But by 2006, and later with the 2013 changes in the *Diagnostic and Statistical Manual of the American Psychiatric Association* (the "DSM-5"), a prominent treatment approach called *gender-affirming therapy* was emphasized.[3] Here, therapists *accept,* instead of *challenge*

---

1. "LH" is a pituitary hormone that stimulates ovulation, and in turn, allows the production of progesterone, the second and necessary female hormone. "FSH" is yet another pituitary hormone essential in both men and women for pubertal development and fertility—in women, to stimulate ovum growth; and in men, to allow sperm development.

2. Histrelin Acetate. Dosing uses one implant every twelve months. Each implant contains 50mg histrelin acetate. The implant is inserted subcutaneously in the inner part of the upper arm and provides continuous release (65 mcg/day) for twelve months of hormonal therapy. If the child/pre-teen needs more than a year of suppression, another implant will be needed—the old one is removed and replaced. Common side effects of Histrelin acetate include irritation at the implant site, mood swings, headache, nosebleeds, tiredness, weight changes, constipation, night sweats, feeling hot or cold, impotence, loss of interest in sex; and in boys, pain or swelling in the testicles. In girls using this medication for puberty suppression, side effects may include temporary breast swelling or tenderness, abnormal onset of menarche (menstruation) or vaginal bleeding, menstrual pain or heavy menstrual bleeding. See: https://www.rxlist.com/supprelin-la-side-effects-drug-center.htm.

3. "Gender-affirming therapies" came about as means to accommodate the need for individuals, especially adolescents and some children, to feel "safe" about their gender-identity conflicts. The therapies are aimed to not dissuade what could eventually be diagnosed as *gender dysphoria*. With such therapies, there is no questioning of the child/adolescent's feelings; to the contrary, they are "affirmed"; the work that is done is largely to stabilize the emotional condition of the conflicted, and move them toward a gender-*confirming* resolution (i.e., accept their feelings and desist from thinking their feelings are incorrect). The biological is secondary to the feelings.

or *work through,* a patient's claim of body/gender incongruity. With this approach and the negation of *gender-challenging* therapies—including a prohibition of gender "conversion therapy,"[4] there were increases in physician referrals of childhood and adolescent clients for assistance with *delaying* the onset of puberty.

In a recent 2017 report published by Drs. Paul Hruz, Lawrence Mayer, and Paul McHugh in *The New Atlantis,*[5] these authors note sizeable number increases in such referrals *world-wide*: In the UK, an increase of 430 percent (2009/10 to 2017); in Canada, four-fold increases 2004 to 2011; and in the US, 40 percent of such patient referrals occurred between 2002 and 2017.

Increases have many reasons, but what seems to predominate is the social awareness of gender-identity disorders in children and adolescents, and the willingness of parents to seek medical help for these children by *pausing puberty.* These therapies and referrals bolstered the popularity of using puberty suppression/puberty blockers during this stated "turbulent time" in a child with identity issues.

Several societies and organizations also began to endorse puberty suppression, among them the World Professional Association for Transgender Health (WPATH), and the (American) Endocrine Society. These also partnered with other organizations to put forth guidelines advocating puberty suppression.[6] It was stated that for the child, puberty blockers would lessen the discordance between their developing body and how they felt about defining their identity.

---

4. In "gender-challenging" or "desisting therapies," the goal is to attempt reconciliation between the *identity* and the *body*, rather than push the biological to the side. The therapy modalities are not *conversion* therapies since they are not aimed at changing the status quo of what "is." Rather, the goal is to *work with what is* and reconcile it—not convert it. The term "conversion therapy" comes from efforts in cases of sexual *orientation,* to help the patient who wants to move "back" into heterosexuality, or "convert" from homosexuality. *The label is wrongly applied to gender-identity therapy.*

5. Hruz et al., "Growing Pains," 3–36.

6. Hembree et al., "Guidelines for Pubertal Suppression," 2. See also Hembree et al., "Endocrine Treatment of Transsexual Persons," 3132–54.

How Do Puberty Suppression/Blockers Work?

Let's briefly review how these operate in the child's body. The goal is to *halt* the progression of natural development that affirms the biology, and the hormones that turn boys into men and girls into women.

Endocrinologists were already aware that *adding more* of the trigger hormone GnRH to what was already being produced naturally to morph the body during adolescence would "desensitize" the pituitary.[7] Then, instead of producing *more* GnRH, providing more LH and FSH, the pituitary would *quiet down these instruction hormones* for the testicles or ovaries to produce more of the corresponding sex hormone. In effect, the pituitary would read the extra GnRH as too much, and shut down instructions for more. With this prompting, the sex glands lower their production of sex hormones—testosterone or estrogen.

As an "even greater benefit," desensitizing the pituitary was said *not to be permanent*—it was "reversible." If a child or adolescent *desisted*, suppression treatments could be safely stopped.[8] After stopping the extra GnRH, the patient's pituitary would resume its normal secretion of GnRH, and the body would return to its normal pubertal development. (This, however, could take up to a year after suppression treatments were stopped . . . a seemingly small delay.) Suppression therapy aimed to provide the perfect stop-gap necessary when time-sensitive decision-making was on the line.

---

7. Crowley et al., "Therapeutic Use of Pituitary Desensitization," 370–72. (LHRH refers to "luteinizing hormone resisting hormone," another term for GnRH.)

8. Desistance in this context means that the child/adolescent is seemingly resolving their gender-identity conflicts, and evidence suggests there is no longer the need to gender-transition. Activists deny that desistance can really happen; but many in the medical community confirm that it does. See, for example, the argument put forth by James Barrett, MD, psychiatrist from the oldest gender identity service in the UK (Charing Cross Clinic, London): "If you wait until puberty has got a little way along, a fair proportion of the children change the clinical presentation. . . . They don't seek a role change any more and will end up with no need for lifelong medical intervention, [no] surgery, and with no loss of natural fertility should they want children." Quote from Lyons, "UK Doctors Prescribing," para. 5.

Is It Really "Reversible"?

The draw for GnRH use has been the "reversibility" assertion. Most of the literature on its use between 2012 and 2016[9] made it seem the best compromise between *not starting medical treatments* for gender identity-conflicted, dysphoric children; or, *moving forward along a treatment path* that would permanently—sometimes immediately—begin to alter the sexual characteristics of the child forever: Hormone-substitution therapy (estrogen for boys; testosterone for girls).

Even earlier than 2012, Dutch researchers Delemarre van-de Wall, Cohen-Kettenis, and van Goozen claimed that children "who will live permanently in the desired gender role as an adult may be *spared the torment* of [full] pubescent development of the *wrong* secondary sex characteristics."[10] Treatment seemed to *save children* from the "horrors" of physical maturation into the "wrong body"—at least for a while—two years, maximum.

However, these claims of "reversibility" have now been challenged by the medical establishment. There are reasons to be very cautious of "reversals" since, for starters, the normal sequence of development would have already been disrupted.

If the developing characteristics would be allowed to "resume" later by stopping GnRH treatment, then it doesn't make sense from a developmental, biological perspective to call this "reversal": *The body that is stunted, remains stunted*; and if allowed to later continue its development, *will really never overcome the deficits in growth or maturation caused by such a period of pause.*

Drs. Hruz, Mayer, and McHugh, writing in their "opus" rebuttal to the new treatment protocols for gender dysphoria in children and adolescents state:

> In developmental biology, it makes little sense to describe anything as "reversible." If a child does not develop certain characteristics at age 12 because of a medical intervention, then his or her developing those characteristics at age 18 is not a "reversal," since the sequence of development has already been disrupted. Given how little we know about gender identity and how it is

---

9. See reports such as Metzger, "Pubertal Blockade Safe"; Kuper, "Puberty Blocking Medications."

10. Cohen-Kettenis et al., "The Treatment of Adolescent Transsexuals." (Bracket and italics mine.)

formed and consolidated, we would be cautious interfering with the normal process of sexual maturation.[11]

Imagine two children, boys age twelve, each physiologically normal, entering puberty. Now imagine one of them being placed on puberty blockers, while the other is allowed naturally to progress into puberty.

The suppressed boy's organs will *not mature*: testicles and penis will remain small; sperm production will not activate; and the body itself will show signs of suppression. Assuming a two-year suppression (age twelve to fourteen), that boy will be several inches shorter than the untreated one; have less muscles mass, smaller genitals; and will be physically more child-like than his counterpart. Even if stopped, and a catch-up year allowed, the effects of the halt will be visible and *irreversible*.

Through this simple example we can understand that the effects of suppression aren't really "reversible," but rather, alter the body *irreversibly*.

Are There Other Problematic Consequences?

Assuming this tween *stops* suppression and desists from gender reassignment, what would be the effects of the pause?

The few studies that have been carried out show that boys who undergo puberty suppression and stop are also at higher risk of developing testicular problems, one being *microcalcifications*, deposits of hardened calcium in the testicles—jokingly called "testicular pearls." But they're not a joke: such may put the adolescent at greater risk for later testicular cancer.[12] Associated with male puberty suppression is also *added weight*, or obesity, since testosterone is a deflector of fat tissue build-up. Suppressing testosterone makes it easier for the body to accumulate fat. We've already mentioned smaller testicles and possibly smaller penises.

We have even fewer studies on girls, but outcomes of suppression that are definitive in girls would be later-onset menstruation,

---

11. Hruz et al., "Growing Pains," 23.
12. Bertelloni and Mul, "Treatment of Central Precocious Puberty by GnRH Analogues," 531–36.

irregular or no ovulation, lessened development of female characteristics: smaller breasts, and atypical body contours.[13] Adding testosterone later to girls who *continue* reassignment, vs. stopping it, ups risks to include elevated liver enzymes; higher cholesterol levels; increased hematocrit (red blood cells) and compromises to her metabolic health; acne, male pattern baldness, and sleep apnea.[14]

In both cases, suppression of natal hormones and any subsequent substitution with hormones of the opposite sex will invariably cause these children to become *sterile adults*.[15] They will also be *shorter* in height than their normal maturation would have allowed, because they most likely will have impaired bone accretion.

We do know about some of the effects of hormones on the developing brain, how these affect brain organization and brain activations during adolescence, a timeframe often called the "critical period."[16]

Postnatal hormones that bathe the brains of boys and girls during pubescence further some elemental differences in structures of the male and female brains (*brain dimorphism*). In both males and females, such effects motivate *endogenous* (i.e., originating from within the organism) body masculinization or femininization, possibly helping to identify the body's genitals with their learned gender.[17]

As well, *hormones are intimately involved in how the brain functions—its neural activity*. We have animal studies that confirm how sex hormone levels in puberty contribute to the final organization of brain structures in mammals.[18] It is during puberty that hormones link the emerging erotics of *body sensations* with the *mind's imagery capacity*, and mental scripting (or in plain English, *erotic daydreams*) then occurs naturally.[19]

13. Fisher et al., "Resumption of Puberty," 3–5.

14. Hembree et al., "Endocrine Treatment of Transsexual Persons," 3132–54.

15. Hormones of the opposite sex compete with natural sex hormones, and over time (less than a year) start to *atrophy* the sex glands of the individual. In men, testicles stop producing sperm, eventually testosterone, and thus atrophy. In females, ovarian cells and ova start to die off, and the ovary ceases to produce estrogen. It will also atrophy in time. The net result in both cases is *sterility*.

16. Money, *Gay, Straight, and in Between*, 7.

17. Cretella, "Gender Dysphoria in Children," 53. See also DeVries et al., "Puberty Suppression in Adolescents," 2276–83; and Fausto-Sterling, *Sex/Gender*, chs. 4–5.

18. Blakemore et al., "The Role of Puberty in the Developing Adolescent Brain," 926–31.

19. Stoller, *Sex and Gender*. See also Stoller, *Sexual Excitement*.

All of this is necessary for adult understanding of sexual feelings and imagination of sexual behaviors and choices. This final hormonal bath is "putting gas in the metaphorical tank."[20]

We can therefore underscore that *puberty suppression could have negative effects on the physiological, neurological, and psychological changes occurring in the pubertal years.* Stopping hormones from doing their body *and brain work* during prolonged periods of peak differentiation could, conceivably, have greater, unknown, and longer-lasting effects than those noted here.

While these are still matters of debate, should children then be subjected to such treatments when there are looming questions? In my opinion, there are simply not enough studies, all around, to establish all the consequences; no controlled and longer-term clinical trials comparing the outcomes of puberty suppression vs. other therapeutic treatments that don't halt puberty for a time.[21] Hruz, Mayer, and McHughes are well worth quoting here, since they consolidate the concerns:

> The claim that puberty-blocking treatments are fully reversible makes them appear less drastic, but this claim is not supported by the scientific evidence. It remains unknown whether or not ordinary sex-typical puberty will resume following an end to suppression therapy in patients with gender dysphoria. It is also unclear whether children would be able to develop normal reproductive functions if they were to withdraw from puberty suppression. It likewise remains unclear whether bone and muscle development will proceed normally for these children if they resume puberty as their biological sex. Furthermore, we do not fully understand the neurological and psychological consequences of using puberty suppression to treat young people with gender dysphoria.[22]

---

20. Money, *Gay, Straight, and in Between.*

21. Mahfouda et al., "Puberty Suppression in Transgender Children and Adolescents," 816–26.

22. Hruz, et al., "Growing Pains," 26.

SEX HORMONES AND SURGICAL TREATMENTS OF DYSPHORIC CHILDREN AND ADOLESCENTS

Mentioned previously, WPATH has set guidelines for the treatment of dysphoric children (pubescent) and adolescents, with progressive levels of *irreversibility*:[23]

- Stage 1: *Puberty suppression*
- Stage 2: *Gender-affirming hormones* (opposite-sex hormone administration)
- Stage 3: *Gender-affirming surgery* (surgical sex "reassignment")

The guidelines are clear that puberty should have begun (medically referred to as "Tanner Stage 2"), with evident physical signs like public hair or breast budding, before *any* intervention is agreed to. (There is recognition that there may be *desistance*, or the disappearance of dysphoria once puberty commences.) Let's be clear, that while the WPATH guidelines don't recommend a specific age to start treatment, the Endocrine Society *did approve* puberty blockers for those *as young as twelve years of age*.[24]

I've already covered the effects and concerns with hormone blockers. I follow with an understanding of *cross-sex hormone treatments*, concentrating on their effects short- and long-term. Next, is a short review of *surgical reassignment*, now "confirmation" surgeries.

CROSS-SEX HORMONAL ADMINISTRATION

Starting *cross-sex hormone treatments* induces either masculinizing (*testosterone*) or feminizing (*estrogen, spironolactone*) physical effects on subjects. The body will start to "morph" into the "phenotypic other sex" in physiological characteristics. See Tables 2.1–2.3 at end of chapter, which delineate the general changes that will occur. In a few months of sex hormone administration, these visible changes will demonstrably show a body in transition; and as explained in the Tables, it may take one to two years to complete most of the transformation.

---

23. World Professional Association of Transgender Health, *Standards of Care*, 10–63.

24. Hembree et al., "Endocrine Treatment," section 2.5.

Changes come with significant adjustment parameters for the pubescent child or adolescent. There are *psychological adjustments* to the morphing body and self-image that need to occur. Insufficient studies, as mentioned, does not help with attempts to clarify these. Moreover, careful monitoring of the effects of hormones on the transitioning body are needed to avoid significant issues, such as cognitive impairments, lack of bone accretion, hematologic issues, and cardiovascular health maintenance.[25] These present as well with sex hormone administration, not just hormone blockers reviewed above.

Along with psychological transitions are the social transitions that must take place for the child/adolescent to accommodate their new typology and role. Some behaviors will need to be "unlearned," while others "learned"; and these need to occur both within, and outside family circles. Here, transitions include changes in external appearances, mannerisms, vocality, and role-related knowledge, not to mention a possible name change.

None of this is simple, particularly in young transgender children who may have already shown mental health problems or adjustment issues due to their dysphoria. Such will not "magically disappear" with transitions in effect—to the contrary, emotional issues may in fact aggravate. It is therefore incumbent upon parents and therapists, with medical professionals involved, to monitor with caution emotional and social elements for successful integration and self-satisfaction.

Surgical Reassignment (Now "Confirmation") Surgeries

Notice the plural in the section heading, above. Depending on the age and maturation of the prepubertal child or adolescent, there will likely be a *series* of surgeries and physical procedures. Following are but cursory lists of what the surgeries involve. They are detailed in medical, but graphic terms.

In *male to female* (MTF) *surgeries*, there is:

- Surgical castration: Removal of testes and internal organs like the seminal vesicles.

---

25. Heneghan and Jefferson, "Gender Affirming Hormone in Children and Adolescents."

Manipulating Biology in Children and Teens

- Penile denudation, skin/nerves salvage for later use, and reconstruction of phallus into a clitoris and hood.
- Re-positioning of ureter and urethra within the newly constructed pudenda.
- Scrotal sac tissue salvaged and reconstructed into labia (*majora* and *minora*).
- Construction of a "neovagina" (a tubal opening which is lined with salvaged penile skin and nerves).
- When of age, breast implants, *if* hormones have not grown breast tissue sufficiently

In *female to male* (FTM) surgeries, there is:

- Bilateral mastectomies, even when there is little pubescent or adolescent breast tissue, to remove mammary glands and reconfigure chest/nipples.
- Complete hysterectomy, removing all internal female organs: Ovaries, fallopian tubes, uterus, cervix, and any ligamental bracings.
- Salvaging ureter and eventual repositioning of the urethra.
- Excision and closure of the vaginal canal.
- Salvaging of labial tissue (*majora*) to form a scrotal sac, where later testicular implants can be housed.

In FTMs, testosterone therapy alone will often make clitoral tissue grow (somewhat or a lot), and elongate. Many FTMs are content enough with this growth. Others will want to enable "standing urination," and undergo a *metoidoplasty*, a procedure that will re-route the ureter, form a urethral opening "through" the newly elongated clitoral shaft, and loosen it from its interior ligaments (for length), thus providing the individual with a potential for upright urination.

(For some adult FTMs the need for a full phallic reconstruction is desirable [called a *phalloplasty*], which can be done later in life. The organ is not functional the same way a natural penis would be, but it may give comfort to the FTM to have a neophallus.)

As is evident even from this cursory listing, the procedures are radical, although now straightforward enough to obtain desirable results for a good majority. As with any surgeries, there are always risks of complications, or outcomes not being what was expected.

Implementing these "interventions" continues, despite ambiguous evidence regarding their effects, making it impossible to draw definitive conclusions about their long-term impact. I take that question up after quoting conclusions drawn by Carl Heneghan, MD, Chief of Evidence Based Medicine at University of Oxford, and colleague Tom Jefferson, who state,

> These interventions remain largely experimental. There are a large number of unanswered questions that include the age of start, reversibility, adverse events, long-term effects on mental health, quality of life, bone mineral density, osteoporosis in later life and cognition. We wonder whether off label use is appropriate and justified for [some hormones] which can cause substantial harms and even death. The current evidence does not support informed decision-making, and safe practice in children.[26]

THE BOTTOM LINE

Today there is very little that scientifically supports engaging puberty suppression, and very little that also supports transitioning children hormonally before pubertal stages. And yet, parents are guided by medical advice that would be *wanton* in other occasions, with little to no substantive "evidence base" to corroborate it. The child is made an authority on their condition, often without extensive psychological work,[27] and parents are left to engage any or all means possible not to traumatize their child: they agree to block puberty, and eventually to start hormonal reassignment. But, certainly, a child's chronologic age doesn't correspond to their level of physical, emotional, or cognitive understanding of themselves (psychological maturity) sufficient to make decisions of this kind; or that they fully understand their particular experiences.

---

26. Heneghan and Jefferson, "Gender Affirming Hormone Therapy in Children and Adolescents," 6.

27. See such accounts in Steensma et al., "How Should Physicians Help Gender-Transitioning Adolescents."

After the Netherlands introduced puberty-suppressing treatment for tweens and adolescents in 2000, the protocol has consistently increased globally,[28] with many treatment centers following the "Dutch protocol," as it has become known.[29]

Somewhere in that global spread, age as a criterion to intervene with puberty suppression drugs, or to start hormone therapy, stopped being applied consistently. Now, age is not always regarded as a primary criterion for hormone mediation,[30] despite it being strictly stated in the Dutch protocol.

Ryan Anderson, introduced earlier, questions the foundations on which suppression and later hormone treatments are based. He states,

> This course of treatment is founded upon a questionable set of beliefs. The first is that very young children can possess a gender identity that may be discordant with the body. Another belief underlying the trans-affirming treatment regime is that puberty may be an "undesirable" and unhealthy condition for children with gender dysphoria. . . . But it isn't clear why the remedy would be to change the body rather than address the disconnection at the psychological level.[31]

Jesse Singal, science writer for *The Science of Us*, in a detailed review of studies made about children and adolescents with gender dysphoria and the need to transition, concludes:

> Every study that has been conducted has found the same thing: At the moment, there is strong evidence that even many children with rather severe gender dysphoria will, in the long run, shed it and come to feel comfortable with the bodies they were born with. The critiques of desistance literature . . . don't come close to debunking what is a small, but rather solid, strikingly consistent body of research.[32]

---

28. Kreukels and Cohen-Kettenis, "Puberty Suppression—The Amsterdam Experience," 4666–72. See also Spack et al., "Children and Adolescents with Gender Identity Disorder Referred," 418–25.

29. De Vries and Cohen-Kettenis, "Clinical Management of Gender Dysphoria."

30. See for example, the number of cases in London that have been treated at one hospital, some as young as ten years, in Manning, "How 800 Children as Young as 10 Have Been Given Sex Change Drugs." In that op-ed, Dr. Gary Butler, lead clinician for gender identity services in London and Leeds, confirms that number.

31. Anderson, *When Harry Became Sally*, 121–22.

32. Singal, "What's Missing from the Conversation about Transgender Kids," 25.

Possibly the best argument questioning the "unscientific gender ideology" of gender-identity hormone treatments in children and adolescents comes from Michelle A. Cretella, MD, herself president of the American College of Pediatricians. Writing an op-ed for the *Journal of American Physicians and Surgeons,* she recently stated:

> Currently there is a vigorous albeit suppressed debate among physicians, therapists, and academics regarding what is fast becoming the new treatment standard for gender dysphoria in children. A review of the current literature suggests that this protocol is rooted in an unscientific gender ideology, lacks an evidence base, and violates the long-standing ethical principle of "First do no harm."

And, in concluding her review, Cretella states,

> The treatment of gender dysphoria in children with hormones effectively amounts to mass experimentation on, and sterilization of youth, who are cognitively incapable of providing informed consent. There is a serious ethical problem with allowing irreversible, life-changing procedures to be performed on minors.[33]

Anne Tamar-Mattis, also worries. She is director of Advocates for Informed Choice, an advocacy organization for the rights of children with intersex conditions. She underscores the legal underbelly of such a complex issue, and the fact that one major result of suppression and later hormone treatment is *sterility.* "Especially when it involves sterilization without a child's possible consent."[34]

What all of this should tell us is that the driving force for use of hormones on children and pre-adolescents isn't good science or evidence, but rather the press from parents, therapists, and doctors who, instead of making evidence-based decisions, forego lack of consensus, good data, or consequences, and move forward with interventions presumed to remedy a problem.

---

33. Cretella, "Gender Dysphoria in Children and Suppression of Debate," 50–54.
34. Tamar-Mattis, "Intersex Babies: Boy or Girl and Who Decides," 6.

GENDER REASSIGNMENT (CONFIRMATION) SURGERIES: DO THEY WORK LONG TERM IN ADOLESCENT TRANSITIONS?

The difficulty in responding to this very needed question is that there isn't sufficient data to suggest specific outcomes in the later life of adolescents. Studies that are long-term and focus on outcomes, such as "quality of life" or "psychological adjustment," generally have no (or a very low proportion of) participants transitioning *young enough* to reach conclusions. Studies that focus on "health outcomes" also have mixed results—some not raising health concerns, while others detailing them.

What we do have data on, I can report, and sadly, results are very mixed! Moreover, results from researchers who *agree* with puberty suppression (i.e., the "Dutch Protocol") and gender-affirming surgeries *report more positive outcomes* in younger populations. Studies available from other researchers who *do not* openly take positions on gender suppression and surgeries, *report mixed outcomes*.

A study by researchers from the Netherlands and Washington State University is one of the few that focused on a young adult sample ($n=55$). These started puberty suppression therapy during early adolescence (mean age, 13.6 years), and were surgically reassigned beginning at 16.7 years. Their conclusions:

> After gender reassignment, the gender dysphoria was alleviated and psychological functioning steadily improved. Wellbeing was similar to, or better than same-age young adults from two general populations [control samples which are not stated in the study]. Improvements in psychological functioning were positively correlated with post-surgical subjective well-being.[35]

The study's "limitations" acknowledge subject teens had *exceptionally close monitoring and medical interventions;* and that these interventions also *contributed to the "success ratio" being reported.* In other words, the sample was *pre-selected* and then given social, psychological, and medical *support throughout the transition and thereafter*, the likes of which would probably *not happen* with an individual teen receiving individual care and not part of a study population. Such a caveat in a small sample matters greatly in clarifying findings.

---

35. De Vries, et al., "Young Adult Psychological Outcomes," 669–704. (Bracketed comment mine for clarity.)

The largest study examining health outcomes for transgenders that includes information for youth ages ten to seventeen was undertaken by Michael Goodman and Rebecca Nash, both MDs from Emory University. The sample examined is *huge*, 6,459 transgenders, and cross-compared with 127,668 non-transgenders. The researchers wanted to learn about the health outcomes for those that had transitioned. They compared numerous health outcomes for people who *did* and *didn't* receive gender-affirming therapies and surgeries. Their results:

> While most young adults [in the sample] felt better about how their bodies looked and how others saw them, depression and self-harm through thoughts of suicide persisted more often than expected for those that began transitioning at 17 years or younger. Compared with young adults who were cisgender, transgenders had a higher risk of cancers that arise from endocrine glands such as the thyroid. Transgender women (MTF) receiving estrogen had a higher risk of blood clots and strokes compared to those who were not transgender. Risks for clots and strokes were particularly pronounced after six years post-surgery. In males [transitioning to females], there were less risks of prostate cancer despite the prostate not being removed in many, possibly due to testicular castration and stopping testosterone production.[36]

Other studies on younger adults (mean ages thirty-one to thirty-seven) confirm that hormone therapies, including sex reassignment surgeries, *elevate certain risk factors over time.*[37] And, while this is not true across the board and in all population groups studied, results of now-available adult studies can help parents of gender dysphoric youth discuss outcomes with their physicians, and be aware of potential health problems in the future should these arise.

In sum, none of the studies of later life effects are conclusive to the point of not recommending hormonal and surgical interventions; but uncertainties and cautions certainly remain. Chris Hyde, MD, from

---

36. Goodman and Nash, "Examining Health Outcomes for People Who Are Transgender." (Brackets mine.)

37. See and compare studies by Kuhn et al., "Quality of Life 15 Years after Sex Reassignment Surgery," 1685–89; van de Grift et al., "Surgical Satisfaction, Quality of Life, after Gender-Affirming Surgery," 138–48; Neto et al., "Gender Reassignment Surgery: A 13 Year Review," 97–107; Dhejne et al., "Long-term Follow-up of Transsexual Persons"; and Jellestad et al., "Quality of Life in Transitioned Trans Persons."

the Aggressive Research Intelligence Facility of Birmingham, UK, undertook a massive sampling of transgender outcomes, and states: "The bottom line is that although it's clear that some people do well with gender reassignment surgery, the available research does little to reassure how many patients do well, how many do badly, and if so, how badly."[38]

The point here is that parents, indeed any adult confronting the possibility of a total sex/gender transition, need to understand the *irreversibility* of such a decision, the short- and long-range benefits and risks it brings. Changing the sexual profile of the body *alters it permanently* to the new status. That means that despite the body morphing, some at the cellular level, it has to still *accommodate* a hormone profile it is not chromosomally geared to. When it does so, it irreversibly changes sexual course.

Bodies can morph successfully when monitored carefully in hormone dosing as well as effects. But that said, anyone on hormonal therapy long-term should be aware of elevated risk factors associated with such use. (Again, refer to Tables 2.1–2.3 at the end of this chapter.)

Ultimately, transgender individuals have to learn to accommodate new sculpted body parts—"neovaginas," "neoclitorises," sometimes breast implants if MTF; and "neopenises," "neoscrota," and flat chests, beards, pattern balding, etc., if FTM. New sculpted features are not functional in the same sense as if these were of natural origin, regardless of how much emotional accommodation and satisfaction they may provide for the person.[39] Learning to live in the new body is yet another challenge, even for those that transition early in life.

---

38. Hyde, "Follow-Up Studies of Post-Operative Transsexuals."

39. Klein et al., "Sexual Functioning in Transsexuals." Klein et al. report from a small, retrospective ("after the fact") cohort study, that reassigned individuals self-report adequate sexual functioning, depending on the techniques used in the surgery. Hess et al. report that sexual satisfaction and function after surgery "depend substantially on functionality [of the organs]." Hess et al., "Sexuality after Male-to-Female [Surgery]," 4. In MTF women, differences noted resulted from the lack of stretching that the "new vaginal canal" (*neovagina*) experienced. (In natal women the vagina can expand centimeters in length and girth when sexually stimulated, a function that is lacking in constructed neovaginas.) In males with a constructed penis (*neophallus*), use of surgical techniques that preserve clitoral nerves and conduction, as well as use clitoral tissue for forming a glans, enabled orgasms after surgery for a majority in this small-in-numbers study. (All brackets mine.)

Gender dysphoria is real, and *it can* and *does* manifest itself in some children—obviously so by the time some of these are adolescents. The critiques and medical cautions cited here I must, however, endorse. These critiques suggest there has been a quick rush to engage interventions of a scope not imaginable a decade ago. With them have come guidelines, but no significant addressing of negatives or side effects, as I've noted. Such negatives are played down or not discussed. Age limits have not been consistently observed, in the US and abroad. Certainly, "evidence based" and objective longer-term research is lagging.[40] And yet, these would provide needed foundations for informed decision-making for everyone involved.

And lastly here, a few words about the ethical issues. Sam Louie, a licensed medical health counselor writes in *Psychology Today*: "The ethical issues that need to be addressed include the following: *autonomy, beneficence, nonmaleficence,* and *informed consent.*"[41] Louie stresses that the individual (in cases we are discussing, children or adolescents) must have autonomy of thought and intention when making medical decisions. "Participants, especially minors, must *understand* that their desires, hopes, and expectations might not correlate with reality."[42] The notion of *beneficence* implies doing only good—what is in the patient's best interest. The question of how to assess "best interests" when the patient is a minor is a big question. Should the age be raised to voting age (in the US, meaning eighteen years of age); or by "proxy," through parents; or much later when the individual has cognitive and sociosexual maturity? *Nonmaleficence* means any treatment(s) won't harm the person, either physically or emotionally, even socially. Finally, *informed consent*—the trickiest to address when dealing with children and adolescents—implies the patient *is aware of the risks and benefits* of all hormonal treatments and surgical procedures. That's a whopping lot of understanding for, as we've mentioned, possibly cognitively unprepared brains of minors.

Parents must therefore guard against facile routes of mediation, and must work diligently to insure that a diagnosis of dysphoria is factual. They must weigh present and long-term risks and benefits of

---

40. Hayes, "Ethical Implications of Treatment for Gender Dysphoria in Youth," 1–14. See also Abel, "Hormone Treatment of Children and Adolescents," S23–S27.

41. Louie, "Trauma and Transgender Identity," 2. (Italics mine.)

42. Louie, "Trauma and Transgender Identity," 2. (Italics mine.)

any hormone suppression, any sex-hormone intervention, and any surgery, for certain.

Parents should engage *time and therapy*, giving these opportunity to verify a gender dysphoria diagnosis; or see the child desist on their own, as some have done.

In the chapter following, we again wrestle with more questions. Coming up, all those religious ones we haven't yet examined. It's a crucible...

Table 3.1 Effects of Estrogen Therapies on MTF Transgender Patients	
Effects of Estrogen Therapy	Comments
Estrogens are the mainstay hormone for trans males wishing to become female. The following changes are expected after estrogen is initiated: • *Breast growth, increased body fat, slowed growth of body and facial hair, decreases in muscle mass, decreased testicular size and erectile function. Decrease in penile mass over time due to the lack of erections.* • *There may not be voice-pitch changes, and depilation of facial and body hair may be necessary to remove these.* Use of estrogen disables testosterone production, but it is often not enough alone. Other anti-androgenic therapies (progesterone, GnRH agonists) may also help to achieve maximum change. The extent of these changes and the time interval for maximum change varies across patients and may take up to twelve to twenty-four months to occur.	While not conclusive, there may be a trend toward an increased risk of heart disease in transgendered women. Estrogenic compounds may affect the vascular system, so there is need to monitor for deep vein thrombosis in long-term therapy. Diabetes may initiate, and therefore blood sugar levels and A1C should be monitored. This comorbidity has been found to be prevalent among transgender populations. There are theoretical risks of breast cancer associated with long-term progesterone use, so if used in conjunction with estrogen, it should be for short term. Liver profiles need to be monitored, as well as mineral density and routine screening for osteoporosis. (Demineralization and bone density loss have been reported.) Male to female patients report improvements in quality of life based on the positive effects of body image and mood.

Sources: Unger, "Hormone Therapy for Transgender Patients," 877–84; Hembree et al., "Endocrine Treatment of Transsexual Persons," 3132–54.

Manipulating Biology in Children and Teens

Table 3.2 Effects of Testosterone Therapy in FTM Transgender Patients

Effects of Testosterone Therapy	Comments
Within three months of initiating testosterone therapy, the following can be expected: • *Cessation of menses, increased facial and body hair, skin changes and increased acne, changes in fat distribution and increases in muscle mass, and increased libido (sexual desire).* • *Later effects in some include deepening of the voice.* • *Most see atrophy of the vagina and increased clitoral size.* • *Male pattern hair loss can occur over time, a result of hormonal effects on the scalp's skin. Some patients find this favorable, as it may be considered masculinizing to have a receding hairline or baldness.* • *In most female-to-male patients (unless testosterone is administered during the peri-pubertal period), there is some degree of feminization that has taken place that cannot be reversed with testosterone. As result, many transgender men are shorter, have some degree of feminine subcutaneous fat distribution, and often have broader hips than biologic males.*	Testosterone has different effects than estrogen in trans men, often increasing muscle mass and thus cutting down on bone loss and demineralization. It is not clear from present evidence whether testosterone increases the risk of cardiovascular diseases. Some studies suggest that over a ten-year period, trans men had elevated cholesterol levels and triglycerides, while others had elevated blood pressure. No studies have found increases in cardiovascular events, such as heart attacks, DVT, or strokes. Female-to-male patients report positive self-esteem and quality of life, but many more FTMs seek hormone therapy from alternative sources than doctors. These "self-medicate" for obvious quicker results (e.g., greater muscle mass, faster masculinization of appearance). It is important not to have this happen. Thus, increased surveillance of hormone therapy is recommended.

Sources: Unger, "Hormone Therapy for Transgender Patients," 877–84; Hembree, et al., "Endocrine Treatment of Transsexual Persons," 3132–54.

Table 3.3 Effects of Hormone Therapies in All Transgender Patients	
Effects of Hormone Therapies in General	Comments
After several months of reverse-hormone therapy, the body will start to alter its phenotypic profile. These changes will increase over the course of time, most often requiring twelve months to two years to reach their full effects. Each body is different, so the change over time is individualized to how each body will respond to the new hormone(s); the timing of treatment in the life course; as well as the overall health of the patient. Changes, particularly the *infertility* effects of reverse-hormone therapy on the gonadal-pituitary-hypothalamic axis, will start to occur within six to eight months of therapy initiation. Suppression of puberty with gonadotropin-releasing hormone agonist analogs (GnRHa) in pubescent transgender patients can pause the maturation of germ cells, and thus, affect fertility potential long term. Testosterone therapy in FTM patients suppresses ovulation and alters ovarian histology; while estrogen therapy in MTF patients can lead to impaired spermatogenesis and testicular atrophy. Hormone therapy plays an integral role in transitioning the body of MTF and FTM transgender individuals. When medically monitored, there are observable morphological transformations, which for many are positive and desirable outcomes. Long-term outcomes need additional and in-depth controlled studies to be conclusive in both MTF and FTMs.	There are important metabolic and health implications, which ought to be considered, and later monitored with care when undergoing reassignment and long-term hormone therapy.

Sources: Unger, "Hormone Therapy for Transgender Patients," 877–84; Hembree, et al., "Endocrine Treatment of Transsexual Persons," 3132–54.

7

Christianity and the Gender Crucible
Revisiting a Theology of Gender

All Christians have theology and doctrine, the question is really whether or not we learned good theology.

—Carol Brookes

Sex is a minefield of discussion and challenges in Christianity, and *gender*, as I've tried to tell, is often misunderstood. We can certainly agree that contemporary issues surrounding gender, the "revolution" at our churches' doorsteps, is as fraught with differing positions as any other deep elements of the human condition.

Consequently, writing this chapter has been difficult and stretching. Reading it will probably transfer some of the difficulty and stretching to you, since the road through a *theology of gender and identity* isn't as well mapped as some may think.

Christian views on the topic are as varied as ever: some denominations outright condemning anything or anyone who veers from what these consider heteronormative and binary: "God's design." Others see gender alternatives beyond the binary, in terms of embodiment as well as identity as not only factual, morally acceptable, but also sinless.[1]

The foci here are those looming questions Christians ought to consider in the "now" of the "gender moment." These questions center on the reality of intersex births; gender as identity and who/what determines it; and whether body modifications to match identity in gender dysphoria is a plausible alternative. Thus, we will confine most of our explorations of theology to these domains and questions.

As we move along, I will review interpretations of biblical foundation narratives that emphasize our male and female origins, as well as theologies that eventually address gender roles. When it comes time to discuss differences between diagnosable conditions and social movements of representation, we take up those questions, as well as how the church ought to respond to gender activism, in chapter 9.

THE GARDEN, AND GENETICS THEREAFTER

"Foundation narratives," as they've been titled,[2] enable biblical writers to draw on rich understandings that eventually focus our view on God's creations. These Old Testament narratives are largely etiological, meaning, their main purpose is to explain why things are the way they are, giving ancients and us moderns a reference point for all beginnings.

---

1. Even *within* denominations and congregations, individuals and groups can hold distinctively different views, and these can also be contrary to views on gender and transgenderism common to Christianity in general. Evangelical denominations, such as Evangelical Lutherans, Evangelical Anglicans, Baptists, Pentecostals, and those considering themselves orthodox Christians, usually do not accept egalitarian positions on gender identity or intersex. Quite a few Christian and Catholic-derivative denominations do have accepting views on gender identities and gender transitions; many even permitting ordination of transgendered individuals. Some, but not all, of the congregations that have egalitarian positions on gender are the Evangelical Lutheran Church in America, the United Church of Christ, Presbyterian Church USA, American Baptist Churches USA, the Alliance of Baptists, Christian Church (Disciples of Christ), the Cooperative Baptist Fellowship, the United Methodist Church, the Episcopal Church, and the Old Catholic Church (USA). What I report here as a list is, however, a "moving target" of change; so be aware as a reader that denominational and congregant positions change, open up, and sometimes close down.

2. Darshan, "The Origins of the Foundation Stories Genre in the Hebrew Bible," 689.

Christianity and the Gender Crucible

Thus, "we may have started in the Garden" . . . but we can't *stay there*.

If there's any general agreement among traditional, conservative Christian denominations, it's the belief that God's design of human beings sets the foundational model for men and women. Many thus insist that the "blueprint" of our sexual design—that of a male and a female—also determines all else about us.

In other words, God created a *man* and a *woman* (Gen 2:4-23), and this sexual differentiation is the determining factor in telling us not only what *physiological sex* we should be, but also what *gender*, what *identity*, and consequently what *gender script* we should act out. "Our anatomy tells us what gender we are," and that "our bodies do not lie to us."[3] Traditional Christian theology thus often argues for the centrality of the anatomical body, the body as the sole determinant of not only our sex, but our *identity*—and even by extension, our *roles*.[4]

What is left out of this determinism are many important elements, and included are presumptions that do not hold when examined. We'll get to these.

Foremost, and in many ways significant, humans reproduce by *procreation*, a very specific conception process also shared by other species—but in this case, essential to the arguments I'll make that impact our theology. Procreation (how we *beget*) enables passing on our DNA through human genetics. And it is in this genetic transmission that we not only see the coalescing of the two sex genes, the X and Y to produce male and female offspring; *but also genetic and physical outcomes beyond XX and XY.* Let's start here.

---

3. Walker, *God and the Transgender Debate*, 54. I will quote several other statements from Andrew T. Walker, below—a passionate but erroneously mined defense of a traditional theology of gender—to illustrate the problem. I urge you to contrast Walker's commentaries with Karl Barth's and like-minded theologians' views of imago Dei. Barth and like others see humans as communitarian males and females, not just sexual bodies and identities. See Barth, *Christ and Adam*.

4. This "concordist" view, a position that needs to *harmonize* all in Scripture, tends to both generalize and project beyond what is possible or certain. Other alternatives are questioned. "If it was this way for Adam and Eve, it is this way for all humans," or so goes the assumption. Concordist views are inherited from Augustine, and his notion that *seminal principles* that began with Adam are continued in all successive human generations. (Augustine, *The Literal Meaning of Genesis*, 235.) The problem with this view, when it comes to Adam and Eve's *children* and *successive generations*, is that these were not "created" in the same way God is said to have created the first humans. Read on.

If genetic instructions and hormones do their job normatively, we will get "one or the other" (male or female) as *differentiated progeny*. But sometimes we get "both" (medically, "hermaphroditism"—a true rarity) or "neither directly" (as in intersexuality). In procreation, the results of biological phenomena don't always fit into the purported binary categories.

Thus, here, in procreation, the theological significance of Adam and Eve ought to be rendered differently, given that procreated results can be, and sometimes *are* different than the binary. Theologian Megan DeFranza has suggested we look at the theological narrative of Adam and Eve as the story of *progenitors* rather than as *paradigms* for human beings.[5] A similar plea comes from Scott Cowdell, a canon of the Evangelical Anglican Church.[6] The plea is for those who look to Adam and Eve as "perfect humans" to understand the processes of human *procreation*, which underscores that the potential for genetic variation found in the human genome was indeed "coded" into the very fabric of human life from its beginning. (This point I'll expand below when I discuss genetic variability.)

DeFranza and Cowdell's option reflects this notion: that within the theological narrative, "Adam and Eve are only the beginning," and as such, an incomplete reading of the text if this part of the story is isolated from human procreation and human history.[7]

Why should this shift in emphasis matter? For several reasons:

First, the Genesis 2 account of this "first couple" emphasizes their most essential functions, which are to *honor God and each other, love God*, and *populate the earth* (Gen 1:28–29). When the intention of the rendering is understood, one then notes that anatomical differences between the pair aren't the main foci; to the contrary, their *similarity* and *complementarity* are emphasized (Gen 2:23–24). This is an essential relatedness if you are to, again, become "one flesh" (v. 24) in your offspring. Ladin's wonderful rendition captures this:

> The moment Adam opens his eyes, he recognizes what he's been longing for: "This," he says, "is bone of my bone and flesh of my flesh" (2:23). It's a complicated form of recognition. On the one

---

5. DeFranza, *Sex Difference in Christian Theology*, 153–85. See also Ciampa, "Genesis 1–3 and Paul's Theology of Adam's Dominion," 103–22.

6. Cowdell "*Gender and Identity*," para. 18.

7. DeFranza, *Sex Difference*, 175.

Christianity and the Gender Crucible

hand, Adam sees Eve as being like him—the "bone of my bone and flesh." On the other hand, he sees her different, a fact he registers by naming her *"isha"* (woman), the feminine form of the Hebrew "man." In other words, Adam recognizes in the creation of Eve the creation of the sexual. Before there was a woman, the universe was a lonely place for Adam, full of animals, full of God, but missing that crucial *other* whose combination of similarity to, and difference from him would enable him to feel at home with himself, and the world.[8]

And the story emphasis continues . . . God apparently also took pleasure in ensuring the couple were reproductively capable, even after they sinned: "Progenitors," filling the earth!

Second, if the human species needs to "fill the earth," it needs a diversity of genes.[9] Procreation allows genetic diversity. It doesn't take too large of a human group to enable necessary genetic diversity for species survival, as we'll see below. Even if we just work with those early lineages in Genesis, as example, we see procreation of sufficient individuals to enable the needed *genetic variegation*.[10]

For instance, the genealogies chronicled in Genesis 5 attest to population differentiation—given all the marrying and childbearing going on. Some appear as intergenerational brother-sister marriages; or extending the lineage, distant cousin unions. We label these *consanguine inbreeding*. Close blood relative unions are proven to force variation probabilities *even further* than mixing random genes from different populations would do on their own. (Inbreeding goes way back in the archaeological human record, and testifies to the practice.)[11] This is one of several sexual arrangements that channel genetic change.

---

8. Ladin, "Torah in Transition," 7.

9. We can't assume that all genetic variations are negative, or the results of original sin (a la Walker). Many are adaptive! Many are beneficial to immunity, environmental accommodation, even brain growth. To suggest all variants of gene expression are "tainted" or "marred" is to not understand God's biology. Moreover, humans needed the genetic wherewithal to populate the earth's different environments successfully.

10. For example, those that lived in the land of Nod (Gen 4), from which Cain took a wife; Lamech's marriage of "two women" (Gen 4:19), their succeeding offspring and their generations, not mentioned except by what their trades were; and, the many "daughters of humans" (Gen 6:2), of which we know little except that these were all "descendants" that had populated the earth (Gen 6:1).

11. Vaesen et al., "Inbreeding, Allee Effects," 1

Other arrangements are those of *interbreeding*—sexual relations between more genetically distant populations. These unions raise the coefficient for variety from that solely inherited from closely related parentages. Interbreeding is also likely to further mingle gene expressions not seen earlier in blood relationships.[12] Following this example, such interbreeding also allows effects from *epigenetics* (acquired inheritances) to extend the range of differences in resulting individuals.[13]

How many individuals are needed to generate a physically, genetically diverse human society? In an interview with BBC News on the subject, Australian geneticist and conservation biologist Dr. Philip Stephens estimated that fifty individuals would garner sufficient genetic variants to keep a human group "going" without becoming victims of extremely high inbreeding—which eventually results in mental and physical disabilities, even death.[14]

He also estimated that 500 persons would offer a gene pool diversified enough to allow offspring to adapt to new environmental situations. Extend that number to 5,000, and one would have enough *genetic resilience* to cover those random losses in genes passed down from one generation to the next.[15]

The important point to recognize here is that, inherent in the genetic material of humans, from their DNA inception, there is the potential for variation. Resulting palettes of human population groups allow them to also *adapt and survive* in different ecologies. Without genetic variation, *we die*.

---

12. Hamamy, "Consanguineous Marriages," 185–92. See also Ben-Noun, *Consanguineous Marriages*; Davidson, "Genetics, the Nephilim," 24–34.

13. *Epigenetics* claims that inheritance of variations (*epigenetic inheritance*) also happens beyond the DNA code, and passes from parents to offspring. Thus, some of a parent's acquired traits can *also* be passed on to future generations in the form of "epigenetic tags."

14. Stephens (quoted in Perry, "Does the Story of Adam and Eve," par. 13). Extreme inbreeding, such as what happened with royal families of Europe, testify to its detrimental effects over a very short time period. See Yong, "How Inbreeding Killed Off a Line of Kings."

15. Gorvett, "Could Just Two People," 15–18. See also the technical article in which Stephens reports these estimates, in Flather et al., "Minimum Variables Populations," 307–16.

Christianity and the Gender Crucible

BINARISM, OR MORE? THE CREATOR'S "CATEGORIES"

How many were born with XYY, XXY, XO genetics? How many hidden from our view in early human and biblical history were born *intersex*? We have no telling, no numbers; but we have the genetic certainty that with increased human population growth, genetic and epigenetic diversity, these individuals *did* come to exist.

In chapter 4, I noted that by the time of rabbinic Judaism and the consolidation of commandments, oral traditions, and interpretations into canonical works (ca. first century CE to the closure of the Babylonian Talmud, ca. 600 CE),[16] Israel acknowledged *intersex and androgynous* individuals. Israel accommodated them without question, and still does today.

Even more significantly, if we go back to Psalm 139, David extolls, "It was you who formed my *internal organs*, fashioning me within my mother's womb" (v. 13)—literally כִלְיֹתָי *(kilyotāy)* "my kidneys"—a metaphor referring to one's bodily organs, and the kidneys as seats of emotion. He follows later with, "Your eyes saw my unformed body . . . when I was woven together" (v. 16).

> The larger context of these passages is that for the Psalmist, an appreciation of God's omnipresence and omniscience rests in understanding that God has created everything and knows everything—even down to how I was crafted in the womb of my mother. This verse is crucial [to understand] because it implies that all of us, no matter who we are, no matter our ability, looks . . . were wondrous to God. And no-one, no preacher or politician has the right to call who I am into question because ultimately, God made me. . . . God's ways are a "mystery" that everyone has to come to terms with, and respect. Moreover, if we take Genesis 1:26–27 seriously, as referring to the entire spectrum of humanity in all its wondrous diversity, then *all* of us are in God's image and "very good."[17]

The point is, *conservative Christianity has not done well here. The church has often refused to acknowledge physical forms that exist*

---

16. Ulmer, "Rabbinic Judaism," par. 1.

17. Commentary from Dr. Robert A. Mullins, Chair and Professor, Department of Biblical and Religious Studies, Azusa Pacific University, Azusa, CA. Directly quoted with permission from mutual correspondence on these verses, Feb 5, 2019. (Brackets mine.)

beyond the binary.[18] As example, let's hear the Evangelical Lutheran Church Diocesan Doctrine Commission's commentary on sexuality, gender, and identity:

> All human beings have been created as either male or female, and it is God's will for us to embrace His good gift even though this can be complex in a sin-cursed world. We can further conclude that however best we categorize the painful experience of gender incongruence, from a biblical point of view, it involves a significant misperception of created reality.[19]

In holding such positions the church is quick to use science: "Biology and DNA matter," because, we are told "it is God's blueprint and design" (to have *only* XX, XY sexes). What can possibly be the alleged "*misperception* of created reality," when we have proof of people being born with sexual forms *outside the binary?* Notice the emphasis on human *creation,* and not a word on *procreation.*

A certain misperception is also found in this statement from Andrew T. Walker, who wrote *God and the Transgender Debate*:

> Our bodies do not lie to us. To misunderstand, blur, or reject the Creator's categories for humanity doesn't just put us in rebellion against the Creator and creation—it puts us at odds with how each of us was made.[20]

The "Creator's categories" certainly apply to the creation of Adam and Eve. These, however, do not remain *binary only* when we witness *procreation*. (Walker is also not accurate in his rendition of what "creates" *gender*—a point we'll discuss shortly, below.)

So, let's reconsider: If God made each of us, and our bodies "do not lie to us," then Walker is unconsciously *affirming, not denying* that intersex, chromosomally or hormonally variant persons are *also* in

---

18. Cowdell again tells us the reason why the church refuses such variety: "Whereas the gender binary has represented a classical and biblical world view 'from above,' it came to represent [as well] a controlling modern materialism 'from below.' In both cases, ancient and modern, I suggest that gender was ideologically freighted in the interest of maintaining a sufficiently differentiated view of reality, which was necessary for preserving social and ecclesiastical stability" ("Gender and Identity," 4). And again, "My issue here is with the . . . unease towards the *hybrid*, the *undifferentiated*, the *unclassifiable*, the *uncontrollable*" (Cowdell, "Gender and Identity," 4). (Brackets and italics mine.)

19. Evangelical Lutheran Church, *Lutheran Introduction to Sexual Orientation*, 6.

20. Walker, *God and the Transgender Debate*, 54.

Christianity and the Gender Crucible

God's blueprint (cf. Ps 139:13). As I hear it, his rationale is not only stretching the science into some warped theology, but stretching theology into some warped science, where it shouldn't be.

When the church *does* acknowledge other than the binary, such as *intersex births*, these formats of humanity are then suggested to be the results of "original sin," the perpetuation of "imperfection" due to the fall.[21] Let's hear Walker again: "What we are seeing here [referring to intersex individuals] is an aspect of creation that has been marred by the fall—a deviation from a norm that reaffirms that a norm exists in the first place."[22] Walker's comments reduce intersex individuals to aberrations stemming from original sin—"marred" is his term here—making them *deviant* from the presumptive norm. Not only is this insulting to the innocent (we do have a theology of innocence for infants and children),[23] but also an ill-informed comment, given what we know through biology *and scripture*. Today, we know these are simply part of the broad spectrum of genetic variations in our species. (Read Psalm 139 again.)

Walker's not the only one. Chuck (Charles) Colson, Nixon's "hatchet man" who found redemption in prison and went on to forge Prison Fellowship, wrote, "The Bible teaches that the Fall into sin affected biology itself—that nature is now marred and distorted from its original perfection."[24] Aside from his many awards and writings, what depth of theological or scientific training did Colson acquire to enable exegeting the complexities of creation and Genesis? I do admire the man and his accomplishments, but I question the ease with which such interpretations are affirmed by Christians, *without hesitation*.

It seems to me that we need to reframe here.

The creation story and the fall of humanity aren't the sole elements in this story. The cosmos is at once "divine" and material, and processes discovered in the world of science aren't in opposition to the grand scheme of creation. Nor are they in opposition to redemption, renewal. God's goodness is fundamental and needs to be factored into

---

21. Walker, *God and the Transgender Debate*, 66–67.
22. Walker, *God and the Transgender Debate*, 158.
23. Bunge, "A More Vibrant Theology of Children," 11–19; See also Dennison, "Do All Children Go to Heaven?"
24. Colson, "How Many Sexes Are There?" 1.

the frame. If we leave it all damned, in pain and death, we discredit redemption and grace.[25]

Nevertheless, negative commentaries are frequently found in Christian critiques of science, many of which are taken at face value, regardless of the individual critic's credentials—or lack of them.

They are so common, that Christian authors Stanley Rosenberg and collaborator Michael Lloyd, both scientists, reflect on this fact in reviewing their own work, *Finding Ourselves After Darwin,*

> [Some Christians] ... want to close discussion [between scripture and science] down too quickly. They want to set firm perimeters perhaps before the appropriate conversations have been authentically held. There's a pressure to assert a position; set up fortifications, and lay out firm boundaries. Is there a place to be willing to take risks and step out?

And:

> [We were] ... thinking about Christian people around the world who are studying science and have been brought up in church traditions that make them think that, to be faithful Christians, they have to reject science entirely. We wanted to offer narratives [from other Christian writers and scientists] that show there is a huge amount of space to relate creatively between the different disciplines of orthodox faith and creative science. They've thought these things through, and they've not found it necessary to reject either the faith or the science.[26]

Theologian DeFranza's well-crafted words should be quoted here:

> Most Christian thinkers continue to uphold the binary sex model in the modern period, emphasizing the significance of sex differentiation as male and female [in creation] and heterosexual relationality for *Imago Dei*, human personhood, and human completeness. Their constructions continue to neglect the presence of intersexed persons within the human community and problematize not only the humanity of intersex persons but

---

25. See Alexander, *Is There Purpose in Biology?* Dr. Alexander, a Christian, genetic scientist and neurochemist, believes that while the cost of human existence includes pain and suffering, it can none the less be squared with the idea of a God of love, whose ultimate purposes for humanity render any cost more comprehensible, ultimately bearable, and redeemable.

26. Rosenberg and Lloyd, *Finding Ourselves After Darwin.* Quotes are from published interview, CCCU, "Finding Ourselves After Darwin," 38–42.

also their legitimacy as images of God.... Ignorance of intersex may account for some of this neglect, but not for all of it. A number... have worked to hide, downplay, or dismiss intersex. [These] must not only reconsider the binary sex model but also consider the theological edifices that have been built upon it. We must find a better way to value sex differences.[27]

Procreation establishes the reality and necessity for human variation, and we now know the reasons why. The resulting physical, sexual "variety" of people do not make these any less as God's creatures. *All are part of the chain of life—not aberrations in a rigid, narrow view of humanity.*

Let's also note, there is no real mention in Genesis that *procreation itself or the human genome* was in some way negatively affected by the fall, other than increasing pain in a woman's child birthing (Gen 3:16). As a matter of fact, as a species, humans have an astonishing similarity *preserved*, as 99.9 percent of humans share genome characteristics.[28] In the adjudication of Adam and Eve, God didn't say *"And your offspring shall be cursed with chromosomes that confound, confuse, and in other ways mean-spirited, damage my binary model."*

No, of course not—that's also modern biological language. So let's restate it: God didn't say, *"And cursed shall be the fruit of your womb, it shall be different than you in ways that will make them aberrations of who they are as men and women."* In fact, it isn't until later in the genealogies of Genesis that God's frustrations with human indignities and sin limit the span of human life (Gen 6:1–5).[29]

Most patriarchs lived long, generous, "fruitful" (read: with lots of offspring into their centenaries) lives.

The point has certainly been made that "all creation groans" with the effects of the fall (Rom 8:20–21), and the ground itself is "cursed"

---

27. DeFranza, *Sex Differences in Christian Theology*, 149–50. (Brackets mine for clarity.)

28. See Marcus Feldman's (Stanford University) cutting-edge research: "People from Distant Lands." (Original research was co-authored under Feldman et al., "Genetic Structure of Human Populations," 2381–85.)

29. God intimated an end to human life *in the* garden when stating, "The man has now become like one of us, knowing good and evil. He must not be allowed to reach out his hand and take also from the tree of life and eat, and live forever" (Gen 3:23). God prohibits humans from living eternally by banishing them. Later God limits the extent of human lifespan.

to bring toil to human labor (Gen 3:17–19). Human physical life and procreation, however, are preserved with great care.

Most births—to be exact, 98.3 percent of all live births—are genetically consistent outcomes.[30] As a matter of record, the hundreds of billions of cells necessary to produce our most intricate human procreation goes on with astounding, astonishing, probability-smashing precision, despite the enormous possibilities for error.[31]

So, if Walker's "marring" of genetic dimorphism means that those *intersexed* are "the result of original sin," then statistically speaking there's a lot of *selective damnation* going on for that 1.7 percent![32] God isn't "knitting" these wrongly, whether through incompetence or on purpose! (cf. Ps 139:13). The only honorable explanation is that in the variability needed for species survival, there is a range of outcomes. Our human *procreation* is close to, but never a perfect "creation," because our genes are not God.

GENDER IDENTITY FROM OUR EMBODIED SEX (ALONE)?

Here's the other theological incorrection I've alluded to: the way many Christians construe sex-differences makes these male and female poles also dictate *gender identity*. In this view, the body anatomical is the *sole* source of what *should be* one's core identity. Any disconnect is relegated to "Satan's devices for deception."[33] To have identity conflicts

---

30. Blackless et al., "How Sexually Dimorphic Are We?" 151–66.

31. See Gerald Callahan's fascinating account, *Between XX and XY*. Callahan, a biologist/pathologist with over thirty years' experience in biomedical research gives insightful evidence of the processes of embryonic differentiation, and underscores the amazing precision it takes to create a normatively formed human being—including their genitals.

32. The notion that all of creation was fundamentally and negatively altered after the fall is called the "cosmic fall" doctrine. Work by some biblical scholars suggests that not all structures of creation were fundamentally changed after the fall. John Bimson, for example, questions that interpretation in "Reconsidering a 'Cosmic Fall'" and gives opportunity for us to query whether "primal sin" has anything to do with intersex births in procreation. This question is especially relevant when considering God's amazing preservation of genetically correct births, and the difficulty of seeing intersex neonates as anything other than part of *imago Dei*.

33. Walker, *God and the Transgender Debate*, 54.

persist insinuates the person is "hardened unto God," and therefore "harboring sin."[34]

Such theology ignores many things and assumes many things. But chief among the mistakes is the notion that *gender identity* is *only derived* from one's *biological sex*.

Let's be clear here: biological sex is—to quote biologists—"*irreducible*," and certainly foundational for male and female functions.[35] This is the essentialism of sexual biology and the *initiating* template for the sexual self-understanding of many.

But *gender*—the role and *identity* part—isn't a product of the irreducible alone. *It is a product of the "sex adjunctive."*[36] And that means the great influences of social factors *outside* the body can have *on one's body, and one's identity*.

What is identified, then, as male/*masculine*, or female/*feminine* is in large part, as we have explained in chapter 4, the product of our cultural scripts and socialization. Conservative theologians ascribe all identities, often including *masculine* and *feminine behavior*, as flowing out of the body proper. *But this is not factual:* much of it comes from *culture, the culture one is reared in.*

Gregg Allison, PhD, Professor of Christian Theology at Southern Baptist Theological Seminary, writes about the "gendered body" [sic] *in ways that confuse this fundamental difference* between what is one's *physical sex* and what is one's *sexual identity*, or *gender*. He states,

> Unlike secondary characteristics such as hair and eye color, height and body type, gender is a primary characteristic. God does not create a generic human being and add on gender [*I think he means biological sex*]; rather, he creates a human being either as a male person or as a female person.[37]

---

34. Walker, *God and the Transgender Debate*, 68.

35. "Sex irreducible": Characteristics of male/female differences that are primary and non-transferable between males and females, namely, semen production, ovulation, menstruation, gestation, and lactation. See Money, *Man, Woman, Boy, Girl*, 224. Also see Fausto-Sterling, *Sex/Gender*, chapter 2.

36. Money, *Man, Woman, Boy, Girl*, 235. The term "sex adjunctive" is introduced by Money to mean "male/female differences that are tertiary or subsidiary, and only peripherally related to sex-hormonal differences with respect to the differences between the sexes" (Money, *Man, Woman, Boy, Girl*, 225).

37. Allison, "Toward a Theology of Embodiment," 4–17. (Brackets and italics mine for emphasis.)

Allison resorts in classic manner to the Christian narrative of having the *body* dictate *all else*, and mistakenly suggests that God is the creator of *gender*, when in fact, gender is *scripted*, after birth, as we state above.

In assigning gender "embodied" as God's creation, Allison concludes, "Human beings are *perspectivally gendered* [sic]—as designed by God."[38] Which then, to Allison, means that our viewpoints *as a man* or *as a woman* are God-instilled—and thus, he claims in rather frustrated tone, "Try as I might, even urged on by my wife, I cannot see life from her—a woman's—perspective."[39]

Sadly, then, Allison and others with these views position the world of experiences, understandings, and motivations as *fundamentally different* for men and women *due to* their "special creation."

Here, we have a *theology of causal difference,* never mind identity, so foundational that one's viewpoint—as a man, or as a woman—can't comprehend the other's! As well, such a theology seems to make one's experience with God and people *fundamentally different* for men and women! Hear Allison again,

> Human *genderdness* [sic] means that a man is conscious of and knows himself as a man, he relates to other human beings as a man, and as a man he relates to God. Similarly, it means that a woman is conscious of and knows herself as a woman, she relates to other human beings as a woman, and as a woman she relates to God.[40]

Initially and superficially, it may all *sound* plausible, until we stop and ask those significant questions about how the effects of *rearing, socialization, social mores,* and *culture's gender scripts* come to bear on how all this self-understanding develops in the person.

How do we then bridge this chasm between men and women, each not being able to comprehend "life from the other's perspective?" What a conundrum! Especially, if one is to be *in complement* and *communion* with one another . . . remember, becoming "one flesh" and (maybe also) "one mind"?

---

38. Allison, "Toward a Theology of Embodiment," 5.
39. Allison, "Toward a Theology of Embodiment," 6.
40. Allison, "Toward a Theology of Embodiment," 6. (Italics mine for emphasis.)

Even more to the point, if it's all locked up into roles and ways of thinking that were *"created perspectivally"* [sic] that way by God, one might as well give up on human rights and justice for gender equity: God would have determined inequalities by default. (These are patently wrong conclusions.)

Things many Christian believers take for granted are more complex than they seem. I suspect many Christians hold interpretive principles as in some way implicit truth. But *theology* and its *hermeneutics* are products of human heads and hearts. These are attempts to understand God's revelation, thus capable of producing differing views, even differing conclusions and interpretations. Walker's conclusions about men and women do not reflect a theology that has been recognized by the churches across the ages as representing core Christian teachings *about men and women*, faithful articulations of and responses to divine revelation given in Scripture—what the Orthodox call dogma.

In discussing these points, we need to distinguish theory and opinion from theology. Canonical and other doctrinal points of agreement should be evidenced in a theology that reflects divine revelation given in scripture.[41] These are the "shoulds." But as we know, theology and theological *theory* embody discourses about, and interpretations of, religious doctrine. In so doing, it often places these in the context of the religious community which it services. In conservative, and especially fundamentalist Christian circles, theological theory and its exegesis is sometimes taken by lay membership *to stand in for doctrine*; a kind of "revealed" theology that then underscores what people believe.[42] It's a brash comment, but one needed here when discussing males and females, God's purposes in their complementarity and relationality.

The argument that counters Allison's conclusions stems directly from scripture itself: God doesn't provide Adam a helpmeet he can't

---

41. See Helmer, *Theology and the End of Doctrine*.

42. Camery-Hoggatt, in *Reading the Good Book Well*, is quick to help us understand that biblical interpretation is no infallible science. In fact, Camery-Hoggatt asserts that when one looks at the history of interpretation, among the discernible patterns is one that often "serves our own predispositions" (25). We also learn that we "interpreters don't come to the Bible as blank books. We come with vested interests, commitments, ideas about what can and can't happen, and ideas about what should and shouldn't happen" (25). Indeed, Camery-Hoggatt's entire chapter 3 aims to help interpretation by revealing how much of a sliding scale it can be, what interpreters can do to discover the biblical author's intention, and any divine truth behind it.

understand—who is so *"perspectivally"* different they can't see God's creation in similar fashion; or experience sin, life after the garden, without understanding it similarly. *Complementarity* and *equality* can't occur between Allison's male and female.

We are committed to scripture. We ought not be committed to particular interpretive traditions, especially when these are patently giving us *wrong answers*. This is especially true of how we go about theologically interpreting the meaning of sex, and the meaning of gender. Here's the follow-up question:

ARE MASCULINITY AND FEMININITY REALLY "DIVINELY SCRIPTED"?

There is no divine script for what a male or female should *be* like, *feel* like, any more than there is a repertoire of *manly* behaviors emanating from Christ himself.[43] We'll get to *that* later in this chapter . . . . But if there *is* a vision of biblical masculinity and femininity, then it, too, must leach out *socio-cultural, adjunctive factors* to reflect well the imago Dei. Otherwise, we remain convinced that our models are as they should be, "divine"; and use our skewed theology to justify our viewpoints.

We can then insist, for instance, that the male patriarchy of the Bible is *the . . . only . . .* correct model: a model that is *not universal*, and historically repulsed—both by males and females burdened under it—due mainly to its many negative effects.[44]

---

43. If one wanted to argue, *"But there is!"* then let's first acknowledge that as "fully human," Christ was subject to the influences of his culture—which was patriarchal and male-centered. Naturally, Christ grew up assimilating the *male role* he learned. But do note . . . he also *voided* numerous stereotypes associated with it: behaviors, feelings, and relationships customary for men of his time. In that sense, Christ displays more *androgyny* than all his male contemporaries. Notice it in Mollenkott, "The Androgyny of Jesus."

44. Steven Goldberg wrote in the early 1970s *The Inevitability of Patriarchy*, a tome that theorized why the biological differences between men and women always produced male domination. It set off a furor of criticism. A decade later, in 1986, Gerda Lerner wrote *The Creation of Patriarchy*. It contests the biological rationale for dominance, and shows clearly that patriarchy and male subordination of women is an intended political, cultural, economic, and ideological *exclusion*, aimed at perpetuating male superiority. Such place women—their status and role—in a subordinate and segregated position. The status of women has little to do with male/female genetics and all to do with how social systems deprive women from information and power, often

Gender as an identity of one's sexual self may early on rely on the physical body as a template. But the *psychological internalization* of that body, what it *means to the person*, is a product of many social scripts and personal experiences, not just the body's anatomy. For instance, a transgender identity isn't just a rejection of anatomy. By default, it also rejects *role*—and this all can get very confused when we discuss, even argue, about it.

BUT ISN'T A TRANSGENDER IDENTITY JUST ANOTHER NAME FOR HOMOSEXUALITY?

The simple answer is, *No, of course not.* And yet, some in Christian denominations feel the "overlap" is such as to warrant them being synonymous: "Even though by definition transgenderism is not the same thing [sic] as homosexuality, there is enough overlap between the two that some regard transgenderism as homosexuality by another name."[45] Please, let's address this "overlap" misstep!

For many Christians, the Bible seems clearly negative on a heteronormative person shifting *sexual behaviors*, such as when Paul addresses sexual *orientation* and uses the term *"effeminate"*— μαλακοῖς (*malakois*)—in 1 Corinthians 6:9 to describe homosexual participants, given that men were giving up their "natural desire for women," and committing "shameful acts with other men" (Rom 1:27). It is conceivable that Paul witnessed effeminacy as defined in his era, or he presumed effeminacy based on the acts. The Greek term (also translated *soft*) could be used to underscore the "reversed" acts men engaged with each other in this passage's acknowledgements.

But the negativity here seems focused on the homosexual *behavior*, lust, and passions that some men and women were given over to—rather than any *gender-identity shifting*—since nothing in these scriptures address *gender identity*. One can remain male/masculine in role *and identity* and still participate in homosexual acts. The same for women: they can remain female/feminine in role *and identity* and engage in same-sex activities. Nothing in these scriptures seems to

---

through their socialization and role ascriptions *as women*.

45. Assemblies of God, "Transgenderism, Transsexuality, and Gender Identity."

allude to gender identity conflicts: men "wanting to be women" or women "wanting to be men."

Assuming traditional interpretations of these biblical texts are correct, Scriptures here and elsewhere are castigating the behaviors, calling these unnatural and shameful; but there is nothing to insinuate gender-identity shifts as we know them or presume them from the historical record in these often-quoted passages.

What Paul stresses appears related more to the phrase "contrary to nature," and the substitution of heterosexual acts for acts considered to not follow "natural relations" (v. 27); *not* a man being "made into a woman," or "ceasing to be a man." This seems to me to be a wrong interpretation, implied early on by John Chrysostom in his *Homilies on Romans* (384–396 CE),[46] which influenced later commentaries on these verses.

In sum, a correct biblical anthropology of *gender* should distinguish it from *behavioral sexual acts*, since the former (gender) relates to *role* and *identity*, and the latter (sex) refers to *what one does physically with one's genitals*.

RECONTEXTUALIZATION OF IDENTITY AND IDENTITY CONFLICTS (DYSPHORIA)

Gender identity needs to be theologically re-contextualized and acknowledged as the product of many influences, experiences, beyond just the body proper. Gender presses beyond biology alone to include the collective narratives of a culture—about men and women—rationales and explanations that include appropriate colors, body contours, behaviors, feelings, and everything learned and transmitted that has

---

46. Chrysostom, *Homilies on the Epistle of St. Paul to the Romans*, 69–71. See also Stevens et al., *Homilies of St. John Chrysostom*, 70. Stevens et al. quote Chrysostom to say "Not only are you *made* into a woman, but you *cease* to be a man" (v.4.2–3), 70. (Italics mine.) Homosexual acts do not "shift" one's gender, since a homosexual man or woman usually does not identify emotionally as the opposite sex, nor sees that identification as a pre-requisite for having same-sex involvements. When effeminacy is displayed by homosexual men, or masculinity by gay women, these behaviors are often regulated by cultural-subcultural *customs* and *roles* in same-sex relationships. But here again, one should not equate these *role shifts* by the person to mean they are, or are wanting to be, the opposite sex in *identity*. Most often, these behavioral shifts are repudiations of the strictures of masculine or feminine *roles*, and not a repudiation of who they are *identity-wise* or *physically*.

Christianity and the Gender Crucible

been internalized. Sometimes, it also includes those social-emotional dissonances people experience *because* they are women, or men.

And, this can also include those disconnects that individuals experience between *their own body proper* and *their mind*. Disconnects imprint on the mind:

> As the years pass refinements of what it means to be masculine or feminine are willingly drawn into him or her from the outside world, or are beat in by the culture's demands. Later conflicts or gratifying reinforcements, physiologic shifts, or life's exigencies will have their effects on gender identity into old age.[47]

Such is also true for possible *conflicts* with one's *identity*. Yet interestingly, theologians often find it easier to embrace concrete physical "facts" to validate acceptances of people differences than *states of mind*.[48]

The fact that science has not clearly identified a body element, gonadal structure, or hormone that "causes" gender identity conflicts in *gender dysphoria*, for instance, does not invalidate the factuality of a brain-body disjunction. Perhaps a case illustration may help to make the point here: when a lower limb is amputated, very often that amputee will experience "ghost limb feelings"—the brain continuing to *believe* that there is a leg there, when there isn't one any longer. Amputees not only report pain sensations, but other normal feelings about their leg, the "chemical memory" of it staying in the brain long after the leg is gone—sometimes forever. There is no limb, but to the amputee experiencing phantom limb syndrome, feeling the leg still there is a reality. So too, is the reality that their brain won't let go of their former leg. What we know about the human brain thus far underscores *the power of imprints*—regardless of where they emanate from.[49]

---

47. Stoller, *Presentations of Gender*, 17.

48. Cornwall rightly addresses traditional Christianity's concern with any shifts or ambiguities in sex/gender as being pathological, "or at least less than ideal" (Cornwall, "States of Mind," 2). Thus, such states are very often assumed by Christians to be changeable; that the mind must be changed, can change: the biological sex is true while what the mind says is false. To say then, there is "real" but also "false" evidence about sex-gender identity, is this view's take-away.

49. Sylvan Tomkins is often referred to as the research psychologist who clearly demonstrated that *affects* (subjective emotional states) are the results of limbic brain information processing, often unconscious, and thus aside from our conscious will. We

To the dysphoric child, adolescent, or adult, the *core imprints of disjunction* are not only real, but determinants of their emotional lives.

The current lack of physical causes for *gender dysphoria* makes it seem that this is a mind-over-matter situation; that it is "all in the mind," and therefore hard to believe that people can't change it. For the person experiencing the reality of a body-brain disconnect, it is as real, powerful, and as persistent as any other human brain-body issue. Regrettably, the science that tries to understand such *sexual imprinting* is still in its infancy. It may be that in the not-too-distant future we discover some physical connection with dysphoria.[50] *But until then*, we should not dismiss diagnosed gender identity conflicts as solely imaginations of body discontent.

Ultimately, for some Christians it may seem *okay* for *intersex* individuals with "ambiguous genitals" to have surgery, even if this surgery is part of a reassignment. But it is *not okay* to have a *gender dysphoric* person undergo hormonal or "gender-affirming" surgery. "*Those who reject God's blueprint and design are rejecting Jesus Christ's authority.*"[51] Where does that leave *eunuchs*?

WHAT OF THE EUNUCHS? A KINK IN BINARY THEOLOGY

Eunuchs present a kink in this theological thinking of the binary, and beyond, to body alteration.

In the ancient world there existed possibly even more rigid divisions between men and women, and what defined these, than in our contemporary world. The social order was often seen as a system of binary opposites, such as slave/free, civilized/barbarian, Greek/

"learn" unconsciously during the formative years of our childhood and adolescence; but also as adults. Here's the kicker: information, feelings, perceptions acquired limbically are motivationally *neutral*; that is, the body responds and the brain *codes* and *imprints*—but it doesn't *care* about where the stimulus, if there was one, came from. People "feel that way" and often there is no perceptual *cause* for the feeling. But this does not deny that the feeling is real to them, often unshakeable. See Tomkins and Demos, eds., "*Exploring Affect,*" 312.

50. Luders et al., "Regional Gray Matter Variation," 904–7. See also Swaab, "Sexual Differentiation of the Brain," 431–44. An excellent summary article on research into gender identity and the brain is Williams, "Are the Brains of Transgender People Different?"

51. Walker, *God and the Transgender Debate*, chapter 5. (Here, my summary paraphrase of the chapter.)

Christianity and the Gender Crucible 157

Roman. The categories into which persons were classed were all-defining. This included roles for men, and roles for women.[52] Despite this, many cultures were open to recognizing and including individuals who didn't conform to male or female physical formats, as already mentioned earlier in this book.[53]

Jesus himself acknowledged three different types of eunuchs in Matthew 19:12, "For there are eunuchs who have been so from birth, and there are eunuchs who have been made eunuchs by men, and there are eunuchs who have made themselves eunuchs for the sake of the kingdom of heaven. Let the one who is able to receive this, receive it."

Most theological commentaries on this verse make it to be figurative of how Jesus underscores celibacy for the sake of the kingdom; or to state it in contemporary terms, not getting married (maybe even dissolving marriage) to avoid distractions from ministry and calling.[54] And so, "the one who can accept this should accept it" (Matt 19:12).

But I want to emphasize the more concrete acknowledgement Jesus makes here of those that are different sexually, or who make themselves different sexually "for the sake of the kingdom."

The Pulpit Commentary rejects the notion that devout men would castrate themselves "for the sake of the kingdom," stating that castration would represent a mutilation and would therefore "contravene the order of nature and the good work of creation."[55] But the Greek used in this passage infers differently—εὐνούχισαν ἑαυτοὺς (*eunouchisan heautous*: "have made themselves eunuchs") seems clear enough as an *act*, not as a metaphor.

In addition, we have extant records from the Middle Ages, when the Catholic Church made great use of castration. Young *castrati* boys and men filled church choirs with angelic voices. And before that,

---

52. Weisner-Hanks, *Gender in History*.

53. Masterson et al., *Sex in Antiquity*.

54. Ringrose, *The Perfect Servant*. See also many Bible commentaries, such as the *Benson Commentary* (1857) or Matthew Poole's *Bible Commentary* (1853), all of which align the passage with marriage and chastity for the sake of doing God's work. None investigate the meaning or intent of the "eunuchs who have made themselves eunuchs for the sake of the kingdom" to mean anything else than their interpretation of it as *celibacy*.

55. *The Pulpit Commentary*, Matt 19:12. The *Commentary* is a *homiletic* commentary on the Bible, an opinion source of theology for many.

some monks cut off their testicles so their sexuality wouldn't interfere with their devotion—Origen of Alexandria (third century, CE) comes to mind here. Self-castrations are well documented.[56] By the fifth century CE, castration is absolutely ruled out of the church, ensuring that male dominance in its clergy wasn't tainted by an absence of genitals to prove it.[57]

The point is, Jesus appears very intentional in his underscoring that the salvation of the soul is of paramount importance; more important than the preservation of the natural body, since Matthew 5:29–30 speak boldly to that fact:

> If your right eye makes you stumble, tear it out and throw it from you; for it is better for you to lose one of the parts of your body, than for your whole body to be thrown into hell. And if your right hand makes you stumble, cut it off and throw it from you; for it is better for you to lose one of the parts of your body, than for your whole body to go into hell.

While again some commentators do not take these verses to mean the literal eye or hand, but rather the thoughts behind them (i.e., that which makes the eye a problem or the hand a soul-degrader), it is the determined language used by Jesus that is the subtext, or *meta-message*: Jesus may be implying he was serious enough about what may cause one to stumble, to stress that the physical body should not be prioritized over the soul.

That said, the Bible also teaches that the care of the body is important, since it is the repository of that soul in this life. In 1 Corinthians 6:13, Paul states "The body ... is but for the Lord, and the Lord for the body." And again, in verse 19, "Do you not know that your bodies are temples of the Holy Spirit, who is in you, whom you have received from God?" God does expect us to take care of the body, manage it, steward it. Taking care of the body, says Rev. Rick Warren, author and pastor, is a matter of spiritual stewardship.[58]

And while taking seriously the care of our bodies, we seem to willingly accept body modifications, even permanent ones, based on

---

56. Tracy, *Castration and Culture*. See especially chapter 3, Collins, "Appropriation and Development of Castration," 73–86.

57. Kuelfer, *The Manly Eunuch*.

58. Warren, "What Does God Say about Your Body?"

Christianity and the Gender Crucible

our contemporary definitions of "care." Thus, Christians today have *no problems* making health or aesthetic determinations that alter the body permanently. Who would refuse surgeries for cancers, or as preventive measures?

Angelina Jolie, in her openly publicized mastectomies, wanted the public to know she had the BRCA genes that made breast and other cancers a future certainty—the ones from which her grandmother, mother, and aunt had died.[59] "Preventative removals" are hailed as life-saving procedures, never mind that they destroy lactating and reproductive organs.

"So what?" we say. "They prolong life"; they "improve the quality of life," notwithstanding that in some cases severe body modifications result. We hail the reasons as respectable determinations. Who should be, could be against them?

What, then, of *aesthetic surgeries* that alter the body for no reason other than, well, *ego?*

We have face lifts, breast augmentations, breast reductions, tummy tucks, "Brazilian" buttock implants; even "penile lengthening" procedures and "testicular augmentations"—all of which do nothing more than satisfy the person's *identity and image concerns,* yet alter the body permanently. Christians undergo cosmetic "improvements" and we laud their good looks, not condemn them to hell because they did them. In 2018, according to the American Society of Plastic Surgeons, Americans spent $16.5 billion in cosmetic plastic surgeries.[60]

We say they are *morally neutral acts:* "Cosmetic surgery is a tool. The question, of course, is how we use it," says Shelly Beach in *Christianity Today.*[61]

But to me, there seems to be some *hypocrisy* at work here, when the church has no significant position on cosmetic body modifications *for the sake of the self,* and yet refuse to acknowledge modifications done by individuals who are intersex or dysphoric, *for the sake of the self.* Conservative theologians call the latter "covetousness," and

---

59. Jolie, "My Medical Choice," 25.

60. American Society of Plastic Surgeons, "2018 Plastic Surgery Statistics Report."

61. Beach, "Cosmetic Surgery to the Glory of God?" para. 7. See also Madueme, "Nip & Tuck," 1.

"falsehood";[62] but don't seem to believe it is covetousness or falsity to want larger breasts, longer penises, or even "total Mommy makeovers."

Let's not forget that God is not a differentiator of persons. Jesus *includes* the eunuchs, whether they are such "by birth," "by human acts," or "by their own acts." Certainly, there is no revulsion or deferral of the Ethiopian eunuch's request by Phillip: the eunuch's desire for conversion and inclusion into God's kingdom is honored (Acts 8:27-39). Perhaps this passage fulfills best Isaiah's prediction, that there would be a time when *even eunuchs* would be included with God's people and receive God's special blessing (Isa 56:3-6).[63]

THE VOICE OF CONSERVATIVE JUDAISM ON TRANSGENDER SURGERIES

Conservative Judaism has grappled with the acceptability of transgender surgeries, particularly for those who aren't intersex by birth, but rather, diagnosed as *gender dysphoric*. We should take a moment to understand Judaism's conclusions, since they address *all aspects* of how Torah (Old Testament) law could be interpreted in such cases.

Writing for the *Committee on Jewish Law and Standards of the Rabbinical Assembly*, Rabbi Leonard Sharzer, himself a medical doctor,

---

62. Thompson, writing as part of the Sydney Diocesan Doctrine Committee, comments: "Among the vices of the 'old self' that all believers are called to discard are *covetousness* (Col 3:5) and *falsehood* (Eph 4:25). These sins are particularly pertinent to the subject at hand [transgenderism]. For many who struggle with gender-identity issues are sorely tempted to desire a body other than the one they have been given. That is covetousness. Likewise, the aim of those who seek to transition gender is to 'pass' as the opposite sex to what they actually are. This is falsehood" (Thompson, "A Theology of Gender and Gender Identity," 7). An alternate response would suggest that diagnosed gender dysphoric individuals don't "covet" another body; rather, they seek alignment *between* their body and their identity. Moreover, any transition's goal isn't to "pass" as the other; it is to align the self-image with the body via a means of resolving body-self dissonances. A lot of Christians aren't *content with the body they have been given*, and improve, change, or in many ways *correct* its perceived or true deficits—many surgeries involve sexual "parts"—without being judged as sinning. Do we have a duality of ethics and morals going on here?

63. Isa 56:3-6: "Do not let the foreigner joined to the LORD say, 'The LORD will surely separate me from his people'; and do not let the eunuch say, 'I am just a dry tree.' For thus says the LORD: To the eunuchs who keep my sabbaths, who do the things that please me and hold fast my covenant, I will give, in my house and within my walls, a monument and a name better than sons and daughters; I will give them an everlasting name that shall not be cut off.'"

Christianity and the Gender Crucible 161

explains that the decisions for an admissible "confirmation surgery" (a male-to-female, or female-to-male transsexual series of surgeries) revolves around the degree of *distress* the dysphoria is causing the person.[64] If the person exhibits *historic distress over gender identity*, or demonstrates a gender identity that historically corresponds to the cross-gender, and is not likely to believe him/herself otherwise, they are considered fundamentally at odds with the gender they've been presumed to be. These would be acceptable candidates for surgery. Sharzer adds, "It is unlikely that someone who has not lived that experience can fully comprehend it."[65]

If the surgery is undertaken in conditions of safety (e.g., in hospitals and with risk mitigation), then the surgery is allowable and justified by the anticipated relief of pain and distress.

Moreover, the *teshuvah halakhah* (a rendering of Talmudic precepts that embody the Torah, or Law), made here to create agreement between religious precepts and contemporary conditions, asserts that the relief of psychological pain or embarrassment is *as valid a justification for transgender surgery as is any surgery for the relief of physical pain*. "Certainly saving a life, would override any halakhic [*legal*, as in religious law] objections to [such] surgery."[66]

This conclusion fits well with the *Diagnostic and Statistical Manual* (DSM 5) of the American Psychiatric Association—as we have noted earlier, the standard for psychological/ psychiatric guidelines, evaluation, and treatment. Conservative Judaism has worked through Talmudic regulations and objections against, for instance, castration, cross-dressing, and more, *since it treats well-diagnosed gender dysphoria as it would any "ailment" (psychological or physical) that needs a remedy to enable full health, and emotional well-being.*

Ultimately, and consistent with the Ethiopian eunuch's example of inclusion into the faith (Acts 8), conservative Judaism recognizes that the "completion" of an identity/body transition may require practical affirmations and considered inclusions: rabbis are thus instructed in required rituals that assist transgendered individuals to change names; re-confirm the person as a Jew through immersion; continue to offer prayers on their behalf; and create public accommodation for

---

64. Sharzer, *Transgender Jews and Halakhah*, 2.
65. Sharzer, *Transgender Jews and Halakhah*, 3.
66. Sharzer, *Transgender Jews and Halakhah*, 20. (Brackets mine.)

them in synagogues, camps, schools, and all public spaces governed by Jewish laws. These accommodations also include a requirement for congregants to recognize the person by their publicly declared gender, name, and appropriate pronouns.[67]

Such accommodations and inclusions do not mean that conservative Judaism is at one with contemporary gender activism, where the complete erasing of gender schemas is a desired goal. In chapter 9, I explore the difference. Here, I underscore that conservative Judaism very much keeps a binary gender schema as Torah creation doctrine; but has, as I illustrate, embraced historically those *intersex*, and now *diagnosed and surgically treated transgender persons*, to enable their accommodations.

ESTABLISHING A "BETTER" CHRISTIAN RESPONSE TO GENDER

We must consider doing better theology in response to our gender moment.

First, as DeFranza and Brown suggest, is to understand that how we interpret sexuality, gender, and sex itself today is *profoundly different* from how those in past centuries and eras did.[68] That means taking care not to replay themes that may be socially and historically distorted when separated from time and context, and thus would need a different rendering.

Such is *not* biblical revisionism: it is not altering the *biblical text*. It is to acknowledge how much of an externally imposed and fixed narrative we continue to carry forward in some of our theology.[69] The theological significance of the creation narratives of Adam and Eve ought to be understood to focus on their shared humanity, their

---

67. Sharzer, *Transgender Jews and Halakhah*, 29–30.

68. DeFranza, *Sex Difference in Christian Theology*, chapter 4; Brown, *The Body and Society*, epilogue, 482.

69. Camery-Hoggatt raises the bar on exegesis in his *Reading the Good Book Well*, by pointing out the importance of situating the *messages of scripture* not only in time and place, but also *culture* (chapters 9–10). In doing so, we entertain *context*. We then learn to "listen to the assumptions that underlay the arguments of the text" (*Reading the Good Book Well*, 122). It is then that we have the *explanatory power* of the message that can transcend time and space—and help us render it anew for a different age.

complementarity, rather than emphasizing just their sexual differences or created bodies.[70]

In this sense, it is evident that the Holy Spirit, by inspiring biblical writers, also *accommodated* inspiration to human languages, cultures, and knowledge of the day, and thus, made use of the "science-of-the-day" as means of conveying inerrant truths.[71]

It would be natural, in this context, to assume Adam and Eve's progeny would be exactly like them; and their progeny; and progeny after that progeny. . . . But if we continue this "concordance" view, we only avoid the discomfort and reality of human history: a history that, despite sin entering the world, has God still working in it! *God preserves the human genome* and yet allows for the *needed variations* to proceed, insuring human survival through procreation.

This is a history that ultimately enables modern science, and with it, the ability to "see" what was made in secret—and understand *we are crafted to produce differences!*

Scripture requires *exegesis*—critical explanations and interpretation—and *that* requires understanding of both the context of time in which it came to birth, and that in which it is now lived out and applied. My friend and colleague Jerry Camery-Hoggatt writes a skillful tome, *Reading the Good Book Well*. His paraphrased comment here implies not that the "revelation needs human help," but rather, that the original meaning of the text in the original context often needs translation to *another context* in *another time*. To Camery-Hoggatt that means "trying to get from what is *said* to what is *meant*," in order to apply any inerrant truth to the now of our lives.[72]

The realities of our human history, human failures and accomplishments, continue to help exegesis by forcing it to be grounded in

---

70. See Eichler's meticulous reading of the creation account, which reveals a fundamentally egalitarian view of the sexes, both nuanced and psychologically sensitive, in "Gender Equality and Creation." (Eichler is a Postdoctoral Fellow at Harvard's Department of Near Eastern Languages and Civilization.)

71. This not a novel idea. Christian interpreters fully acknowledge that in the writer's language, the message of what is ultimately conveyed is inspired. These also acknowledge the role of human writers of the Bible, their words often reflecting the form of their culture and experiences, contemporary ideas about nature, etc. Some even give opinions (such as Paul does at times), these comments falling outside the scope of their teaching. All of this is not only conceivable, but probable. See Warfield, *The Inspiration and Authority of the Bible*, 166-67.

72. Camery-Hoggatt, *Reading the Good Book Well*, 72.

present realities, not just the past. Such grounding does not devalue God's inerrant message. On the contrary, it opens it up to be the living word of God for every generation. Isn't it wonderful to understand genetics and "get" a lot of how we've come to be?

Second, the importance that we place on the body as the definer of who we are, personally and emotionally, has its limits; and *identity* is subject to other influences outside of it. Theologians need to protect themselves "from asking more of human sexuality [i.e., the sexual body] than it can possibly bear."[73] DeFranza thus adds, "What should be clear by now is the inadequacy of the simplistic binary model and its naïve repetition in theological anthropologies. Conservative theologians cannot continue to speak about sex differences in ways that avoid scientific studies of sex, gender, and sexuality."[74]

And this is where the rub is acute: many theologies remain insistent that science brings us false information; that modern scientific findings about *our body, our psychology*, and the social influences from *outside the body*, influences that *imprint* on our minds, are patently false. These theologies also seek to discredit biological information, information that hints at other possibilities beyond the historical explanations theologies have given. But the studies continue to pile up.[75]

We need to approach matters differently. "The letter kills, but the Spirit gives life" (2 Cor 3:6), and "where the Spirit is . . . there is freedom" (v. 17). The horizon opens up.[76] The Spirit is the Spirit of Christ, and Christ is the Lord who shows us the way. In this modern world, Christ does so not through an ancient science but a modern one, in which we can better understand the forces that *move the body, the mind*, in ways unknown to our forebears. It would thus be a continuing error to think that the body proper determines all our being.

---

73. DeFranza, *Sex Difference in Christian Theology*, 267.

74. DeFranza, *Sex Difference in Christian Theology*, 268.

75. For instance, see three separate studies over five years: Kruijver et al., "Male to Female Transsexuals," 2034–41; Zhou et al., "A Sex Difference in the Human Brain," 68–70; and Herbert, "Is Gender Identity in the Brain?"

76. Being clear here, the scriptures are the *letter*, but it is the Holy Spirit that helps us find *revelation* in it. Matthew Henry's Commentary thus suggests, "The gospel so much exceeds the law in glory, that it eclipses the glory of the legal letter. But even the New Testament will be a killing letter, if shown as a mere system or form, and without dependence on God the Holy Spirit, to give it a quickening power" (3:1–11).

Third, and possibly most important, in God's economy the body's priority is to not get in the way of the soul's health. If it gets in the way of your salvation; if it so encumbers your capacity to focus on God so wholly that it becomes a problem unto itself, then the core biblical message is clear: remove from it what is a hindrance.

THE BODY AS "NOT OUR OWN"

Some Christians argue against changing one's body to match one's gender identity, grounding their objection on the notion that our body does not belong to us. Often quoted is 1 Cor 6:19-20. When we "belong to Christ," we should certainly and fully be his; yet the greater truth in these verses is often omitted—that being the importance of *de-centering the self*, not obliterating our physical identity when "in Christ." The Corinthian verses cited may well be an actual call to deaden our *will*, not do away with our *identity*. Our will is the most intimate aspect of personal control we need to let go of, the apostle Paul illustrating his own decentering as a symbolic *crucifixion* of his will: "I have been crucified with Christ and I no longer live, but Christ lives in me. The life I now live in the body, I live by faith in the Son of God, who loved me and gave himself for me" (Gal 2:20).[77]

Deadening the will does not necessarily mean that we lose our *self-concept*. Rather, if "Christ lives in me" *my will is decentered*, not that *my self-identity is obliterated*. The gifts of the Spirit mentioned in Romans 12:6-8 certainly *identify* personal pronouns that embed themselves in the self-conception of the Christian so gifted: *prophets, teachers, encouragers, givers, etc*. Each of those who receive keep their identity, and other self-identifiers are added by the Spirit's giftings. Rather than putting to death my *identity*, theologian Volf suggests Christ ought re-center my *self* (two words):

---

77. It would be easy to argue we are transformed through the "renewal of our minds" (Eph 4:24), and that is obviously true. But Paul himself arguably struggles after his conversion with the imprints in his mind (Rom 7:15-20). He thanks God for Jesus, who despite our mortal and sinful body, our second-guessing mind, enables us to be worthy of God's salvation. We "groan inwardly as we wait eagerly for our adoption" (Rom 8:23), and we "wait for it patiently" (Rom 8:25). Meanwhile we remain fully human—and consequently live in this "body of death." "Christ will eventually rescue me from all this" (Rom 7:24-25).

Re-centering entails no self-obliterating denial of the self that dissolves the self in Christ. To the contrary, re-centering establishes the most proper and unassailable center [Christ] that allows self to stand over and against persons and institutions that threaten to smother it. . . . For if Christ lives in me, as Paul says, then I must have a center that is distinct from Christ the Center.[78]

It is the case, then, that some diagnosed *gender dysphoric* individuals, and some *intersex* individuals, see modifying the body as a necessary step in freeing them from its interference with identity, devotion, and ultimately their service to God. In their view, such an alteration remains instrumental to working out their salvation "in fear and trembling" (Phil 2:12). Moreover, this *kenosis*,[79] this "emptying" of what may be intrusive to full psychophysical and spiritual health, seems *necessary* to them in decentering the self to the full will of Christ.[80]

This was, in a way, Sister Michelle's story: her transition freed her to think more holistically, to see that her life had meaning and purpose beyond the struggles of dysphoria. Once she transitioned, she had no problems listening to that ancient tug, to become invested in the life she had felt Christ was now calling her to. Let's also underscore here, her *kenosis* involved giving up her sexual life: her vowing to a life of celibacy, as a nun, would "empty out" vestiges of what would become unnecessary after her transition.

And like Kyler, most gender-reassigned persons aren't attempting to *erase* the gender binary as much as *find their place in it*. Joy Ladin, a male-to-female transgender, describes it:

> I grew up thinking I was the only one of my kind—someone, something—whose genderlessness (I was a boy who felt like a girl) meant I was alone in the universe. . . . Since the birth of my gender, my inclusion, however tentative and problematic on the female side of the gender binary, I have started to feel that

---

78. Volf, *Exclusion and Embrace*, 70–71.

79. "Kenosis" is the corresponding noun to the Greek *"ekenōsen"* (ἐκένωσεν), the "emptying out" of certain attributes, such as is referred to Christ's incarnation and his "letting go" of godly attributes, as in the translation of Philippians 2:7.

80. Read how nine transgender Christians explain their physical transition as facilitating a full commitment to Christ, in The Christian Century, "How Do You Hold Together Your Trans Identity and Your Life of Faith?"

there is in fact a place for me in the world. Becoming a woman has made me feel human. . . . You may be oppressed, you may be crushed by circumstances, you may feel trapped in a life in which there seems to be no possibility of God or redemption, but if you open your eyes, mind, heart, you will see that God is right there, in the circumstances that seem to make the idea of God absurd.[81]

The conversations in this chapter are not meant to convince anyone that priority should be given to gender-altering surgeries, *fiat*. It is to underscore the importance of situating the conversation about intersex, gender, gender identity, and gender change in a theology of personhood that challenges improper understandings about human *procreation*, and doesn't make "the body" more than it is.

And yet, most conservative Christian denominations cannot accept gender transition as a valid option, even if it is *just* for the well-diagnosed *gender dysphoric* or *intersexed*.

To accept gender transitions in dysphoric individuals "in Christ" will require opening our theology of the person to accept Christians who transition, who see their bodies "as a living sacrifice," and as "reasonable service" (Rom 12:1). No such narrative, which rearranges what we presume to understand, can be readily accepted without examination—and some resolution—of what theologians call *the problem of particularity*.[82] Camery-Hoggatt explains,

> Whenever we read scripture we are builders of bridges between [the] there and then, and [the] here and now. If this is so, the bridges we build are almost always buttressed on both ends by real-life situations and not by general [theological] principles. . . .The Bible is also about real life; . . . the very purpose of our theological thinking involves coming to terms with the messiness, or rather, coming to God in the middle of the messiness. People make life-changing decisions based on what we say—or do not say—in the name of the Bible. The bottom line is about real people, often trying to do what's right—what's Christian—in difficult and confusing circumstances.[83]

---

81. Ladin, "Torah in Transition," 3, 7.
82. Camery-Hoggatt, *Reading the Good Book Well*, 18.
83. Camery-Hoggatt, *Reading the Good Book Well*, 17–18. (Brackets mine.)

We may not untangle this Gordian knot to please most conservative Christians here and now. But let's remember all theology is curated, or monitored, or given to us by gatekeepers—and we feel good that those we entrust get it right. The "if it's good enough for Jesus, it's good enough for me" mindset doesn't settle the problem of particularity. Multiple factors shape theology, since it is a human enterprise attempting to unravel the implications of biblical truth.

What we can rest on, at least for now, are the testimonials of Christians who are transgender or have transitioned. A feeling of freedom and completeness that enables a deeper relationship with Christ may not be every transgender Christian's experience, but testimonials here certainly attest that for some, this has indeed been their truth.

Ultimately, as we seek a better context for our theology of gender and identity, our task is to recognize that in the end times—the *eschaton*[84]—all bodies *will be transformed:* "Flesh and blood cannot inherit the kingdom of God, nor does the perishable inherit the imperishable" (1 Cor 15:50). In the end, there will be no distinctions or worth in binary or *other* models, since in Christ "there will no longer be male nor female." Susannah Cornwall states it well when she argues,

> The "no more male-and-female in Christ" then, means no more taxonomies of goodness or perfection attached to the successes or otherwise of how a given body meets certain criteria for maleness or femaleness. . . . The end—the cessation—of male-and-female is *the* end—the *telos*—for humanity [as we know it].[85]

Making much ado about polarizing sex and the identity of persons is ultimately futile work if the person is "in Christ." Paul, instructing believers in Colossians 3, aims to remind us that our life is now "hidden in Christ." Doing so should set our minds on "things above" (v. 2), having put on this "new self" (v. 10) where, in God's view and acceptance of our variegation, "there is no gentile or Jew, circumcised or uncircumcised, barbarian, Scythian, slave or free, but

---

84. In Christian theological language, *"the eschaton"* is a ready stand-in term for the end of the ages/world, and the coming kingdom of God, wherein the resurrection of our bodies will have new forms, "as the angels." Sexual distinctions are not important, or may be obliterated altogether, since "in Christ there is neither male nor female."

85. Cornwall, *Sex and Uncertainty in the Body of Christ*, 73–74.

Christ is all and is in all" (v. 11). Already, in Christ, there is an erasing of differences. How much more in the *eschaton!*

JUDGING THE OTHER

Hopefully I've presented rationales that address essential theological issues. I add one more: Pope Francis uttered the unimaginable sentence—coming from a pope—when he said, *"Who am I to judge?"*[86]

Francis' overarching response was to questions about sexual differences, questions that implied possible critique and judgment of others' experiences. In his recent book, *The Name of God Is Mercy*, Francis explains that before all else comes the individual person, his/her wholeness and dignity. People should be treated with delicacy and not be marginalized: "People should not be defined only by their sexual tendencies: Let us not forget that God loves all his creatures and we are destined to receive his infinite love."[87]

As Christians, we should then carefully distinguish how an individual has come to a position of gender-identity conflicts. If there are *persistent* and, often, *immutable cross-identity issues*; or if the individual is *intersex* and wishes genital modifications to enable living life without the constraints they may feel they have, then these seem legitimate venues for ultimate hormonal and/or surgical considerations. (Conservative Judaism thinks so.)

Who are we to judge? It is a private matter between the person and God.

Let's remember the scriptural injunctions against judging others in Matthew 7:1–5, below (and nearly all of Romans 14):

> Do not judge, or you too will be judged. For in the same way you judge others, you will be judged, and with the measure you use, it will be measured to you. Why do you look at the speck of sawdust in your brother's eye and pay no attention to the plank in your own eye? You hypocrite, first take the plank out of your own eye . . . .

---

86. McElwee, "Francis Explains *Who Am I to Judge?*" 1. And well that neither Francis, nor us, should judge. There are significant admonishments in both Testaments against humans judging other humans: Matt 7:1, 3; Luke 6:37; Rom 2:3 and 3:9, as injunctions. For the entire slap on the head, re-read Romans 14.

87. McElwee, "Francis Explains," 1.

Lisa Salazar, a transgender Christian and author of *Transparently: Behind the Scenes of a Good Life*, echoes Pope Francis' admonitions in her strong caution:

> I know there are many Christians who will discount everything I've said and done as heretical and completely unscriptural. But I warn them to be careful. I have the witness of the Holy Spirit in my life and in the same way I cannot judge anyone's standing in the Lord, no-one except the Lord can judge my standing in him. To attribute what I have experienced and how God has worked in my life to the works of Satan, is to run the risk of attributing the work of the Holy Spirit in my life to Satan. Do not blaspheme the Holy Spirit by declaring my experiences as counterfeit and invalid. As was the case for the early church, when the Holy Spirit was poured out among uncircumcised gentiles and Jewish believers alike, and the church had to change its theology to accommodate this new God experience, we need to be careful today that our theology is not so inflexible that we run the risk of putting God and the Holy Spirit in a box of our own design.[88]

ULTIMATELY, A BETTER HUMAN ESSENTIALISM AS IMAGO DEI

Our theology may also need more work on those *human* characteristics it sees as essential for the imago Dei.[89] As I see it, the traits that Jesus himself displayed are *androgynous, not sex-typed*, regardless of his male body.[90]

And yet, there are theological interpretations that extoll Jesus' incarnation *as a male*, as if his masculinity needed a coda. In doing so, what is admired is not only his ancestry and lineage, marking him Jewish for the Jews and the greater Roman world to note; but the precedence of his *maleness*:

---

88. See Salazar interview by Rachel Held Evans, in "Ask a Transgender Christian," last paragraph.

89. Pyle, "Man Enough."

90. See Jewett, *Man as Male and Female*. By *"androgyny"* I mean the best characteristics that men *and* women bring to the table, which are, in themselves, *gender neutral*. Jesus was a model of blending these for all to see—even when he was criticized for breaking role boundaries, loving his disciples openly, welcoming women, crying, and also yelling. This is not "unisex"—it is an answer to sexism in the church.

He grew to a certain height with specific features that made him identifiable to all who knew him. He became a carpenter. He had a sexual make-up that identified him as male. . . . What is described reveals Jesus as a fully embodied human male, with all that goes with a male body, from genetic heritage, musculature, to daily hunger.[91]

Having a male Y gene is, indeed, the greater miracle of the incarnation.[92] Genetics itself is breached in this miracle birth, since Mary could have only contributed an X gene, not a Y.[93]

But *assigning masculinity* to Jesus, with the attributes perceived to be *manly*, whether in his own or our culture, is patently wrong. Jesus did more to break free from any masculine stereotype than any other biblical persona. He does not need masculinity to make him *Immanuel*.

Jesus weeps as he comforts Martha and Mary after Lazarus dies (John 11:35). He didn't take a wife, as per male Jewish custom. He traveled with both male and female followers. He is homosocially intimate with his beloved disciple John, who rests on his chest. He spoke directly to women; healed women; he addressed women like he would address any man. He is anointed by women, and appears to his women followers first. Hear it well from Virgina Ramey Mollenkott:

> But although limited to a male body, he refused to be limited to "masculinization" to the fulfillment of only half of his human potential. . . . He cooked for his disciples; he openly cried for his dead friend; he served food to crowds; he was gentle with children; he taught the so-called feminine virtue of submissiveness to males as well as females. He refused to define blessedness in terms of biological functions; he said his mother was blessed not because she bore and nourished the divine child, but because she heard the word of God and carried it out (Luke 11:27-28). When he healed the menstruous woman, he specified that the healing should be located not in a male Savior but rather within the woman's own faith (Luke 8:48). Thus, he healed not only her

---

91. Assemblies of God, "Transgenderism, Transsexuality," 7.

92. If one thinks carefully about this miracle, the noteworthy fact is that in the male "XY" combination there is complementarity embodied: X *and* Y, not XX, or YY! God's embodiment in the male format *is itself a genetically complementary act* which fully embraces male and female genetics into one human form. Recall our discussion in chapter 4, where I note that in the womb, we are "both" before we become "either."

93. Genesis and Genetics.org, "Eve's DNA."

issue of blood but her attitude about herself, and he demonstrated a selflessness which has not been part of male socialization.[94]

To me, the following traits are the essentials for *any sex, any gendered person* of faith: *wisdom, perseverance, generosity, compassion, faith, servanthood; being loving, forgiving, prayerful, committed, patient, and humble.* All else, or anything else, are the additions and subtractions that our societies and cultures pile on us, and that includes our Christian cultures. Godly *people* ought to aspire to emulate Jesus regardless of their sexual form or gender identity. The family of God has no room for sex-stereotyping Jesus, or anyone else.[95]

But, *would it have mattered if Jesus had incarnated as a woman*—aside from obvious cultural-religious and political constraints? Would it have made a difference if God Incarnate would have taken on the "opposite sex" format?[96] It wouldn't have worked in the culture and time Christ lived, nor likely in our own era even. But the question shouldn't repulse us as much as make us think about the nature of God as *divine* and as *incarnate*.

Imago Dei—human creation "in the image of God"—isn't about the *God-image* being male and female, *since God has no sex, no gender;* but rather about the *complementarity* it holds: in the Old Testament, YHWH uses both masculine and feminine metaphors and self-refers as both a *mother* and a *father* to Israel (cf. Isa 42:14; Num 11:12). God self-revealed is the "I am that I am" (or "I will be what I will be," depending on the Hebrew rendition), a pure Becoming—a "restless verb that refuses to stand still or be fixed."[97] God certainly has no preference for one gender over the other. But humans do.

The model of God as Father and Jesus as Son is scripted male-centric so the incarnation can fit the culture into which Jesus was born; not because there is some mystical, patriarchal rationale for it

---

94. Mollenkott, "The Androgyny of Jesus," 3.

95. "In all of this," writes Mollenkott, "we have the support of the whole New Testament, not just the nature and behavior of Jesus. Paul taught males as well as females that 'the harvest of the Spirit is love, joy, peace, patience, kindness, goodness, fidelity, gentleness, and self-control' (Gal 5:22)—virtues society has labeled as feminine. Paul also taught females and males to "instruct and admonish" other Christians and to put their whole hearts into whatever they were doing (Col. 3:16, 23)—virtues society has labeled masculine" ("The Androgyny of Jesus," 4).

96. Ritchie, "What If Jesus Had Been a Woman?"

97. Ladin, "Torah in Transition," 4.

in God. It was God's timing for it to be at that moment and in that place—as planned from the beginning of time and revealed by the prophets: in that form and format (1 Pet 1:19).

To underscore the focus here, the church should acknowledge that much of its historical gender schemas come from *cultural models,* not God, and not from Adam and Eve, not even from Jesus himself.

We also can't *bend* Jesus' resurrection to imply the Risen Lord's body is a testament that keeps us *just the way we are* when we rise again—that gender reassignment just won't work itself into the resurrection, as I've heard it argued.[98] At some point, *we will all be transfigured,* and become as the angels.

Thus, we should stop trying to fit all masculinities and all femininities into the "biology of the first creation"; or if that doesn't satisfy, argue for a male-female polarity only, and Jesus' own masculinity as evidence of God's preference for the masculine. If we stop this, we open the door for greater understanding of our *procreated* variegation, and greater acceptance of Christians by those outside the church, who may feel all Christians are inescapably caught up in perpetuating the strength of men and the secondary status of women.

Moreover, we are freed to revise our gendered *roles,* and reflect more on what imago Dei really means. We can extend grace and mercy instead of verdicts to those intersex, or those with gender identity conflicts—both in our churches and outside of them.

---

98. There isn't consensus among conservative evangelical denominations like the Assemblies of God in arguing for gendered bodies in the resurrection, but most do imply that the "creation duality" of male/female is to be preserved in a glorified body. Referring to Matthew 22:30 and Mark 12:25, where Christ teaches that in the resurrection humans will be "as the angels," the interpretation centers around not being given in marriage (since angels do not marry), and minimizes any emphasis on a renewed and spiritual body. The Assemblies' position paper states, "It is the resurrection even more than the doctrine of creation that highlights the sanctity of the body, as it is clear that God's final intention for humans is existence as embodied beings." And: "The difference between the natural and glorified bodies is a difference of mortality, not a difference of embodiment" (Assemblies of God, "Transsexualism, Transsexuality," 8). This is a "theology of the body" that preserves sexual bodies despite sexuality being *of no use,* and *plays down resurrected bodies being transformed into celestial bodies.* First Corinthians 15:41: "They are buried as natural human bodies, but they will be raised as *spiritual bodies*" (italics mine). Let's *correct* our theology: flesh and blood and sexuality *as we know these* do not inherit the kingdom (1 Cor 15:50).

8

Pastoral and Church Leadership Responses to the Gender Moment

> "How should we approach the problem of identity and otherness and of the conflicts that rage around them?"
>
> —MIROSLAV VOLF

If you've picked up this tome with the hope of not only getting an overview of the gender "moment," but insights into how to respond to the many voices now coalescing on the issues, this chapter is especially for you.

Here, I provide suggestions for clergy, lay leaders, as to *how to respond* when facing others with gender conflicts or reassigned gender. In addition, I suggest ways and means for clergy and leaders to educate themselves, and their congregation, to enable compassion and social justice. Lastly, I offer suggestions on how to mediate any dissonances with congregants; and in chapter 9, following, with gender activists. None are easy tasks.

If you are a pastor or lay leader in the church, you are in a role that requires significant humility and service. Dealing with gender issues will test both requisites and more, your knowledge of all the parameters surrounding gender. Thus, the first order of business is getting yourself readied emotionally, informationally, as well as prayerfully, to address individuals with gender conflicts.

PRECONCEPTIONS, GENERALIZATIONS, AND STEREOTYPES

I attended a Christian university in Florida during a portion of my undergraduate education, one in which "Christian service" was a required part of the student agenda, regardless of one's major. The university courted students from Southern states, particularly. In contrast, I was from New York City.

When it came time to enjoin Christian service, I readily volunteered for "jail ministry." There was a nearby county jail that, despite the Civil Rights Act, still had *separate sections* for African-Americans and whites. In New York, we had no such.

I had volunteered in gang member recovery and drug detox programs during the then-fulminating heroin epidemic in New York. I had no preconceptions of what jail was like—*I knew*—I had encountered them, visited in them. I also didn't have a "color filter difference" given my variegated ethnic, racial, and cross-cultural experiences growing up in Manhattan.

I share this because as we prepared for ministering at this county facility, all I heard were comments of who to watch out for: "Watch out for Blacks," I was told. "Be careful not to let anyone—especially Blacks—endear themselves to you." Mind you, these were genuinely Christ-seeking young adults and academic leaders wanting to not only share the gospel, but also bring some "good news" to those incarcerated.

And yet, here we were—getting cautionary and preconceived notions of how *different* these two sets of inmates were; and how much we needed to insulate ourselves from being manipulated by one group, and (the assumption was) not so much the other. Those moments illustrate how often, and subliminal, entrenched preconceptions of people groups can be; how much we tend to generalize and sometimes outright stereotype, despite best intentions and our religiosity.

A diversified society doesn't limit unconscious bias.[1] Ives Erickson pointed out that "these biases exist in our minds [often] without our knowledge or consent,"[2] noting that the mind forms "strong alliances with things and people that are familiar while developing subtle biases against those that aren't."[3]

We would like to believe we are somewhat beyond the racial in the twenty-first century, but recent US social and political history certainly disavows that notion! Likewise, we would like to think that religious leaders (lay or otherwise) have worked on being less influenced by generalized preconceptions of people groups, social groups, social movements, and individuals themselves. But we are all human, to a fault.

To minister effectively to individuals and/or families facing gender- and sexual-identity issues, your first step is to take a close look at what *preconceptions, generalizations,* and *stereotypes* you may hold about such individuals or conditions.[4]

The challenge here is to be ruthlessly honest about the ways in which *our own socialization, our own set of reified postulates about people,* and especially about *how we go about unpacking our gender theology,* may get in the way of mercy and reconciliation:

---

1. *Unconscious bias* I define here as our hidden blind spots—ones we have difficulty seeing but which influence our beliefs and behaviors toward others. These are often acquired and sustained implicitly, and automatically shape our responses to others in both positive—but most often—negative ways. We tend to think of ourselves as good people, good Christians, and resist the idea that our unconscious biases can influence our behaviors toward others.

2. Erickson, "Blind Spot," 1.

3. Erickson, "Blind Spot," 2.

4. You may know these terms outright, but let's ensure we are on the same page. A *preconception* is an aforethought, a presumption that forms a conceptual frame about a person or group, condition, or problem. We can "inherit" these preconceptions, or they can form as we collect and assemble factoids about people or things. A *generalization* is a belief—often manifest as a statement—about a person or group that may hold some truth but needs to still be tested in the individual case. Not all generalizations are *false,* but most overreach and overdo without testing the applicability to persons or groups. A *stereotype* is like a generalization, but oftentimes worse, since it may contain tidbits of truth mixed in with false assumptions. Most often when articulated, it is such a stretched generalization that it winds up hurtful to the person or group in question. All need reworking, and in many cases purging, if we are to go beyond them in our care and facilitation of *the other.*

- How do I think about sex and gender? What is my take on people with gender conflicts?
- What do these individuals and their conflicts "challenge" in me that may make me move to positions of generalizations or stereotypes? Do I have these? If so, what do these tell me about such individuals that may be false—or a *pre-judgment*?
- Has my *theological position* made me a *rejecter first*, as opposed to *one who listens and welcomes exploration*? Can I be an *accompagnateur* to someone with gender conflicts despite whatever my theology says about such conflicts?[5]
- What needs changing in my theology (perhaps doctrine!) that may make me more *available and open*?

Jesus called us to be non-judgmental and non-condemning (Matt 7:1–3), and we want to be that way—it is just human nature to insist that the filters we have are adequate for this moment. Working through them, reformulating them sufficiently to allow us open hearts and open ears is the fundamental first step we take to assist in earnest.

EDUCATE YOURSELF ABOUT CONTEMPORARY GENDER ISSUES

As previous chapters try to make clear, issues of sex, gender, and identity are complex and cut across many disciplines. The need for pastors and church leaders to be conversant with and knowledgeable about transgender and intersex conditions is a pre-requisite for ministry with such people: we have much to learn if we are going to be of use to God and fellow congregants on these matters.

Three major areas of information needed, and underscored in previous chapters, revolve around the *medical*, the *psychological*, and the *sociocultural*. Certainly, there are myriad good sources in print now that can assist pastors in obtaining unbiased, medically and

---

5. Philippians 2:12 and 1:6 come to mind. Here is that term again, *accompagnateur*—from the French "to be another's accompaniment or sojourner"—first used in the sense I am using it here by my colleague and friend Paul Farmer, MD. Farmer founded Partners in Health as a response to Haiti's persistent epidemics, eventually HIV/AIDS; and turned that effort into a worldwide "accompaniment" movement for the sick and marginalized.

psychologically sound information. Additionally, I've made the point earlier that our theology on gender needs attention, some of it requiring a rethinking based on physiology, genetics, and culture. I hope the many references in chapters 4 and 7 help to facilitate these critical areas for you.

There are numerous other resources that can aid in revisiting theological positions on gender, and make these more amenable in application to God's love, mercy, and reconciliation.[6] It would befit a pastor or church leader to familiarize her- or himself with these types of specific knowledges before attempting to facilitate for congregants.

LISTEN–LISTEN AGAIN–THEN LISTEN AGAIN

Of course, we know that being *attentive* and *listening* is a requisite for any facilitation. Even more here, where individuals falter and quiver in their attempts at unpacking with another a set of feelings that they themselves may be conflicted about.

This is no ordinary element: as we've noted, gender identity goes to the core of the self, and there is nothing more overarching about one's being than what one "feels" about one's identity and body. To do justice to this unpacking, we must listen, and listen *attentively*, and listen *actively*.

In *attentive listening*[7] (sometimes called *active listening* in psychology), Grohol suggests the listener isn't just "listening" audibly—one ought be applying a skills-set that helps facilitate rapport-building, understanding, and ultimately trust. Here are some of Grohol's key points (the commentary is mine):

---

6. Again, a "must read" for serious theological inquiry is Megan DeFranza's *Sex Difference in Christian Theology*. Whether you agree or not with DeFranza's meticulously researched and well-written study, the many deductions and recommendations in her volume will certainly stir up a broader understanding of humanity, and what it means to be made in the image of God.

7. Sharing can be overwhelming if one is hearing only one's own voice. Techniques of active or attentive listening lessen that possibility by subtly engaging the individual, making the sharing seem more like a conversation than a disclosure. Ensuring that one does not take the lead or "over-state" helps keep the individual in *telling mode*, and at the same time eases their angst over being the only voice. See Grohol, "Become a Better Listener," from whom I've parsed some key points to reiterate here.

- *Attentiveness:* the listener is actively engaging the other via eyes, body posture, and kinesthetics (such as nods, smiles, or other facial gestures that tell the other you are getting what they are saying). Be self-aware as you attend: if your kinesics send a message that you are uncomfortable, that you are thinking distinctively different thoughts rather than listening, any of these can stop the communication dead on. Monitor yourself discretely.
- *Re-stating:* in active listening you repeat what the person said that appears important. This is not "parroting" but rather re-stating, re-wording in short what the individual has said. You can begin with, "Let's see if I'm getting correctly what you are saying . . . ."
- *Prompting:* keeping the individual engaged *and* talking *about what their gender feelings are all about is critically important.* You can assist with brief prompts, such as, "I understand," and "Go on . . ." or even, "This [point] seems really important [to you] . . . ." People generally respond by adding more—and the more elaboration, the more information you will have on how the person feels, and how they are processing what is being shared.
- *Use silence, with caution:* one can allow for moments of silence to help individuals recompose, "reframe" feelings, and help them process what is being said or what you are stating. If the sharing seems to move into unproductive territory, a brief pause will usually assist before making any other comment.
- *Validate:* I mean by this genuinely communicating with empathy and care, saying such as "I really value and admire your willingness to talk about such a difficult issue . . . ." Shame is a significant emotion with gender-conflicted individuals in the church. You will need to do your utmost to help them relieve themselves of shame. Professionals, inclusive of clergy, have often unwittingly *contributed* to shame—sometimes by their reactions, and other times by a fixated insistence that this "gender-identity problem" is patently wrong or sinful. Be aware of how shame enters the sharing moment, and help to do away with it by affirming *the person.* They are God's child.

IS THERE A GOAL HERE?

Gender conflicts can challenge faith experiences at very foundational levels, and as we have explored, bring into question myriad formulations of what gender means and how it is to be contextualized. I believe for the pastoral counselor, *not the therapist*, the best facilitation one can provide a gender-conflicted or transitioning individual, and their family, is the ethical and personal support that Jesus displayed with those marginalized and cast off.

I thus challenge you to consider being an *accompagnateur*, in the most pastoral sense of the word, "going the second mile" with the person in question rather than attempting to formulate responses that only they and God can settle. Let's remember: there is no "prescription" to offer—every person struggling with gender conflicts is different. You may deal with one person; but that experience can't be translated to another. Formulaic reasoning does more damage than good. I say this because a word of caution is needed here: Clergy are taught to view information provided them through those learned lenses of *pastoral counseling*, which in some ways mirror therapeutic interactions of behavioral therapists and psychologists. *However*, differences here are two-fold:

(1) Clergy may not have the specialized training required to deal with the myriad issues involved in the clinical aspects of sexual/gender conflicts.

(2) Clerical lenses can include theological positions often affirmed by the cleric's denomination and/or their theological training, coloring their understanding of issues such as dysphoria. Theological views aren't necessarily problematic. But without the clergy first addressing *in themselves* how these may in fact steer the received understandings, clergy responses may embody wrong assumptions, or formulaic solutions. We've dealt with some of these in earlier chapters.

If you do attempt to inform, emphasize Jesus' love and empathy for those who are going through tribulations; make sense of the science and integrate it with the theology in a correct, yet biblically faithful way; and most of all, underscore that Christ's love and sacrifice focused itself on saving the *soul* rather than just the body.[8]

To be compelled to *walk alongside* a person is to open oneself to sharing the agony and, yes, sometimes the ecstasy, as it unfolds in the real lives of people. Christ beckoned some of the most repudiated individuals to walk alongside him; and he in turn walked alongside *them* (Matt 4:18–22).

That does *not* mean quickly taking on the role of "teacher" or "advisor": only in the most fundamental way should we attempt to take on such roles, regardless of one's training or theological position on the issue. Yes, of course, Jesus debated the Pharisees and Sadducees, and overturned moneychangers' tables in righteous zeal. Yes, of course, Jesus taught all over Galilee. He also spent thirty years in preparation for a three-year ministry.

Our commission is not to usurp the Holy Spirit and try to "educate to change people." Rather, our commission is to help our brother, our sister; go with them the second mile, give them our coat, and sup with the pariah. If we are asked to instruct, it is then our role to assist the person in allowing the Holy Spirit to guide them into all truth (John 16:13). For some so gifted, teaching as the Holy Spirit guides them is part of what these can offer (Rom 12:7). *But you can't teach what you don't know.*

Ultimately, the overarching pastoral goal here is to exercise the "embrace" Volf proposes as the best theological response to the problem of exclusion.[9] "Exclusion" may cause us to react *not-so-well* to all those who are different, with different views—even different theologies of being—so much so, that we hinder the work of God.

---

8. This is *not* to mean that Jesus disregarded the body, nor that his teachings as well as those of the apostles disavowed the importance of the body. It *is* to emphasize that a proper theology of salvation must regard the *priority* Jesus gave to the soul vs. the body, in that while both are partners in salvation, the latter *will be transformed* (Phil 3:21) for it to enter the kingdom. Moreover, the stark hierarchy of soul and body in its importance to obtaining the kingdom cannot be disputed after reading Matthew 5:29–30. In contemporary medicine, we often choose to save the life of a person by cutting off a limb. Unfortunate, yes, but we say it is "necessary" to save the life. We do not condemn the surgeon's recommendation nor doubt its probable efficacy in saving a life. *Think about this.*

9. Volf, *Exclusion and Embrace*, 20.

Volf suggests we practice using "double-lens" vision—seeing things from both "our here" and "their there."[10] This enables one to treat the other with equality, and dissuades us from delineating their differences. Seeing from the perspective of the other gains us the ability to step outside ourselves, cross any social boundary, and move into the world of the other to *know it*. Most important, it enables the other to come into our world, and *know it too*.[11]

Taking the step of opening ourselves up to the other, enfolding him or her, *they* or *ze*, with the same embrace that God enfolded us with, generates in us all the kind of selves we need to be to live in harmony with others. Volf ultimately recommends we "concentrate . . . on fostering the kind of social agency capable of envisioning and creating just, truthful, and peaceful societies, and on shaping a cultural climate in which such [persons] will thrive."[12]

THE CHURCH AS A SAFE SPACE: TEACH CIVILITY TO YOUR CONGREGANTS

Gender-conflicted, transgender, and intersex individuals need a safe space in the evangelical church. Truthfully here, they haven't really had one! There are few conservative Christian churches I know with opportunities for people struggling with a secret gender identity, transsexual individuals, or families with gender-conflicted or intersex children, to risk "outing" their situation. *Being in a position of authority enables pastoral leaders to take the opportunity to show the congregation what it means to walk humbly with those that crave authentic relationships, regardless of who they are.* Again, Romans 12:9–16 come to mind:

> Love must be sincere. Hate what is evil; cling to what is good. Be devoted to one another in love. Honor one another above yourselves. Never be lacking in zeal, but keep your spiritual fervor, serving the Lord. Be joyful in hope, patient in affliction, faithful in prayer. Share with the Lord's people who are in need. Practice hospitality. Bless those who persecute you; bless and do not curse. Rejoice with those who rejoice; mourn with those who

---

10. Volf, *Exclusion and Embrace*, 25.
11. Volf, *Exclusion and Embrace*, 25.
12. Volf, *Exclusion and Embrace*, 22. (Brackets mine.)

mourn. Live in harmony with one another. Do not be proud, but be willing to associate with people of low position. Do not be conceited.

Without any mention to the congregation, my pastor had been communicating with and befriending a local Muslim imam of a nearby mosque, an encounter brought about by a congregant's community drive to donate shoes for needy kids in poor countries. A few Sundays ago, as our service was beginning and people were standing for the first worship song, in enters a 6'4", thawb-clad, serwal-panted, and skullcap-topped Imam with a large walking stick! He proceeds to the front row, and quietly sits. Our worship leader finished the song and our pastor took over the microphone, stating nonchalantly, "I want to welcome Imam [name], who is joining us today." No other mention or introduction until much later at dismissal.

Business as usual? Not entirely; but then, not an extraordinary moment either for a congregation that has found hospitality, a communitarian spirit, and room for welcoming sundry varieties of human identities without losing oxygen. So, what's the point?

Here, the example *is to lead by example.* Welcome those that have differences! Showing grace and truth requires a level of authenticity on the part of those who lead that then becomes an example for others to emulate.

In different ways, political and social, *we are losing civility.* Twitter, Facebook, and Instagram are consistently used as put-down tools, and the position of others with differences serves as fodder for denigration. Our country is in the middle of a campaign of *distrust.* The many, many narratives being presented lack the authoritative backing of fundamental institutions, so now we need to "fact-check" everything and anything.

Church folk aren't immune to this trend, especially when confronted with out-of-the-ordinary situations and out-of-the-ordinary-people issues that seem to challenge *our* theology. We lose trust in each other. Anthropologist Tanya Luhrmann, who studies Christianity and Christian churches, writes in a *New York Times* op-ed, "This sense that the human church isn't always to be trusted crops up frequently. . . . People talk about being *church wounded.*"[13] Perhaps we all need a

13. Luhrmann, "C. S. Lewis, Evangelical Rock Star," para. 5.

refresher course on Christian civility and politeness. Which get us to the need for *alterity*.

When the church becomes insular, it loses its ability to openly meet with people of different geographies of being. The estrangement rises from the way our Christian culture and evangelical subculture configure our experiences, pushing for similarities and distancing differences.

I know this is a bold statement. But consider: We engage insularity at several levels. The church may have its therapy groups, outlets for coping and expressing suffering, yet these meet out of sight from the main congregation and the general fray of congregants. When it comes to the sexual, especially, the larger congregation and its leadership shy away from open discourse. People with issues are left to feel their "otherness." This was not the model for the first-century church, nor should it be ours today.

We need a larger ethic of recognition, as spoken of by Emmanuel Lévinas, a Jewish philosopher and ethicist, who reminds us in his life's work of the importance of opening ourselves up to the "other" in ways public;[14] in ways that acknowledge their being and their struggles without excuses; and that allow us open hospitality, care, and concern for their humanness and their difference. This is *alterity*—a recognition of the other "just as they are," giving them the human and spiritual legitimacy these deserve.

In fact, it's been argued by Lévinas and others that when we practice alterity, the "other" in many ways not only becomes equal to us, but precious to us. "Alterity is a precious and transcendent element—its loss would seriously impoverish a world culture of increasing sameness and arrogant, insular narcissism."[15]

CREATING A CULTURE OF GRACE AND CIVILITY

Clergy of larger congregations should consider developing adult learning opportunities including readings and discussion on issues of sexuality, being gendered, gender identity, and discussion of gender conflicts, transgender, and intersex experiences. *This is a great*

---

14. Lévinas, *Alterity and Transcendance*.
15. Baudrillard and Guillaume, *Radical Alterity*.

Pastoral and Church Leadership Responses to the Gender Moment

opportunity to also teach civility and non-judgmentalism: include in the teaching some of the "courtesies" we expect and ought to extend to others. Among them:

- Treating everyone courteously.
- Acknowledging others and listening respectfully to them.
- Listening actively (as per above recommendations).
- Speaking kindly and not taking positions.
- Exercising self-control.
- Focusing on the issues and not personalizing debate.
- Respecting other's opinions.
- Giving open-minded consideration to viewpoints other than one's own.
- Generating inclusiveness.
- Avoiding shifts of responsibility and blaming.

In these points, we find the essence of what Paul was attempting to teach the church in the book of Romans. Haven't read it lately? Here is its essence, culled from Romans 14. Paul is engaging a dialogue full of illustrations and sharp questions on how we view and treat each other: admonitions about avoiding quarrels "over disputable matters" (v. 1); not judging others, but allowing each to be "fully convinced in their own minds" (v. 5), because what they do, "they do so for the Lord" (v. 5).

By mid-chapter of Romans 14, Paul is driving the pointed questions home: "You, then, why do you judge your brother or sister? Or why do you treat them with contempt? For we will all stand before God's judgment seat." (v. 10.)

Ouch!

If that's not enough, verses 13–14 further push the point home: "Therefore let us stop passing judgment on one another. Instead, make up your mind not to put any stumbling block or obstacle in the way of a brother or sister." And, "I am convinced, that nothing is unclean in itself. But if anyone regards something as unclean, then for that person it is unclean."

Here, Paul is using Jewish food restrictions in the Law to underscore that, in the new covenant, the more important fact is to not let another stumble by your accusations. And, in Paul's final commentary, the point of all of this is clearly evidenced: *"So whatever you believe about these things, keep them between yourself and God. Blessed is the one who does not condemn himself by what he approves"* (Rom 14:22). Let's preach and live *that!*

Mid-week services and sermons can also serve as effective means for opening explorations of culture and gender issues. They can become catalysts for a series. Matthew 19:11–12 can easily become launching verses for sermons on the topic of intersexuality, or the biological reality of people born with an anatomy that is clearly undifferentiated.

Teaching civility and some form of gender awareness ought to also include separating out tabloid sensationalism, activism, and stereotypical Christian responses based on fear, from the truth of how intersex and transgender people live their lives.[16]

Most transgender and intersex individuals lead rather normal lives. Most are not congregating *en masse* to parade for justice; nor are they weird looking; nor child-molesters; nor mentally ill. The variegation is, exactly, akin to the lives of other people in other groupings.

Pastors and clergy need courage to enter this discourse and lead their congregations in the rightful exploration of these topics. There are rich opportunities here to minister, as well as to engage contemporary realities of difference now at the church's doorstep.

DEALING WITH OBJECTIONS

I focus here on two major threads—when congregants raise objections to either an individual transitioning among them or to statements by clergy that congregants feel violate *their* interpretations of scripture. Naturally, there is a lot more that can, and does happen; but "these two strands" need special attention.

---

16. A saddening read is Hida Viloria's *Born Both: An Intersex Life.* For data and life histories based on a nationwide survey of transgender and intersex individuals, see Beemyn and Rankin, *The Lives of Transgender People.* This is a "textbook" in its comprehensiveness, and shatters stereotypes!

As we read in Kyler's history, persons who disclose their transgenderism, or who may start to transition while being a member of a congregation or religious worksite, often face indirect and direct discrimination. It can be subtle avoidances, or outright face-to-face derogations. Those doing the put-downs often feel justified, in one way or another theologically, to call into question why this person is being "allowed" to "be(come)" in the midst of congregational life. And, the pastor will hear it directly from them!

I don't need to underscore here the "hows" of dealing with such complaints—but I do want to emphasize the necessity for any response to also be a *teachable moment*.

Here is where clergy can offer insight to individuals who object, but who often do not have accurate information, and are therefore threatened by the situation. I thus urge you to turn such a complaint into a moment where contested spaces can be turned into shared ones. I mean by that, enabling the individual with significant worries room to see that they or their personal beliefs are not at risk because of this other person's issues. *Teach them: There is no leper in the room. There is no contagion effect going on.* Educate them on what transgender and intersexuality actually embody for people.

I follow here with some interesting findings that could account for viscerally negative reactions. In a 2017 poll by the Public Religion Research Institute (PRRI), a non-partisan, nonprofit organization, data collected show most evangelical Protestants have *not* had close contact with any transgender person (only 9 percent have). Similarly, mainline Protestants fare no better (only 15 percent have). If one broadens the categories to "all Americans" (a random sample here of 36,465), only 21 percent of the sample had any contact with a transgender person. Unfamiliarity can breed misinformation, fear, and contempt.[17]

Addressing theological discrepancies is of course much more difficult, particularly when clergy members themselves embrace theological positions that may disagree with the transitioning individual's theological anthropology, or that of another congregant. I see the role of a minister-servant *not* as a means of providing opportunity to interject one's theology or position, but rather one that can turn the argument to another element of essential theology: how to show

17. Piasenza and Jones, *Americans on Discrimination Against*, 2.

love and respect, humility and benevolence, *even to those with whom we may theologically disagree*. If as a pastor one can do this—show by example that exploring the "rightness or wrongness" of someone's theology doesn't lead to unfruitful communications or misconnections—then we all benefit. "To do this, we must put our identity in Christ, so that we listen, think, and act with love, joy, peace, forbearance, kindness, goodness, faithfulness, gentleness, and self-control."[18]

Andrea Tornielli, Vatican correspondent who wrote the introduction to Pope Francis' tome *The Name of God Is Mercy*, aptly writes there,

> We live in a society that encourages us to discard the habit of recognizing and assuming our responsibilities: It is always others who make mistakes. It is always others who are immoral. It's always someone else's fault, never our own. And sometimes we even experience the return of a kind of *clericalism*, always intent on building borders, "regulating" the lives of people through imposed prerequisites and prohibitions that make our daily lives, already difficult, even harder. An attitude of being always ready to condemn and much less willing to accept. Ready to judge but not to bow down with compassion for mankind's sufferings. [A] message of mercy . . . sweeps all those stereotypes away.[19]

The value of pastoral care and counsel rests on the opportunity to provide moments that further *compassion*, that acknowledge we come to Jesus "just as we are," and that he in turn loves us regardless of our issues (Mark 19:17; Luke 19:10). We would do well to refrain from attempts to discredit the other person's feelings or viewpoints.

And while these moments may seem as opportunities to "correct" views and *"teach what the Bible says,"* I urge restraint on these points.

We help most when people feel heard, accepted, supported; not debated, or needing to be persuaded to think otherwise. You may find that knowing your gender-questioning parishioner has a strong faith in God helps you to accept their reality. And, although you may not interpret biblical passages in the same way, you can find comfort in knowing that God is not excluded from your parishioner's problems. Recall that for many with gender conflicts diagnosed as dysphoria, the disconnect with the body won't simply "just go away" with novel thinking.

---

18. Parler, "How Should Christians Navigate," par. 9.
19. Tornielli, "To the Reader," 8. (Bracket mine.)

In such cases, pastors would also do well in helping parishioners and families obtain credible therapy partners.

THE POLITICS OF CARING

This overview would not be complete without touching on the political ramifications for a pastor, clergy, or church leader when these take on controversial topics. Pastors risk their likeability, reputation, sometimes even their position when they move outside the comfort zones of their denomination or congregation. And, I am *not* referring to clergy who move into "queer theologies" or who stretch well-established *doctrinal* positions. I am underscoring that the mere fact of "allowing" a congregant or family to work through their gender issues *while a member of the church*, or accompanying them through the rough times, can cause ripples of dissent for the pastor.

But if Jesus is the model, then we must note he certainly pushed people beyond their comfort and constantly questioned interpretations by those in religious power positions as to what God expects of them in relation to their brothers and sisters. He also engaged many whom even his own disciples felt were discrediting to him and his work.

On one occasion, I was asked by a staff member to help her disclose to our academic administration that after decades of struggle, she had been diagnosed with gender dysphoria. She had decided to transition hormonally and physically to male. I agreed to accompany her.

She disclosed first to the university president, who graciously and without hesitation supported *the person*. With his consent to disclose, she told her superiors. Such disclosures would also require the university's governing board to be notified and advised quickly. I was asked by the president to also engage in that process: I was to prepare a document—a type of *Amicus Brief*—that would inform and educate the governing board on being transgender, as well as provide my advice on how to proceed in this particular case.

Upon writing the *Brief* and meeting with the governing board, the elephant-in-the-room moment came when a board member openly asked whether *anyone* (on the board) had considered the *consequences* of *allowing* this individual to transition while an employee of an evangelical institution of higher education.

And then the big question... *"How do we think our membership [church and community, alumni and families of students] will react to our allowing such a transition to happen among us?"*

The silence in the room was overwhelming. The matter quickly got referred to a sub-committee. And as predictable, the subcommittee's recommendation was that the individual be offered a generous severance package *stat*, and counseling support. To note: these were *not* my recommendations.

The staff member took the severance with great disappointment, feeling vulnerable and dejected, but not wanting to further her grief in what was already becoming a hostile work environment. She felt this was a "buy-out" that would avoid the governing board taking a position on gender dysphoria (even by default).

Worse, the decision would not appear to support one person's struggle to *become emotionally whole*, since it could have opened a can of worms theologically for the institution: gender reassignment was not condoned outright by the evangelical denomination with which the university was affiliated. In fact, and at the time, the denomination had not addressed gender-identity issues formally nor taken a position on it, or explored it theologically in any open forum. (It did so in 2017.)

Moreover, she couldn't handle a prospective legal, human resources battle with the university proper—although the thought of a lawsuit crossed her mind several times.

Certainly, there could have been a better resolve to the case than a quick severance option, and all that it implied. And yet, many in positions of power who were also clergy on the board of regents felt they were *supporting the person* through the severance; when really, these were supporting their fear of repercussions and shunning their own need to work through the subject—if only by default. Some felt that if they didn't go along with the normed sentiment, that they, too, would fall out of political grace. And my suggestions, well, these were given thanks, but not considered in earnest.

How the institution and denomination would have reacted to the person completing their transition *in situ*, we'll never know. We also won't ever know how a challenging situation might have surfaced our compassion and care in ways that mended, rather than furthered the break in a believer's heart.

It costs to care.

Clergy need to be willing to bear the cost of such caring in return for helping enable their congregations to reach a communal place where *every person* is worthy of dignity, God's love, and *our* understanding. Congregants need the pastoral example to push through complicated medical, relational, and theological questions related to intersex and transgender individuals. To be successful as a congregation that loves and reaches out to others—even though not everyone agrees on the issues—is to have engaged a communal project. Such requires the pastor to lead congregants *to be engaged*, not just in raising issues, but in *accommodating them*. Are we our brother's keeper?[20]

Pushing care practices out of the private, personal realm and into the congregation as a public sphere is at once to cultivate a community of learners who can also teach each other to care for one another. Dialogue by and through pastoral individuals and lay leaders can generate empathic conversations that ultimately center us on our capacity to channel God's love, and seek social justice through interpersonal connections.

A pastoral response to transgender or intersex persons cannot even begin if these experience unloving environments that do not welcome them in the congregation.

"The temptation pastors must face down is the reduction of transgendered persons to their gender dysphoria, as if the adjective *transgender* exhausts the meaning of the noun *person*."[21] Hospitality and love address some of the most fundamental needs in the lives of *all* persons. And after all is considered, the essential is whether they are "in Christ." Then, "if anyone is in Christ, the new creation *has come*. The old *has gone*, and the *new* is here!" (2 Cor 5:17).

---

20. In Romans 14:19 Paul admonishes the church to pursue "things which make for peace and the things by which one may edify [build up] one another." Paul follows with the golden exhortation that love is even greater than faith and hope (1 Cor 13), and even uses the human body to drive home the "many members" idea, which make up the church. While love must sometimes correct and admonish (2 Thess 3:13), one should foremost demonstrate the "tender heart and humble mind" scripture also exhorted us to pursue (1 Pet 3:8). We are our brother's keeper when we refrain from "quarreling . . . outbursts of anger . . . factions, slander, gossip, arrogance, and disorder" (1 Cor 12:20).

21. Assemblies of God, "Transgenderism, Transsexuality," 13.

I urge you to respond to transgender persons—among you or who come to you—by embodying an exemplar Jesus in action, in humility, and in love. Suggestions on how to deal with the social "revolution" surrounding gender—a different challenge altogether—are in the chapter that follows!

Table 4. "Punch List" of Suggested Questions and Conversations on Sexuality and Gender the Church Should Address

Topical	Questions/Conversations/Audience
Understanding our sexuality	Age- and gender-appropriate discussions can be initiated with youth, young adults, and adult groups that focus on themes understanding sexual development, managing sexual unfolding and sexuality, sexual attraction, biblical precepts and body, mind, and behavioral responsibilities: • Sexuality as "God's good gift" vs. our downfall. • Seminar for parents on "You and Your Sexy Teen." • Discussion with youth on attraction, sexual attraction, and sexual behaviors. • Study groups on gender, gendered roles, complementarity vs. hierarchicality between men and women. • Adult sexuality—responsibilities as singles, as marrieds, as divorced, as parents, as grandparents.
Gender, gender identity	Conversations and audiences: • Mid-week adult collaboratives on understanding gender identity and gender-identity conflicts; Christian responses to individuals with conflicts; and on addressing social movements revolving around gender identity and gender roles. • Youth seminars on gender, gender identity, the transgender "moment"; dealing with gender questions. • Sermons on church civility and Christian responses to the gender movement, individual congregants with gender conflicts. • Discussion groups on congregational accommodation of people with gender differences. • Board positions and policy statements on sexuality and gender that reflect mercy and reconciliation, inclusion. • Sermons on being "thy brother's keeper" and applications of Pauline doctrines for mutual care.

continued on next page

Topical	Questions/Conversations/Audience
	Table 4. "Punch List" of Suggested Questions and Conversations on Sexuality and Gender the Church Should Address
Gender, gender identity	Questions to explore as congregation and sub-groups: • How to prepare youth to address the gender issues in society from a Christ-like perspective. • Youth experiencing transitions: how to support them despite possible differences of positions theologically. • Gender neutrality vs. gender bipolarity in public spaces such as bathrooms, church facilities. Can single loaded bathrooms work? • Accommodations for gender beyond male-female in church activities and venues such as Camps, retreats, and overnighters?
Church leadership training	How much do we know? What don't we know that we ought to know? • Do we know the distinctions between intersex, gender-identity conflicts, gender non-conformity, gender dysphoria, transsexual, transgender? These and homosexuality? • How do we develop and deploy training for staff and leaders on gender issues and responses? • How do we deal with "outs" in the congregation; how do we manage congregational angst, responses? • What are the best means of developing and utilizing supportive counseling referrals for individuals with gender conflicts, or who are/are considering transitioning? Who discover themselves intersex? • How do we align congregational positions and policy with positions and policies of an affiliated denomination, if so required? • Which church leaders/lay leaders should take responsibility to oversee some of these charges? • How do we coordinate agreements, responses, support so that we are of "one mind, one accord" when it comes to serving our brethren? Our community members?

9

The Church and Transgender Activism

This book's introduction tries to make a point clear: for the Christian, especially, there needs to be an understood and well-defined *distinction* between what is *intersex*, what is a *diagnosable gender-identity disorder*, and what is now a *social movement of expressive individualism and self-representation*.

These distinctions are important at three levels: for how we understand others; for how we act and react to others; and for what is or is not acceptable in biblical and canonical contexts.

Our current "transgender moment" has certainly increased awareness of those who are intersex, and of those who struggle with gender and identity from early life forward. If such efforts end up inspiring us all to consider their reality, their struggles; helping us to respect and sympathize with the intersex or dysphoric; it'll be good for us all.

What is less noble, sometimes pernicious, is an offshoot activism that, while proclaiming worthwhile aims, dismisses any historical elements of sex and gender, and labels them as *transphobia*.[1]

Such reactions from some individuals are now part of a *social venue* of *expressive individualism*, where any gender essentialism is simply tossed out and a new repertoire of gender options is taken as a birthright. In such cases, we may be seeing a form of rebellion that is neither socially constructive in the end, nor, as many Christians

1. Linker, "The Egregious Overreach of Transgender Activism."

would see it, aligning with God's purposes. I'll explain this commentary and my reasoning below. But first, we need a little history.

THE BIRTH OF GENDERQUEER ACTIVISM

All social movements have a long history, and offering a brief summary of the history of our present gender activism will allow us to connect it to the sparks that may have started our now flaming fire.

In 1990, queer theorist Judith Butler published *Gender Trouble*,[2] and fast-forwarded the notion that gender isn't what we *are*, but what we constantly *do*. In that sense, Butler, who became "pop" through the tome, unleashed a theory of gender that basically says gender is *fluid* and results from our constant interaction with cultural configurations of sex and gender. That, in simple English, means that we *perform gender*, or to use her label, "gender as performative."

Which meant that this new definition of what gender *was* could "confound the very binarism of sex, and expose its fundamental unnaturalness," since people could "perform gender" beyond the boxes these were given. Butler thus pushed the idea that any gender *category* or "boxes" become themselves "instruments of regulatory regimes," efforts to "normalize oppressive structures." To Butler, the binary especially, but any label really, become "rallying points" to contest "oppression."[3] (Note the need to destabilize linguistic categories, since these are modes of "oppression.")

By 1992, Leslie Feinberg, a self-identified transgender herself, printed and circulated *Transgender Liberation: A Movement Whose Time Has Come*.[4] In it, she called on those identifying themselves as "transsexuals" to come together and invoke *language as a tool*, using it to compose *their own definitions* of who they were. She claimed language labels that limit self-identity to the gender binary were tools of oppression by those in power, enforcing the binary at the expense of liberal gender expression. The gender binary, she emphasized, was a contrivance of Western civilization and class societies.[5] (Note the alignment here with Butler's ideas of identity politics.)

---

2. Butler, *Gender Trouble*.
3. Fischer, "Think Gender Is Performance?"
4. Feinberg, "Transgender Liberation."
5. Feinberg's rationale and historical documentation presents significant information,

This agenda was a new kind of revolution, one that could be achieved *on one's own terms*—at the time, without a mass movement of supporters, and without the individual doing much more than re-labeling/redefining themselves. They could then take their new selves into the open air of the public square. Of course, one voice became many.

Thus, through personal testimony, a printed memoir, or through blogging, those that felt they were refused entrance to nontraditional representations of self were suddenly being heard. And it changed popular culture. It also made everyone an *expert*: "When logic that fixes bodily form to social practice comes undone; when narratives of sex, gender, embodiment loosen up and become *less fixed in relation to truth*, authenticity, originality, and identity, then we have the space and the time to imagine bodies otherwise."[6]

Fast forward to 2005. The advocacy and lobbying group Human Rights Campaign (HRC) underscores that gender *identity* ought to disavow *any* relationship between it and the sexual body; indeed, *any* connection to *any* history, insisting that *identity* is *only* rooted in personal subjectivity and social conventions—thus the two can be misaligned.

HRC's reasoning: "Sex is arbitrarily assigned at birth,"[7] so naturally it can, maybe *should be* manipulated by the person later. Or maybe, even earlier in life; no matter. It follows that there needs to be unwavering acceptance and affirmation by *everyone* of what *anyone* says they are, feel they are, or act as they would. And this is the voice of genderqueer activists, who by the way, aren't representative of most transgender persons. (In fact, per gathered testimony, many transgender persons *reject activism*, and some even claim being victims of it.)[8]

---

some of which cannot be ignored. Her conclusions are like those of Michel Foucault, French philosopher-activist of the 1960s–80s, who believed the ones who set out on the path to *be themselves*, to *express themselves* in "authentic gestures," were the ones fighting "for all of us" against the lies and distortions of the bourgeois order. Those who challenge the "normal" were, to Foucault, the real heroes.

6. Halberstam, *Trans: A Quick and Quirky Account*, xi. (Italics mine for emphasis.)
7. Human Rights Campaign, "Resources."
8. Anderson, "Transgender Ideology Is Riddled with Contradictions."

ACTIVIST CLAIMS

Activists claim that despite you being normal in birth sex, your "assigned sex" doesn't have to stay that way if you don't want it to. More to the point of *gender:* activists state your gender is "also assigned" at birth, and it, too, doesn't have to stay true to its assignation. It's all up to you.[9]

The position taken is not only to recognize *intersex*, or individuals who may have *gender-identity conflicts*, all well and good; but—as we've noted in earlier chapters—the aim is to erase *all* restrictions on gender identification save what the person says about themselves, "no matter what." Most significant is *not* individual rights here, but rather the notion that sex—biological sex—exists *only* in the mind of the beholder; and following from this, so does gender.

At first glance it may seem liberating—that we need *no boxes*. But there are numerous problems with the argument, problems that make it internally incoherent and ultimately, biologically and politically untenable.

For one, most people are born with genitals that determinedly fall into one of two biologically binary categories (again, excepting here, momentarily, the intersex minority). How can these categories not matter in determining *at least some fundamental part of one's identity?*[10] Moreover, none of us was "assigned" a gender *identity* in fact. We were identified as one of two sex categories based on our genetics and genitals. We were then instilled with *role socialization* as males and females, even before we understood them. Based on our internalization of those roles *and* our experiences, gender is being socially encouraged all through us. Eventually, however, *how we understand ourselves* and *how we play our roles* truly varies from person to person, despite their assignations at birth and cultural scripting.

So, defining genderqueer individuals as "those who were not assigned the correct place on the sex or gender category" in fact creates a false "binary" between those who conform (to whatever degree) to

---

9. See www.transequality.org for details of this perspective. See also Anderson, "The Philosophical Contradictions."

10. Biologist Anne Fausto-Sterling, in *Sexing the Body*, argues pointedly that sexual biology is foundational to sex and identity; and while she *also* acknowledges sociological and cultural processes in the development of sex and gender, sexual biology to her remains fundamental, of great import in understanding the sex/gendered person.

sex of birth and gender and those who do not. This enables the self-defined non-binary person to claim they have the right to reassign, *no matter what*, because they have been misunderstood, and thus politically oppressed.[11] Sex of birth doesn't matter. Gender rearing doesn't matter. Society doesn't matter. What matters is what *I* believe.[12]

As a lobbying group, HRC's website logs "Our Victories," among them actively utilizing social media networks (especially Facebook, Instagram, and Twitter) to launch "iconic viral campaigns" for those "affected and marginalized" to influence others and "challenge skeptics": "Through the combined use of revolutionary hashtag campaigns backed with community action and social media takeovers that spread awareness and center important narratives, HRC has been able to maintain a leading presence in social media, digital communications, and beyond."[13]

This is not gender dysphoria. It is not intersexuality. It isn't even a person searching for identity, "questioning" their gender. Persons embracing this repertoire of self-options seem to want, demand, *only* self-affirmation—body politics included—more than a reconciliation of self *and* body.

We must respond with compassion and sympathy, yes; *but make a distinction* between this type of gender-identity activism and gender conflicts that have been identified through medical research, corroborated as individualized and often painful histories. Acknowledging the factuality of intersex persons or those diagnosed with gender dysphoria is only one part of the ongoing cultural change; individuated issues there are often beyond the person's capacities to change them.

---

11. See Rude, "It's Time for People to Stop Using the Social Construction of 'Biological Sex' to Defend Their Transmysogyny" again.

12. Reilly-Cooper writes, "None of us was assigned a gender identity at birth at all. We were placed into one of two sex classes on the basis of our potential reproductive function, determined by our external and internal genitals. We were then raised in accordance with the socially prescribed gender norms for people of that sex. We are all educated and inculcated into one of two roles, long before we are able to express our beliefs about our gender identity, or to determine for ourselves the precise point at which we fall into a gender label. So defining transgender people as those who at birth were not assigned the correct gender has the implication that every single one of us is in essence, a cisgender person. There is no spectrum" ("Gender Is Not a Spectrum," 8).

13. Human Rights Campaign, "Our Victories" (2019).

For the Christian caught up in trying to understand all of this, the distinctions here are significant. Several questions should help to clarify:

- Is the motivation behind the gender conflict one mediated by *social currents and political correctness*, or one that has developed naturally from either malformed genitalia or mind-body disjunctions? I've argued we need to make space for the latter two, while resisting cultural ideologies that, on the whole, denigrate sex/gender distinctions.

- Is there a difference? *I would argue there certainly is.* Dealing with gender dysphoria or intersexuality means dealing with significant, individuated, and historical facts, often causing pain, disjunctions of body-self, and self with others. Dealing with a social movement in which the subculture seeks to neutralize altogether any algorithms of sex or gender, including concordances between anatomically normed bodies and identities, is, in my estimation, to deny basic humanity its due place. That includes the sexual binary as the baseline norm, which science itself confirms.

- If the person is Christian, *is Christ at the center of their lives?* It seems inane to single this out—but for the purposes of ministry and compassion, it is essential to understand whether Christ has been deeply brought into the fray. Why? Because "centering Christ" is an essential feature of following Christ, and a witness to be heard by others: to get Christ and faith in him as one's central compass is an essential part of the Christian walk. If they do/do not participate in the faith, how is that position an influence on their ideology?

HOW THEN SHOULD THE CHRISTIAN UNDERSTAND AND RESPOND?

Many in the church are calling for compassion, mercy, and some aspect of reconciliation—myself included—between the Christian church and those caught up in the social movement surrounding gender. However, the trajectory forward is not to just engage the popular "diversity framework," nor an "integrated framework" of inclusion, although both have something beneficial to offer.[14]

We must start by acknowledging intersex births, realigning our theological anthropology to the truth that *procreation* can result in a variety of sexual forms beyond the binary. These people are also God's children! From there, and acknowledging the spectrum of our *procreated* humanity, we can go on to make room for less judgment and more of what Mark Yarhouse has called "walking alongside the suffering."[15] I credit Catholics in doing a better job at this than Protestants, given all their historical leprosy asylums, hospitals, and the crowned legacy of Mother Teresa's work among the poor and sick of India. (This is *not* to insinuate a comparison between people with gender conflicts and lepers, or those suffering! It is to underscore mercy and compassion.)

We are not talking about the homeless or the sick here, although these seem to find a more generous welcome than those with gender conflicts in our Christian congregations these days.

Aside from making theological and pragmatic, in-person room for intersex persons and those with medically diagnosed gender-identity conflicts in our congregations and ministry, we must also address the growing pressure from the social world to make admissible this rebellion against *any* gender or sex label that is *not self-defined*. How do we respond to that?

Responding to a "Culture-bound Syndrome"

One of the first steps is to avoid the politics and media-driven polarizations that promote accusations. Any such approach reinforces position-taking: that there can be only winners and losers, and any form of mutual understanding or accommodation is impossible.

Gender rebellion today appears to me as a *culture-bound syndrome*.[16] As I explained in chapter 3, we face a society and culture

---

14. Yarhouse, *Understanding Gender Dysphoria*. Yarhouse proposes upholding the "created genders" (I think he means *sexes*); demonstrating compassion and hope; appreciating the complex issues of "gender confusion" and walking alongside those who suffer. All the diversity frameworks that abound underscore the dignity and worth of differences, and denounce in one way or another all forms of discrimination, bias, and stereotypy.

15. Yarhouse, *Understanding Gender Dysphoria*, 137

16. This is my "cultural diagnosis." The term is borrowed from medical anthropology,

in which expressive individualism, becoming one's "authentic self," moves one to create one's own identity—free of rules, constraints, and even obligations beyond those one imposes on one's self. *You are, and are entitled to be, the creator of your own self.*

Thus, within the larger awakening spurred by identity politics, there's a growing number of younger people who are now accepting of *gender fluidity* and *gender ambiguity*. These can find themselves believing gender doesn't matter at all, or not that much.[17]

Social media has inflamed such sentiment, to the degree that adolescents in increasing numbers can manifest sudden symptoms of gender dysphoria, even though parents had not previously seen any signs of identity problems, or confusion. In chapter 2, I introduced researcher Lisa Littman, who likened this trend to a socially mediated "contagion," and called such symptoms *rapid onset gender dysphoria*.[18] For her research and coining the term, she was severely chastised and derided.[19] No matter. The phenomenon she describes has all the bona fide qualities of a culture-bound syndrome, fed by the politicized faction of our gender moment.

As to the movement itself, Jaquelle (Crow) Ferris, author and creator of *The Young Writer's Club*, writes,

> This is a cultural vs. biblical catechism. . . . This movement teaches some true and beautiful things Christians would affirm, such as the inherent worth that flows from being an image-bearer of "truth." But in much of the *ra-ra mentality*, there exists a deeper craving for self-fulfillment. It doesn't matter what the haters say. You've got to be loud and proud, and no, don't just love yourself, . . . worship yourself. Be whomever you want to be

---

where it means a combination of symptoms that identifies a condition, all of which only occur within a specific, bounded cultural realm. Here, I am referring to the series of social actions that affirm expressive individualism above any social or other obligation, and that are therefore "symptomatic" of a culture's belief that you are your own [best] maker; and no other criteria matter as much. These manifestations deviate from the usual behavior of the individuals of that culture, and are a reason for distress/discomfort.

17. Fischer, "Think Gender is Performance?"

18. Littman, "Parent Reports of Adolescents." See also Kay, "An Interview with Lisa Littman."

19. Melchior, "Peer Pressure and Transgender Teens."

and find your happiness in that self-realized identity. Embrace the true you, and shame anyone who doesn't.[20]

Add to this moment decades of political correctness, the cultural necessity to legitimize every distinctive and erase every conformity, and you have all the makings of the present social moment—a gender *revolution*. As much as the moment has promoted the rights of intersex and gender-dysphoric persons, for many genderqueer activists it has also become a rigid orthodoxy.[21] Activists and allies protest all other possibilities. Many Christians and others, who maintain *any* binary model, are called bigots, trolls, and worse names.

Responding by Teaching Your Children Well

In this venue, you are a "first responder": Our children need a *correct* biblical catechism for this era:

- It's worth repeating: Whatever we say and teach, "it should be age-appropriate," keeping in mind that this is the 2020s and we all have TVs and Google; kids and teens seem to have been born with smartphones and tablets; and most also learn about sex early, from media and peers. Kids know *much more* than you and I did when we were their age—but that doesn't mean they know in truth.

- Start with the fact that God created human beings, and that first creation was of a man and a woman. God created two sexes, *not two genders* (as Mark Spansel mistakenly writes in his Gospel Coalition article for parents);[22] and explain *procreation* as the

---

20. Ferris, "How Youth Like Me." Ferris states, "This is a new, radical politics that is entirely self-centered: It is politics *against* the other, whose presumed, staid morality stands as a barrier to individual fulfillment, and dissuades the real 'me' from becoming '*me*'—whose right to self-determination has been stolen" (ibid., 2).

21. By "orthodoxy" in this context, I mean a set of beliefs which are rigid and whose adherents "hold tight" to them as the only truth. This novel gender orthodoxy proposes (a) that biological sex isn't to be a determinant part of gender identity; (b) sex *assigned at birth* is really a social construction (only), and therefore amenable to being changed as the person matures into a "true identity"; (c) biological sex itself can be medically *changed out*, yet still hold the same meaning—presumably function—in its new composition; and (d) that any vestiges of a *gender schema* is tantamount to an act of injustice, and any critique of gender/change is necessarily bigoted and phobic.

22. Spansel, "How to Talk to Your Kids."

process human beings employ to make humans. When you do, don't extend *binary sex* in the biological creation of Adam and Eve to also mean the same genotypic outcome for all progeny. Understand and teach that there are *variations to the binary in reproduction*, even if these numbers are small by comparison. We are *all* God's children.

- This is an opportunity to add the notion that while there are two biological sexes, in the unfolding of human genealogies we see some *genitally intersex individuals* being born into the human line. Credit that to elements in the process, or in kid's language, "things sometimes turning out differently." Variegation is also true in other species.

- Add to that a "however"—*However*, all of humanity is in God's image, and that means all humans have the capacity to express God's will and God's nature, especially when Christ is their savior. That even those who do not have Christ as savior need our love and attention, care and respect, because God gave all of us life and souls.

- When age-appropriate, have a conversation about *gender identity*, and frame it within the context of everyone at some point coming to terms with who they are physically, emotionally, and why they feel the way they do about themselves; that it is normal to wrestle with issues of identity.

- That as a young person or teen, some individuals struggle more with feelings that they aren't who their bodies say they are; and that we have a term for that—it's called *gender dysphoria* when it significant and persists over time. As Christians, teach that we should equally comfort and love these individuals, and should *not judge* them based on what some believe is "right" or "wrong." Judgment is reserved for God, not us.

Respond by "Walking with Your Neighbor" (This is the Hardest)

- Jesus was called out as a "friend to sinners" (Matt 9:11; 11:16–19), and indeed he did eat, drink, and go into common individual's homes. People followed him everywhere—and I am certain, there were many different *types* of people walking with him, and he with them. The notion "walking with," implies that we all assume some cadence, even if not the same strides.[23] Do not let a politicized, glamorized, or defended position dismiss the person wholesale. Offer to "walk" *with them;* and,

- *Listen to them.* Listen to their stories and don't commiserate out of some need for righteous pity. This is not something that, if told to you, you can fix by arguing or denying their feelings. Listening to *them* opens the door for them listening to *you.*

- *Show compassion.* This is easily misunderstood, so I will share what I believe compassion means: opening one's self to the situations of others (Prov 31:8–9). Compassion, as a response to those that espouse gender activism, should mean we approach with acts of kindness and not scorn. Compassion overcomes anger (Hos 11:8). Compassion as a response to gender rebellion implies that you understand it as a social movement in a world full of turbulence, not as you being conscripted to change a mindset.

- *Speak truth when you are well informed.* That doesn't mean outright telling people they are in error. You may be tempted to do so, and proclaim righteous confrontation as your Christian mandate; but this seldom changes minds or situations, especially for individuals who have espoused a movement and identified themselves with its philosophies. I would prefer you learn to speak *in* truth. That means *your conviction* of what is true, *when you've read and informed yourself well of facts beforehand.* Jesus prepared himself for thirty years for a three-year ministry. If enabled, be correct biblically, scientifically, and ethically. Remember, it's the *Spirit of God* that leads people into truth (John 16:13). It's not your job to change minds.[24]

---

23. Here's that French term *accompagnateur* again, reminding us we can accompany people in their journey—whatever it may be. Here, it would be a good term to use as we "accompany" someone with a different philosophy or agenda by listening to them and their challenges, as opposed to arguing with them.

24. Volf, in *Exclusion and Embrace*, has a good discussion of what "truth" entails in Christianity. Briefly summarizing it here: "truth" is used to define things *reliable*, as in "the truth of God's faithfulness"—so well expressed in human history. Truth isn't just *factual* as elements go; truth is what stands the test of time and is counter to falsity and deceit. God's truth is both in revelation and in divine action. Truth is also found in *doing true things*, "telling the truth," as the disturbing case of Ananias and Sapphira

- *You can agree to disagree and still receive your "neighbor."* Such is especially key when there are gender-transitioning individuals as your "neighbor," with whom you may disagree; when there are gender-reassigned individuals in your congregation, or when there is activist philosophy present. Welcoming arms are always better than stares of disapproval. And, if you need to explain people to your children, do so with compassion and care.

- *Stand in opposition to bullying.* Interesting that *bullying* is a term we now relegate only to school or media environments; but I have seen it in churches, sometimes in the name of Christ. Another term for bullying is *negative persuasion*. Be keen to stand opposed to any form of discrimination. Jesus did not discriminate, and in Jesus, there is "neither Jew or gentile, male or female, circumcised or uncircumcised" (Gal. 3:28). All are welcomed to become part of God's family.

The Christian's answer to activism should thus be one that first increases one's own understandings of the depth of the issues; that teaches our children well; that provides us understandings that can help us separate the different voices; and then—only then—render a compassionate response.

A compassionate response—once again—does not dismiss the person; does not insult the person (even if *you* feel insulted). It recognizes wrongs done to them, and at the same time, acknowledges that some of the motivational factors behind their actions and feelings may not be correct; may be stretched; may be, from a biblical perspective, wrong. A compassionate response sets *conversation* above *confrontation*. It allows for *dialogue* and for a welcome. Ultimately, a compassionate response sets the venue for God to be allowed in.

To facilitate such a response, read Ed Stetzer's *Christians in the Age of Outrage: How to Bring Our Best When the World Is at Its Worst*. "Instead of Outrage, Engage."[25]

---

demonstrates wasn't done (Acts 5:3–4). The relationship of truth and trust are, to Volf, complementary. Thus, truth is revealed, in Christ as Truth; and in scripture as trustworthy items are pointed out; in the nature of God; in the nature of people, and in nature itself. Ultimately, truth "embodied" is God's Spirit—"the Spirit of Truth"—which leads us into *all truth* (John 16:13). See Volf, *Exclusion and Embrace*, 233–73.

25. Stetzer, *Christians in the Age of Outrage*, 3.

WHEN IDENTITY POLITICS PUSHES . . .

Genderqueer identity politics now focuses on who determines someone's sex and gender, since the argument is that only an individual can know their true sex and gender.[26] Christians should not validate any gender theory stemming from a politicized agenda that attempts to *erase* realities about biological sex, gender, identity, any more than we should deny the truth of sexual and gender differences in people.

Understanding this politicized agenda is essential to maintaining an alternative, *that there are two complementary, binary sexes*, even when sometimes the result of procreation is intersex. *That there are irreducible reasons*—biological, physiological, reproductive, interpersonal—for this binary schema occurring in most births and culture histories. There are reasons (as stated in chapters 4 and 7) why assignations of sex at birth are given, even as we recognize possible issues if dysphoria or intersexuality enter the picture.[27]

As Christians, we can't erase the truth of sexual baselines. Remember, biologists, endocrinologists, and assuredly theologians too, agree these are *sex-irreducible* realities. Christians are in profound ways influenced by the biological complementarity of male and female forms—and, even when these forms enjoin in intersex outcomes, the baselines are there to note.

Activists' claims that any baselines are inconsequential goes against a fundamental truth for Christians: at its core, biology matters. It matters to the biologist, too![28] It matters to the male, the female, the intersex; *and it matters to the gender dysphoric*, who wishes binary gender change! Dysphoria is not to be treated lightly, nor the issues involved for those so diagnosed. Gender-dysphoric individuals are often confused with those supporting an expressive individualism that dismisses all else about gender as inconsequential. Gender dysphorics are not arguing that.

---

26. The Economist, "Briefing: Transgender Politics Focuses on Who Determines Someone's Gender." The article, a "briefing," is both historical and political. It situates the debate between genderqueer claims and their critics in a way that raises the concern of how gender politics is beginning to segregate rather than unite.

27. See Andrea Long Chu's personal narrative and counterpoint, "Surgery, Hormones, but Not Happiness."

28. Fausto-Sterling, *Sexing the Body*.

We also can't erase the truth that the sexual binary is *still* the majority's life course. One ought *not be judged* because one acknowledges that 98 percent of humanity fits a binary sexual schema, with corresponding binary identities. A concordance of sex and gender, however "constructed," is a majority's experience. Culturally and across the continents, people are *not changing their minds* about their biological sex in large numbers, nor about how they perceive themselves *as gendered*. To say that, ought not bring critiques of *transphobia*, presumptions of *oppression*, or complaints that one is reinforcing a *stereotype*.

We should separate these facts from the tired, historical wrongs that *genderized role ideologies* have produced. Such ideologies are even a larger problematic! As Christians, we should acknowledge that many of our historical ideas about men's and women's *roles*, notions of *hierarchy* and *power*, have their basis on *ideologies about gender* that are patently misguided, and that have made many lives suffer needlessly. We've covered those points in chapter 7.

So, let's not confuse things: gender *roles* are total social constructions; and yes, they are slowly changing to be less restrictive, constrictive, of both behaviors and identities. This type of change in *role ideology*—so necessary—isn't to be confused with *biological sex*, although connected. Almost everyone modern and thoughtful recognizes *role problematics*. We can change the ideologies, behaviors, and expectations of roles and yes, influence who we become ("Rosie the Riveter" comes to mind); but for this to happen we do not have to dismiss biological sex as inconsequential to who we are.

We should discourage the idea that gender politics entitles every individual to do as every individual wants to do for him- or herself without social impact. Social philosopher Jean-Jacques Rousseau (1712–78) cemented the individual's right to pursue their destiny, but put it well when he stated that "life is a social contract."[29] We give up some of those individuated freedoms for the sake of participating in the larger social construction we call society. And this is also biblical: 1 Peter 2:13–17 puts it like this:

> Submit yourselves for the Lord's sake to every human authority. . . . For it is God's will that by doing good you should silence

---

29. See Rousseau, *The Social Contract*.

the ignorant talk of foolish people. Live as free people, but do not use your freedom as a cover-up for evil; live as God's slaves. Show proper respect to everyone, love the family of believers, fear God, honor the emperor.

The idea, then, that personal rights ought not affect others, and that we should make all others yield to an individual's self-declared will, puts into jeopardy the distinct tenor of what society is built on: agreements, not *just* individuations or political spaces for accommodations. While such are particularly important, so are social agreements; and these include parameters that a majority will to keep, and truths nature still guards. Opening up gender-role strictures ought not produce gender-identity politics.[30]

Such politicking can lead us—indeed, *is leading us*—into becoming a nation of tribes, tribes that divide humanity into either monolithic dominants or subjugated others; who then see any interaction between them only in terms of power relations. Why shouldn't someone "be who they want to be" without contestation? The right to sex/gender self-identification has become a political *cause célèbre*.[31]

Of course, for many well diagnosed gender-dysphoric individuals, the need to live as their psychological gender and not their sex of birth is paramount. This self-definition and right is legally called

---

30. Western thinking is heavily influenced by concepts of individual selves, and personal autonomy as central to our moral philosophies. From Descartes to contemporary theorists, Western philosophers consider "the self" as independent, individualistic, and in rightful self-control. In many ways, this "rugged individualism" contrasts and often refutes the inherent ties in relationships that are characteristically seen in social collectives. Social collectives and the ties that they bring to the equation of self-in-society are a lot messier than the view that individuals are steadfastly in control of their own destiny. Gender-identity politics disregards the will of the collective to have some say over individuation, the rights of others, and even biology.

31. Reilly-Cooper, a political philosopher at the University of Warwick (UK), wrote in 2016 a piercing but insightful view on the politicized claims of gender activists. Her retort: "So if you want to call yourself a genderqueer femme demigirl, you go for it. A problem emerges only when you start making political claims on the basis of that label—when you start demanding that others call themselves cisgender, because you require there to be a bunch of conventional binary cis people for you to define yourself against; and when you insist that these cis people have structural advantage and political privilege over you, because they are socially read as the conformist binary people, while nobody really understands just how complex and luminous and multi-faceted and unique your gender identity is. To call yourself non-binary or genderfluid while demanding that others call themselves cisgender is to insist that the vast majority of humans must stay in their boxes, because you identify as boxless" (Reilly-Cooper, "Gender Is Not a Spectrum," 9).

"self-identification." In most adult cases of gender dysphoria, the justification for self-identification is *objective evidence*: a clinical diagnosis of historic gender dysphoria, and the volume of medical diagnostics—psychiatric included—to validate it. "The desire on the part of many who suffer gender incongruence to find resolution by changing their body is a sign of the importance of the body to human identity."[32] Like conservative Judaism and Pope Francis, in such cases, we ought not judge.

But, as calls for gender self-identification grow to become an *eraser* for *any other* gender schema, even biological sex determinants in biologically normed individuals, the implications for the welfare of many grow as well: as example, children especially, their development and even safety.[33]

We've already covered the worry over a rush to treatment of the young with gender conflicts. Beyond this, gender-identity activism is affecting *what children learn*: if children can't use their biological sex to tell whether they are a boy or a girl (assuming normed genetics and development), the new paradigm suggests the education system come to their "rescue."

As example, the California State Board of Education is revamping its *Health Education Framework* to include elements of the *California Healthy Youth Act*—a 2016 law that requires sex education include lessons on gender identity. On the surface, not so bad; except that the new framework asks teachers to engage discussions about gender identity beginning in kindergarten, and notes emphatically "some kindergartners may be transgender . . . ."[34]

---

32. Assemblies of God, "Transgenderism, Transsexuality, and Gender Identity," 11.

33. Dyer, "Federal Policies: Serving Neither the Community, the Family, Nor the Transgender Student."

34. California Family Council, "California Elementary Teachers Directed." Some California school districts and teachers have already begun changing curricula and using these materials; but many believe they are not age-appropriate, nor should it be the role of the school to unfold gender: "Children who are beginning to read don't understand gender dysphoria, nor do they understand being trapped in the wrong body, gender change operations or any notion of a 'gender spectrum'" (ibid., 2). However, *parents can't "opt-out"* of this instruction as they can with sexual health education or HIV prevention. Instruction on materials that discuss gender, sexual orientation, but do not discuss human reproductive organs or functions, are not subject to parental opt-out laws in the state.

There are new workbooks and teaching materials, such as *Who Are You? The Kid's Guide to Gender Identity*, whose cover flap reads:

> This brightly illustrated children's book *helps anyone ages 3+* understand and celebrate gender diversity, with straightforward language and illustrations for talking about how we experience gender: our body, our expression, our identity. It includes an interactive wheel on "Body, Identity, and Expression," and a guide for adults/teachers.[35]

This positioning of the need to define gender has spread quickly. Activist groups, some that also include parents of children deemed *genderfluid*, have promoted the idea that children may be "born in the wrong body." Another especially popular notion is to say, "God made a mistake with me."[36]

Clearly, many other examples could be given.[37] The social necessity to aright historical gender transgressions becomes a new imperative to deconstruct *all of gender and sex* for the sake of individual rights. In doing so, it *overreaches*—beyond the responsibility of parents for their children's sexual education and children's own age-appropriate understandings and self-knowledge. It trumps the social will of the majority to keep some semblance of binary gender and certainly sex distinctions alive and well.

LIVING AND LEADING THROUGH THE "MOMENT"

We humans live in social constructions, societies that are complex and have rules about behavior, dress (you still can't go out on the street naked, as you were born, without a social ruckus). The many items Rousseau alluded to in our social contract are there for good reasons.

---

35. Pressin-Wheedbee and Bardoff, *Who Are You?*
36. The Economist, "Transgender Politics," 4. (Brackets mine.)
37. I use a footnote here to highlight the fact that women's groups have actively campaigned and cautioned against the idea that the definition of "woman" ought to include trans-men, i.e., transgender women. This opens yet another debate on the effects of *self-identification*, its legalities and implications. Some transgendered females agree: "It would be better to abandon the push to self-identify legal sex, and look for progressive changes. . . . More generally, we need to be intellectually honest. I am not female and I know that I cannot become female; but I can and do live in a way analogous to the way that women live. I make no claims I cannot justify and my life is better for it," states Debbie Hayton in an *Economist* op-ed ("Gender Identity Needs Objective Evidence," 4).

The apostle Paul found himself in a toxic environment when visiting the church at Corinth, later documenting it in his first letter to them. Not only was the Corinthian church a mess, but the intersection of it with Corinthian society proper, the church's failures in considerate social acts—arrogances both in theological reasoning and social posturing—made the situation factional and political in the larger community.

We learn many things from the way Paul deals with the Corinthians, both inside the church and out. Corinth exposes the countercultural challenges generated by politics, gender, and sex. They accost us as well today. Campbell writes:

> Paul's ethic of Christian love was deeply countercultural and highly demanding. Heterogeneous communities mask how tough it is to practice this kindness and consideration across social divisions [racial, ethnic, sexual, gender], where it needs to bridge and heal and not merely to fit into a group.... Corinth exposes the countercultural challenge.[38]

Paul's admonitions to the Corinthians to be kinder didn't necessarily stop their condescension towards different people. To the point: they were competing in terms that their surrounding culture dictated—rather than following Paul's example as a servant leader who welcomes marginalized converts and cares for those who were shamed in society. Paul points out that such self-promoting acts are a betrayal of what Christianity stands for, a theme he consistently returns to in 1 Corinthians. For both individuals and leaders, it is the Christian who *reaches into the lives of the other*, who *values and engages the marginalized*, that is truthful to their faith. The ethic of kindness and "embrace" is a much tougher challenge for Christians than that of exclusion and critique, especially when applied to social activists.

The Middle We Need to Find

We should not be contentious. We do need to speak truth as we see it, *and it needs to be a dialogue*. Where, then, is the beginning of this

---

38. Campbell, "Paul Wrote to a Community in a Culture War," 6. (Brackets mine.)

conversation, between genderqueer activism and the church? And, where does it lead? Somewhere, there is a middle we have yet to find.

Perhaps the church can help itself to find that middle by lending a listening ear, being less judgmental, relating appropriately, being more accepting of intersex and gender-dysphoric persons; and helping those with different opinions *want* to enter places where God is worshipped.

Are there such strides being made by conservative Christians? I believe there are.

One example comes from the Assemblies of God, an historical Pentecostal, conservative evangelical denomination formed around a revivalist period in the US (the Azusa Street Revival, 1906–9). The AOG, as it is called, is now the largest Pentecostal denomination globally, and in the US, with over three-and-one-half million members, with thousands of minsters and congregations in all fifty states. In 2017, its General Presbytery issued a position paper on transgenderism, transsexuality, and gender identity, from which I've quoted in prior chapters. Here, and from it, I cite evidence of how the denomination encourages one to respond to transgender individuals—and by extension—to *correcting prior wrongs and negativity* towards these and others of the LGBTQ community.

While a long-term "discipleship goal" is stated as helping the person experience increasing *self-integrity* (not defined in the document), it

> ... is not the only discipleship goal, nor even the first issue that needs to be addressed in the lives of transgender persons. The most fundamental issue is, after all, whether they are "in Christ," to use the apostle Paul's term. "Therefore, if anyone is in Christ, the new creation has come: The old has gone, the new is here!" (2 Cor 5:17).... [And even if they are not "in Christ"] the practical question, then, is how to create an optimal environment for transgender persons.[39]

And again:

> Jesus' famous saying regarding the speck and the plank (Matt. 7:3–5) is germane.... However, there is often a failure to address unloving attitudes toward people with views and practices that are different. Ministry to transgender persons—and LGBTQ

39. Assemblies of God, "Transgenderism, Transsexuality, and Gender Identity," 13.

> persons more generally—acknowledges and repents of unloving words and deeds that have been spoken or done toward them. ... A pastoral response to transgender persons cannot even begin if they experience an unloving, unwelcoming environment in the local church. Hospitality, by contrast, welcomes people at the point at which they are met. The temptation pastors must face down [then,] is the reduction of the transgender person to their gender dysphoria and related behaviors, as if the adjective *transgender* exhausted the meaning of the noun *person*. A pastoral response to them must be patient, encouraging, and forgiving all along the way.[40]

And finally:

> This does not mean that those who struggle with gender incongruence are sinning, nor does it mean that attempts to resolve the incongruence against the body should be regarded as intentional rebellion against God rather than as a fight for survival. ... This is [also] not to say that there should be an entirely rigid and unreasonable standard for expressing a particular gender based on cultural stereotypes.[41]

The position paper goes a long way toward embracing those with differences. It does not outright endorse surgical gender transitions, but neither does it judge those who do. In my estimation, the *substance* of the message is clear: a forward move to welcome trans individuals who wish to engage with the denomination, and not judge these as "living in sin."

It also provides a more flexible understanding of *gender expression* than the "cultural stereotypes," meaning, rigid masculinity and femininity. Moreover, insertion of the comment on LGBTQ persons, which ... "acknowledges and repents of unloving words and deeds that have been spoken or done toward them," is affirmation that the denomination is open to kinder treatment of *gay persons*, even if same-sex behavior remains doctrinally incompatible.[42]

---

40. Assemblies of God, "Transgenderism, Transsexuality, and Gender Identity," 13.

41. Assemblies of God, "Transgenderism, Transsexuality, and Gender Identity," 15–16.

42. Distrusting activists will claim, *"Here we go again, accepting the person, but not their lives."* Notions of inclusion in commentaries that embrace and welcome vs. judging and excluding are a welcomed alternative to conservative Christian positions, which have often denigrated the person *along with* any behavior deemed doctrinally incompatible. Let's be fair—all this is a step forward, toward what Volf called "inclusion

Responding with Care

How one responds to the "moment" should model Christian détente towards ideas that clearly rebuff basic understandings about the biology of humans, or longstanding biblical doctrines. Christians should no more go along with those who reject biblical and biological realities than challenge them *unfairly* (without dialogue or kindness). In de-escalating any hostilities, we should also look to ourselves, acknowledge and repair *our* biologically wrong views, uninformed theologies, and refrain from judgments. We should right wrongs against people who are distinct, so we don't repeat history and respond incorrectly. Acts 10:34 should be kept on our sightline: "I now truly understand that God does not show favoritism."

I have stressed understanding the distinctions *in and about gender*, here and in earlier chapters, because we need an informed church; a church that speaks with clarity, not suppositions or wrong "facts." I've tried to point out where our theological interpretations in the past have reified ideas that don't hold in *procreation* and beyond—in relation to *identity*, *self*, and *roles*.

Mark Yarhouse has called the church to engage a more relational ethic,[43] and I believe he is correct in suggesting the church open itself to a more pluralistic audience, giving opportunity for people to hear the gospel without feeling they are being judged for who or "what" they are. This seems to me to be the present AOG position, showing love and understanding despite differences. It is a big, courageous move forward for this evangelical denomination. Such simple acts of compassion and friendliness go miles in enabling all—visitors and members alike—to feel the inclusion Jesus modeled. Our churches and congregants need to be open to and engage differences. Doing so generates those safe spaces alluded to earlier.

How then to respond directly to activists? Our response should sound something like this: *I understand. We were once myopic. While I may not agree with you totally, I can agree to hear you and understand*

---

and embrace." It does *not* mean conservative Christians are changing doctrinal positions. It *does* mean greater openness to embracing the person, less judgment, and a show of love—much as Jesus did. See chapter 7.

43. Yarhouse, *Understanding Gender Dysphoria*, 153.

you, and not judge you. And I hope you can hear me and understand me, and not judge me, either.

The gender revolution won't go away any more than the sexual revolution did. As Christians, we must live in the world, engage the world, but not be *of the world* (John 17:14–15).[44] If we are to emulate Jesus, then we must find a compassionate route to communication and embrace that can ultimately reveal the Spirit of Truth.

That means responding to the transgender moment with compassion and an open door, ultimately working out any possible conciliations with those that have determined and different views. We can enable conversations that provide a listening ground where we can both stand. We can welcome, include, and embrace. We must open wide the doors of mercy and grace, so the Holy Spirit can do God's work *in all of us.*

---

44. It's important to understand the distinction between being "in the world" and "not of the world" to address the gender "moment." We can recognize injustices done against people based on prejudices. We can understand the global turmoil of modern life—predicted in scripture. We can understand how the Christian who takes a position may be seen as contributing to some unnecessary social impediment. And we can extend mercy and reconciliation, precisely, because "we are not of this world" any longer. The emphasis is not on being *better than others*, but being *different from others*—in that, for Christians with Christ at the center, the main goal is to serve God's purpose on earth. And that means not setting up roadblocks that shield us from the world, or the world from us. Intentional openness to hear, understand, and attempt some reconciliation *is the work of God through us for this age.* Responding to the transgender moment requires us to be more than citizens of the world. It requires us to be a pathway out of it.

Conclusion

"If not us, then who? If not now, then when?"
—Rep. John R. Lewis

When I first told a colleague in our Religion Department that I was going to write a book on the "gender moment" for Christians, he jokingly said, "Why? We have the Bible." After a long pause, a frown, then a smile, he added: "Go for it, and I pray what you say gets read."

Mind you, I love this guy—he's one of my best friends.

But I couldn't get over the underlying pause, that if there was something to say about the issues of gender to Christians, it wouldn't be coming from a *sociomedical scientist*, one who was also a *sexologist*. Did it have to be from a theologian?

Why in the world would I open myself up to the scrutiny of Christians and theologians, who would probably *eyebrow* some of the explanations I had in my head as to what was going on, and what our Christian positions ought to be? After all, I *was* this "paradoxical" professional: a sexuality scientist, educator, counselor, *and also a trained clergyperson*. Wasn't this enough of a variegation to address a complex issue? I took courage from this melded background, the Holy Spirit's urging, and the histories I've shared here, to forge on. This book is the result, and I hope it's been helpful. But we're not done yet.

Conclusion

A TRAJECTORY FORWARD

Certainly, the gender revolution is upon us and life will be different here. Gender as not just a construct by which we classify people and ourselves, but now as a force of our identity so big it is a *movement*, a *moment*, a *revolution*, which the church of Jesus Christ must contend with. It's about time we do so.

This moment is not about bathrooms and lockers and agendas or bigotry. It's not about homosexuality this time, or homosexual marriages, or even about fake news.

It's about realizing that there are people born intersex whom the church has omitted from existing by insisting solely on a binary model. It's about *people*—sometimes children, other times adolescents, and many times adults—who struggle with gender identity in the most personal and inscrutable ways. It's about recognizing *their* existences, *their voices*, and making room to hear them—hopefully to love and include them.

It is also a moment for distinctions. No doubt there is a tangible ideological divide that separates those involved in gender-identity politics from those that resist it. But as I said, this "moment" should not lead to, nor remain, a schism. Recognizing that there are distinctive differences, including goals, on both sides of the spectrum ought to help us as believers separate that which needs correction and adjustment from what needs to be kept and validated; *and then talk about it*. If as a church we cannot get ourselves to that middle, where we can sustain cogent conversations about gender and gender ideology, we are missing a fundamental opportunity to learn about, and engage the other. *If not us, then who? If not now, then when?*

Your Parental Engagement

Parents, you may not be teaching your children enough.[1] Recognizing intersex, and particularly gender dysphoria as realities shouldn't be simple statements of approval or disapproval. As such, Christian

---

1. Anderson is illustrating the "transgender catechism" through the work of Transgender Student Educational Resources (TSER), who put out graphics such as the "Gender Unicorn" and the "Genderbread Person," now part of many school curricula, to promote a "highly subjective and incoherent worldview [on gender]." Anderson, "The Philosophical Contradictions," 8. (Brackets mine.)

parents should engage their children's understandings—age-appropriate for certain—in doing justice to individuals born with intersex genitals, or who are transgender. The former, remember, are often reared in gender-conforming ways, and may be same-gender friends to your children and adolescents. The same holds for those questioning or in transition—they are in our schools and lives.

Schools should not be delegated the responsibility for teaching children *who they are*, nor should they allow special interests to override parental responsibilities. And parents, well, parents shouldn't allow their children to be told in school, "maybe God made a mistake with you," or provided literature that cancels out any of the biological understandings we've explored.

Intersex births are real, and they need explaining. Acknowledging the reality of intersex and transgender persons as the church reviews its binary model is a necessary engagement for the church to consider and parents to engage.

If you have an intersex child, that makes matters personal to you as a parent, and it should move you to model that beneficent stance found in historical Judaism, in its acceptance, support, and love of people of all sexual formats. Dealing as a parent with a child who is gender-conflicted or diagnosed dysphoric challenges all the resources of our heads, hearts, and hands. But you must move through the tunnel, making prayer and godly wisdom your hallmarks of decision-making.

Children with gender dysphoria require parents with wisdom and sound information. More, parents need to allow *time* to enable probable desistance, versus moving forward quickly with hormone suppression (which I have not at all recommended), or eventual hormonal and surgical options. You'll find resistances at many levels if you "wait." But waiting doesn't mean not *listening*, *caring*, or *doing*. You can move through the necessary steps to understand, be supported and supportive, while working with therapists that align with the ultimate goal of doing no harm.

Your Personal Engagement

Gender dysphoria and transsexual shifts as realities of the day are here to stay. How we as Christians understand transgenders *in toto*, and people individually, should mark us as caring, loving, Jesus-emulating

Christians who are here to understand, walk alongside, and not judge people. This stance is a recognition that the way forward for many gender-dysphoric persons is a difficult road of decision-making about self, and about *self-in-society*. No person should be an island.

For adults with gender dysphoria who elect gender reassignment/confirmation, let's recognize this is a totally individuated decision that ought not be judged by those standing outside *that body* and *that mind*. We should remember a gender transition is *exceptionally difficult*; surgeries are complex, often medically problematic in some results; and may not always yield desired long-term outcomes. People in such situations need accompaniment.

We ought to also recognize that for many, gender transitions *do* work, allowing individuals a move to a life-course they had dreamed about but never thought possible. In these, there are successes in becoming the person they deemed they were. Recognizing that such transitions need not impede the personal relationship these have with God and Jesus as Lord, but may even enable them for some, is imperative to quell our minds (our judging minds!) from doing harm by default. We need to hear their testimonials and not judge *their* truth. Again, apostle Paul admonishes, "Keep your belief about such matters between yourself and God. Blessed is the one who does not condemn himself by what he approves" (Rom 14:22).

Separating out what are real, diagnosable dimensions of personhood for many, from those that are based on sociocultural trends and politically correct stances is also a necessity for the church. I've recommended not participating in contestations with activists, but rather, *conversations* with them. In doing so, I've pressed on our distinguishing what are medically diagnosable conditions, from those that appear to be supporting a culture-bound syndrome. These, I feel, are especially important distinctions, not just for church leadership, but also for every Christian with a serious mind and conscience.

A TRAJECTORY FORWARD FOR CHURCH LEADERSHIP AND CHRISTIAN THERAPISTS

To the Church Leadership

A friend of mine, a church pastor, recently approached me wanting to discuss "this whole transgender issue." He said, "I don't know enough about this, but I'm hearing it all the time now in the news, so how do I prepare?" This need for preparation, for knowledge, is in large part the reason why I wrote this book.

Church leaders need to become interested in, *and part* of the larger social discussion. The discussion has already filtered into our congregations; questions about gender ideology, about gender transitioning, about our children being exposed early, often prematurely, to questions childhood isn't ready to answer. And questions arising from Christian individuals wanting answers about their own gender feelings.

Pastors need to learn to care for what's going on in their church, but also in their communities and in their communal spheres of influence. I'm not generalizing a judgment when I say "need to learn" or "care"; I am underscoring a fact: with busy lives and sundry church projects and ministries to attend to, pastoral life and responsibilities often become choices to make. We feel justified in having addressed transgender topics if we've done a sermon on what we think about it, maybe confirming what a denomination's position is. After all, trans people aren't showing up in our congregations *en masse*. We care very much about what affects our families, our church projects, ministries, and outreaches in more *normative* ways.

Well, guess what's going on in our families, our church ministries, and outreaches!

We can't dismiss the social wave of transgender ideology. We can't dismiss actual stories of people and congregants, ministers, missionaries, church leaders who are "outing," and are all around us. We need to get informed. We need more than the essentials to enable us to respond with understanding and compassion.

If we want to be current and offer compassion and care for those in the transgender moment, *a network of informed and caring clergy is needed*. Such can then collaborate to learn together, respond to those intersex; those with gender dysphoria; and yes, to those outing their nonbinary choices as influenced by the social movement of reimagining selves. Why not start a network among your pastoral connections?

We need provisions of good data, good readings, conversations with those who are intersex and trans; plans for educating *ourselves* and *our communities of faith*. We also need to engage community care, and by extension, plan for continuing quality improvement of *how* we care.

To the Christian Therapeutic Community

We need informed clinicians who can effectively deal with gender issues, and who are also Christian—who render that label without prejudice. Clinicians who understand there are distinctions between theological positions and clinical ones, and who can reconcile these in the clinical hour. Moreover, we need clinicians trained in sexological sciences, with an informed and nuanced understanding of the biological and the hormonal; of what accounts for the substrates of sex and gender as these play themselves out in our psyche, and in our sociocultural world.

There are healthy options therapists could engage for patients if they had the right training. Throckmorton and Yarhouse have already provided a substantive baseline in their practice framework for managing sexual-identity conflicts.[2] Sexuality therapy and sexual counseling are specialties, and there is significant lack of Christian therapists who have engaged such training. I suspect this is because most of such training comes from "secular sources." As one trained in sexological sciences, there is nothing in such training that a Christian cannot negotiate. Good training respects religious sentiment, and that has been my experience.

A great resource for training to consider is that provided by the American Association of Sexuality Educators, Counselors, and Therapists (AASECT). AASECT also offers certifications in sexual therapy, counseling, and education. Not only will such certifications expand the Throckmorton-Yarhouse practice framework, but situate those

---

2. Throckmorton and Yarhouse state, "The purpose of these recommendations is to develop professional consensus around appropriate mental health responses to those individuals seeking assistance due to sexual identity conflicts" ("Sexual Identity Therapy," 8).

with augmented sexuality/sexual therapy expertise within a network; elements that can help tailor sexual counseling, therapy, and education appropriately. In addition, those of faith so certified can also help Christians who transition adjust to their new life.

But we aren't there yet with Christian therapists and counselors. A network of sexologically trained therapists and counselors would support added knowledge and modes of care; add expertise; all strengthening therapists' abilities, and referral options for patients. Ultimately, let's not forget therapists work with not only their direct clients (children or adults), but also with their families. Even more reason to stretch the knowledge-base and skills to manage gender/identity issues in the context of family dynamics.

A TRAJECTORY FORWARD FOR US ALL

I've emphasized our need to learn more about *the other* as now rendered, not only as we've been taught; also, as we learn through the sciences *and* through a theology that "reads the good book well." Christians, we can't ignore good science, nor should we want to. Evidence-based science can help us distinguish facts from trends, basics from probabilities, truth from ignorance. Science is not anti-faith, but can coexist with it. Pope John Paul II wrote, "Science can purify religion from error and superstition; religion can purify science from idolatry and false absolutes. Each can draw the other into a wider world, a world in which each can flourish."[3]

God *is* revealed in nature, since "the heavens declare the glory of God" (Ps 19:1). Likewise, faith, as Dr. Francis Collins demonstrates, is not the enemy of scientific reason: rather, it is its perfect complement.[4] Collins came to faith *through* science, himself the leader of

---

3. Pope John Paul II, "Letter to Director of the Vatican Observatory."

4. Collins writes, "Many will be puzzled by these sentiments—assuming a rigorous scientist could not also be a serious believer in a transcendent God. This book aims to dispel that notion, by arguing that belief in God can be an entirely rational choice, and that the principles of faith are, in fact, complementary with the principles of science" (*The Language of God*, 3). Dr. Collins was head of the Human Genome Project, and is today one of the world's leading scientists on the cutting edge of DNA research—one of the world's genius geneticists. In this work, he explains his own journey from *atheism* to *faith*. It is through his studies of chemistry, physics, and biology that Collins discovers the hand of God.

the International Human Genome Project. "For me, the sequencing of the human genome, and uncovering this most remarkable of texts (which President Clinton called *learning the language in which God created life*), was both a stunning scientific achievement and an occasion of worship."[5]

I have tried to illustrate, simply, how the science of genetics and our understanding of hormones "opens up" our understanding of how "fearfully and wonderfully" we have been made. Science and its technologies show us much more of God's creation than was known in biblical times, to biblical writers, revealing even more of God's glory today than in earlier human history. Our current frame of reference also needs exegesis that enables our Christian pilgrimage in the here and now, as much as in the past. Scriptures speak to all generations and in all situations; and the heavens still declare God's glory.

Let's admit, we also haven't done very well in the gender category, either—we've been myopic. Our myopia doesn't have to continue. Everyone can become better informed, help to correct misperceptions—biblical or otherwise. We can all bear witness to the fact that "Jesus on board changes everything." That means our judgments, our expectations, our abilities, as well as our capacity to understand the depth of what it means to be human, and to care. Ultimately, to do no harm to our neighbor.

> *Let us stop saying we love people. Let us really love them, and show it by our actions. Then we will know for sure, by our actions, that we are on God's side; and our consciences will be clear, even when we stand before the Lord.*
> 1 John 3:18–19 (NLT)

---

5. Collins, *The Language of God*, 3.

Bibliography

Abel, B. S. "Hormone Treatment of Children and Adolescents with Gender Dysphoria: An Ethical Analysis." *Hastings Center Report* 44 (2014) S23–S27.

Alexander, Denis. *Is There Purpose in Biology? The Cost of Existence and the God of Love.* London: Monarch/Lion Hudson, 2018.

Allison, Gregg R. "Toward a Theology of Human Embodiment." *Southern Baptist Journal of Theology* 13 (2009) 4–17.

American Psychiatric Association. *Diagnostic and Statistical Manual of Mental Disorders*, 5th ed. Arlington, VA: American Psychiatric Publishing, 2013.

———. "Gender Dysphoria." (Section 302.85 [F64.9]). In *Diagnostic and Statistical Manual of Mental Disorders*. 5th ed. Arlington, VA: American Psychiatric Publishing, 2013.

———. "Position Statement on Therapies Focused on Attempts to Change Sexual Orientation (Reparative or Conversion Therapies)." (2000) http://www.apa.org/Downloads/Position-2000-Therapies-Change-SexualOrientation%20(2).pdf

———. "Transvestism" (Section 302.3 [F65.1]). *Diagnostic and Statistical Manual of Mental Disorders*, 5th ed. Arlington, VA: American Psychiatric Publishing, 2013.

American Society of Plastic Surgeons. "2018 National Plastic Surgery Statistics." *ASPS Plastic Surgery News*, 2018, https://www.plasticsurgery.org/news/plastic-surgery-statistics.

Anderson, Ryan T. "The Philosophical Contradictions of the Transgender Worldview." *Public Discourse* (2018). https://www.thepublicdiscourse.com/2018/02/20971/.

———. "Transgender Ideology Is Riddled with Contradictions." *Commentary: The Heritage Foundations* (February 9, 2018), https://heritage.org/commentary/transgender-ideology-is-riddled-contradictions.

———. *When Harry Became Sally: Responding to the Transgender Moment.* New York: Encounter, 2018.

Arnold, Arthur P. "A General Theory of Sexual Differentiation." *Journal of Neuroscience Research* 95 (2017) 291–300.

Assemblies of God. "Transgenderism, Transsexuality, and Gender Identity." Position paper of the General Council of the Assemblies of God, 2017. https://ag.org/Beliefs/Topics-Index/Transgenderism-Transsexuality-and-Gender-Identity.

Augustine, St. *The Literal Meaning of Genesis, Vol. 1, Ancient Christian Writers.* Edited by John Hammond Taylor. Mahwah, NJ: Paulist, 1982.

Bader, Lee. "Third Genders: New Concept? Or Old?" *The Evolution of Human Sexuality*, February 2014. https://sites.psu/edu/evolutionofhumansexuality.

Barlow, Dade. *Electric Dade* (YouTube channel). https://www.youtube.com/user/ElectricDade.

———. "FTM Transition: One Year on Testosterone" (YouTube video). *Electric Dade* (YouTube channel). November 29, 2012. https://www.youtube.com/watch?v=wvAClyCwZvU.

Barth, Karl. *Christ and Adam: Man and Humanity in Romans 5*. Translation by T. A. Smail. Eugene, OR: Wipf and Stock, 2004.

Baudrillard, Jean, and Mark Guillaume. *Radical Alterity*. Translated by Arnes Hodges. Los Angeles: Semiotex/MIT, 2008.

Beach, Shelly. "Cosmetic Surgery to the Glory of God?" *Christianity Today*, April 2010. https://www.christianitytoday.com/women/2010/april/cosmetic-surgery-to-glory-of-god.html.

Beauchamp, Scott. "The Kids Aren't All Right: What the Gender Identity Revolution Has in Common with 1960's Drug Culture." *The Public Discourse*, February 2017. http://www.thepublicdiscourse.com/2017/02/18781/.

Beemyn, Genny, and Susan Rankin. *The Lives of Transgender People*. New York: Columbia University Press, 2011.

Ben-Noun, L. *Consanguineous Marriages from Antiquity to the Present*. Beer-Sheva ISR: B.N Publication House (Ben Gurion University of the Negev), 2017. https://www.researchgate.net/publication/315756235_consanguineous_marriages_from_antiquity_to_the_present.

Benson, Joseph. *Commentary of the Old and New Testaments*. Amazon English Services LLC, 2018. Kindle Edition. https://www.amazon.com/Joseph-Benson-Commentary-Old-Testament-ebook/dp/B07L5NL9QW.

Berenbaum, Sheri A., and Adriene M. Beltz. "Sexual Differentiation of Human Behavior: Effects of Prenatal and Pubertal Organizational Hormones." *Frontiers in Neuroendocrinology* 32 (2011) 183–200.

Berenbaum, Sheri A., et al. "Gendered Peer Involvement in Girls with Congenital Adrenal Hyperplasia: Effects of Prenatal Androgens, Gendered Activities, and Gender Cognitions." *Archives of Sexual Behavior* 17 (2018) 1112–14.

Bertelloni, S., and D. Mull. "Treatment of Central Precocious Puberty by GnRH Analogues: Long-Term Outcomes in Men." *Asian Journal of Andrology* 10 (2017) 531–36.

Bimson, John J. "Reconsidering a 'Cosmic Fall.'" *Science and Christian Belief* 18.1 (2006) 63–8. https://www.scienceandchristianbelief.org/serve_pdf_free.php?filename=SCB+18-1+Bimson.pdf.

Blackless, Melanie, et al., "How Sexually Dimorphic Are We? Review and Synthesis." *American Journal of Human Biology* 12 (2000) 151–66.

Blakemore, S.J., et al. "The Role of Puberty in the Developing Adolescent Brain." *Human Brain Mapping* 31 (2010) 926–31.

Boylan, Jennifer Finney. *She's Not There: A Life in Two Genders*. Portland: Broadway, 2013.

Brooks, John. "The Controversial Research on 'Desistance' in Transgender Youth." *KQED Science*, May 2018. https://www.kqed.org/futureofyou/441784/the-controversial-research-on-desistance-in-transgender-youth.

———. "Is Three Too Young for Children to Know They're a Different Gender? Transgender Researchers Disagree." *KQED Science*, August 2018. https://www.kqed.org/futureofyou/440851/can-you-really-know-that-a-3-year-old-is-transgender.

Brown, Peter. *The Body and Society: Men, Women, and Sexual Renunciation in Early Christianity*. New York: Columbia University Press, 1988.
Bunge, Marcia J. "A More Vibrant Theology of Children." *Christian Reflection: A Series in Faith and Ethics* (Summer 2003) 11–19. https://www.baylor.edu/ifl/christianreflection/ChildrenarticleBunge.pdf.
Butler, Judith. *Gender Trouble: Feminism and the Subversion of Identity*. London: Routledge, 2006.
California Family Council. "California Elementary School Teachers May Be Directed to Teach Transgender Lessons." *Education Magazine* (October 2018). https://californiafamily.org/2018/california-elementary-school-teachers-may-be-directed-to-teach-transgender-lessons/.
Callahan, Gerald N. *Between XX and XY. Intersexuality and the Myth of Two Sexes*. Chicago: Chicago Review, 2009.
Camery-Hoggatt, Jerry. *Reading the Good Book Well*. Nashville, TN: Abingdon, 2007.
Campbell, Douglas A. "Paul Wrote 1st Corinthians to a Community in the Middle of a Culture War." *Christian Century*, January 3, 2018, 6.
Carlson, Alison. "Essay: Suspect Sex." *The Lancet Medicine and Sport* 366 (December 2005) 539–42.
Carter, Joe. "From Agender to Ze: A Glossary for the Gender Identity Revolution." *The Gospel Coalition* (May 13, 2016) https://www.thegospelcoalition.org/article/from-agender-to-ze-a-glossary-for-the-gender-identity-revolution/.
The Christian Century. "How Do You Hold Together Your Trans Identity and Your Life of Faith? Nine Trans Christians Tell their Stories." *The Christian Century*, January 2017. https://www.christiancentury.org/article/how-do-you-hold-together-your-trans-identity-and-your-life-faith.
Chrysostom, St. John. "Homilies on the Acts of the Apostles and the Epistle to the Romans." In *A Select Library of the Nicene and Post-Nicene Fathers of the Christian Church*, vol. 11, edited by Philip Schaff. Buffalo, NY: The Christian Literature, 1886.
Chu, Andrea Long. "Surgery, Hormones, But Not Happiness." *New York Times*, November 24, 2018.
Ciampa, Roy E. "Genesis 1–3 and Paul's Theology of Adam's Dominion." In *From Creation to New Creation: Essays on Biblical Theology and Exegesis*, edited by Daniel M. Gurtner and Benjamin L. Gladd, 103–22. Peabody, MA: Hendrickson, 2013.
Cincinnati Children's Hospital. "Mixed Gonadal Dysgensis." https://www.cincinnatichildrens.org/health/m/mixed-gonadal-dysgenesis.
Coalition of Christian Colleges and Universities. "Finding Ourselves After Darwin." *Advance Magazine*, Fall 2018, 38–42.
Cohen, A. "Tumtum and Androgynous." *Journal of Halacha and Contemporary Society* 38 (Fall 1999) 1–11.
Cohen-Kettenis, P. T., et al. "The Treatment of Adolescent Transsexuals: Changing Insights." *Journal of Sexual Medicine* 5 (2008) 1892–97.
Collins, Francis S. *The Language of God*. New York: Free Press, 2006.
Collins, Jack. "Appropriation and Development of Castration as Symbol and Practice in Early Christianity." In *Castration and Culture in the Middle Ages*, edited by Larissa Tracy, 73–86. Rochester: Boydell & Brewer, 2013.

Colson, Charles. "How Many Sexes Are There?" *BreakPOINT* (1996). www.breakpoint.org/1996/10/blurred-biology/.

Cornwall, Susannah. "'State of Mind' versus 'Concrete Set of Facts': The Contrasting of Transgender and Intersex in Church Documents on Sexuality." *Theology and Sexuality* 15 (2009) 7–28.

———. *Sex and Uncertainty in the Body of Christ: Intersex Conditions and Christian Theology*. London: Equinox, 2010.

Cowdell, Scott. "Gender and Identity: Freeing the Bible from Modern Western Anxieties." *ABC Network, Religion and Ethics* (September 17, 2017). https://www.abc.net.au/religion/gender-and-identity-freeing-the-bible-from-modern-western-anxiet/10095390.

Cox, J. A. *Intersex in Christ*. Eugene, OR: Cascade, 2018.

Cretella, Michelle A. "Gender Dysphoria in Children and Suppression of Debate." *Journal of American Physicians and Surgeons* 21 (2016) 50–54.

Crowley, W.F., et al. "Therapeutic Use of Pituitary Desensitization with a Long-Acting LHRH Agonist: A Potential Treatment for Idiopathic Precocious Puberty." *Journal of Clinical Endocrinology and Metabolism* 52 (1981) 370–72. https://www.ncbi.nlm.nih.gov/pubmed/6780592.

Darshan, Guy. "The Origins of the Foundation Stories Genre in Hebrew Bible." *Journal of Biblical Literature* 133 (2014) 689–709.

Davidson, Gregg. "Genetics, the Nephilim, and the Historicity of Adam." *Perspectives on Science and Christian Faith* 67 (2015) 24–34.

Davis, Georgiann. *Contesting Intersex: The Dubious Diagnosis*. New York: New York University Press, 2015.

De Vries, Annelou L. C., et al. "Young Adult Psychological Outcomes After Puberty Suppression and Gender Reassignment." *Pediatrics* 134 (2014) 669–704.

Deaux, Kay. "Psychological Constructions of Masculinity and Femininity." In *Masculinity/Femininity: Basic Perspectives*, edited by June Machover Reinisch et al., 289–303. New York: Oxford University Press, 1987.

DeFranza, Megan K. *Sex Difference in Christian Theology: Male, Female, and Intersex in the Image of God*. Grand Rapids: Eerdmans, 2015.

Denison, Jim. "Do All Children Go to Heaven?" *Christianity Today*, May 2013. https://www.christianitytoday.com/ct/2013/may-web-only/do-all-children-go-to-heaven.html.

DeVries, Annelou L. C., and Peggy T. Cohen-Kettenis. "Clinical Management of Gender Dysphoria in Children and Adolescents: The Dutch Approach." *Journal of Homosexuality* 59 (2012) 301–20.

DeVries, A. L. C., et al. "Puberty Suppression in Adolescents with Gender Identity Disorder: A Prospective Follow-Up Study." *Journal of Sexual Medicine* 8 (2011) 2276–83.

Dhejne, Celcilia, et al. "Long-Term Follow-Up of Transsexual Persons Undergoing Sex Reassignment Surgery: Cohort Study in Sweden." *PLoS ONE* 6 (2011) e16885. https://doi.org/10.1371/journal.pone.0016885.

Diamond, Milton, and Keith Sigmundson. "Management of Intersexuality: Guidelines for Dealing with Persons with Ambiguous Genitalia." *Archives of Pediatric Adolescent Medicine* 151 (1997) 1046–50.

Docter, R. F., and Virginia Prince. "Transvestism: A Survey of 1032 Cross-Dressers." *Archives of Sexual Behavior* 26 (1997) 589–605.

Donaldson James, S. "Intersex Babies: Boy or Girl and Who Decides?" *ABC News* (March 16, 2011). www.abcnews.go.com/Health/intersex-children-pose-ethical-dilemma-doctors-parents-genital/story/?id=13153068.

Dreger, Alice. "Ambiguous Sex—Or Ambivalent Medicine? Ethical Issues in the Treatment of Intersexuality." *Hastings Center Report* 28 (1998) 24–36.

Drescher, Jack. "Five Myths on Being Transgender." *The Washington Post Opinion Section*, May 13, 2016. https://www.washingtonpost.com/opinions/five-myths-about-transgender-issues/2016/05/13/eca17dbc-177e-11e6-9e16-2e5a123aac62_story.html?

Dyer, W. Justin. "Federal Policies on Transgender Students: Serving Neither the Community, the Family, nor the Transgender Student." *The Public Discourse*, June 6, 2016. https://www.thepublicdiscourse.com/2016/06/17211/.

The Economist. "Briefing: Transgender Politics Focuses on Who Determines Someone's Gender." *The Economist*, October 27, 2018. https://economist.com/briefing/2018/10/27/transgender-politics-focuses-on-who-determines-someones-gender.

Ehrhardt, Anke, and Heino F. Meyer-Bahlburg. "Effects of Prenatal Sex Hormones on Gender-Related Behavior." *Science* 211 (March 1981) 1312–18.

Eichler, Raanan. "Gender Equality and Creation." *The Torah* (website). https://thetorah.com/gender-equality-at-creation/.

Erickson, Ives, "Blind Spot: Do Unconscious Biases Affect Our Hiring, Firing, Work Relationships, and the Care We Provide?" *Caring Headlines* (2015) 4. https://www.mghpcs.org/caring/Assets/documents/issues/2015/February_5_2015.pdf.

Evangelical Lutheran Church. *Lutheran Introduction to Sexual Orientation, Gender Identity & Gender Expression*. St. Paul, MN: ReconcilingWorks, 2019.

Evans, Rachel Held. Interview with Lisa Salazar, "Ask a Transgender Christian." September 11, 2012. https://rachelheldevans.com/blog/ask-a-transgender-christian-response?format=amp.

Fausto-Sterling, Anne. *Sexing the Body: Gender Politics and the Construction of Sexuality*. New York: Basic, 2000.

Feinberg, Leslie. *Transgender Liberation: A Movement Whose Time Has Come*. New York: World View Forum, 1992.

Feldman, Marcus. "People from Distant Lands Have Strikingly Similar Genetic Traits, Study Reveals." *ScienceDaily* 20 (December 2002). www.sciencedaily.com/releases/2002/12/021220080005.htm.

Ferris, Jaquelle (Crow). "How Youth Like Me Learn Expressive Individualism." *Christian Living*, January 2017. https://thegospelcoalition.org/article/how-youth-like-me-learn-exrpressive-individualism.

Fischer, M. "Think Gender Is Performance? You Have Judith Butler to Thank for That." *New York Magazine, The Cut*, June 13, 2016. https://www.thecut.com/2016/06/judith-butler-c-v-r.html#_ga=2.199745966.1806084098.1585947944-1859312516.1585258375

Fisher, M., et al. "Resumption of Puberty in Girls and Boys Following Removal of the Histrelin Implant." *Journal of Pediatrics* 164 (2014) 3–5.

Flather, Curtis H., et al. "Minimum Variables Populations: Is There a 'Magic Number' for Conservation Practitioners?" *Trends in Ecology and Evolution* 26 (April 2011) 307–16.

Francis, Pope [Jorge Mario Bergoglio]. *The Name of God Is Mercy*. New York: Random House Translation Editions, 2016.

Gardner, M., and D.E. Sandberg. "Navigating Surgical Decision Making in Disorders of Sex Development." *Frontiers in Pediatrics* 6 (2018) 1–9.

Genesis and Genetics. "Eve's DNA." Genesis and Genetics (March 2014). http://www.genesisandgenetics.org/2014/03/31/eves-dna/.

Genetic and Rare Diseases Information Center, National Institutes of Health. Bethesda: US Department of Health and Human Services. https://rarediseases.info.nih.gov.

Gil, V. E. "To Feel or Not to Feel: Framing and Clarifying the Debate on Sexual Orientation in the Church." Paper presented at the Evangelical Missiological Society Annual Meeting, Dallas, TX, October, 2017.

Goldberg, Steven. *The Inevitability of Patriarchy*. New York: Steven Morrow and Sons, 1974.

Goodman, M., and Nash, R. *Examining Health Outcomes for People Who Are Transgender: Comparative Risks and Benefits of Gender Reassignment Surgeries*. Washington, DC: Patient-Centered Outcomes Research Institute (PCORI), 2018. https://doi.org/10.25302/2.2019.AD.12114532.

Gorvett, Zaria. "Could Just Two People Repopulate the Earth?" *BBC Future's "Best of 2016"* (January) 2016. http://www.bbc.com/future/story/20160113-could-just-two-people-repopulate-earth.

Green, R. "Robert Stoller's Sex and Gender: 40 Years On." *Archives of Sexual Behavior* 39.6 (2010) 1457–65.

Grohol, John M. "Become a Better Listener: Active Listening." *Psych Central* (2018). www.psychcentral.com.

Guarnaccia, Peter J., and Lloyd H. Rogler. "Research on Culture-Bound Syndromes: New Directions." *American Journal of Psychiatry* 156 (1999) 1322–27.

Gutierrez, M. "Bill Stirs Intersex Rights Debate." *Los Angeles Times*, March 25, 2019. https://enewspaper.latimes.com/infinityarticle_share.aspx?guid=012719a6-eb8b-4d69-a0ba-921d131f0e721.

Halberstam, Jack. *Trans: A Quick and Quirky Account of Gender Variability*. Oakland, CA: University of California, 2018.

Hamamy, H. "Consanguineous Marriages. Preconception Consultation in Primary Health Care." *Journal of Community Genetics* 3 (2012) 185–92.

Hayes, Kelsey. "Ethical Implications of Treatment for Gender Dysphoria in Youth." *Online Journal of Health Ethics* 14.2 (2018). http://dx.doi.org/10.18785/ojhe.1402.03.

Hayton, Debbie. "Gender Identity Needs to Be Based on Objective Evidence Rather Than Feelings." *The Economist*, July 3, 2018, 4. www.economist.com/openfuture/debbie-hayton-oped/.

Helmer, Christine. *Theology and the End of Doctrine*. Louisville, KY: Westminster John Knox, 2014.

Hembree, W. C., et al. "Endocrine Treatment of Transsexual Persons: An Endocrine Society Clinical Practice Guideline." *Journal of Clinical Endocrinology and Metabolism* 94 (2009) 3132–54.

Hembree, W. C., et al. "Guidelines for Pubertal Suppression and Gender Reassignment for Transgender Adolescents." *Child and Adolescent Psychiatric Clinics of North America* 20 (2010) 725–32.

Heneghan, Carl, and Tom Jefferson. "Gender-Affirming Hormone in Children and Adolescents." *BMJ Online: Evidence Based Medicine Blog* (February 25, 2019). https://blogs.bjm.com/bmjebmspotlight/2019/02/25/gender-affirming-hormone-in-children-and- adolescents-evidence-review/.

Henry, Matthew. *Matthew Henry's Commentary on the Whole Bible.* Peabody, MA: Hendrickson, 2008.

Herbert, J. "Is Gender Identity in the Brain? What Does This Tell Us?" *Psychology Today* (August 2016). https://www.psychologytoday.com/us/blog/hormones-and-the-brain/201608/gender-identity-is-in-the-brain-what-does-tell-us.

Herek, G. M. "On Heterosexual Masculinity." *American Behavioral Scientist* 29 (1986) 563–77.

Hess, J., et al. "Sexuality After Male to Female Gender Affirmation Surgery." *Biomedical Research International* (May 27, 2019). Doi: 10.1155/2018/9037979.

Hines, Melissa. *Brain Gender.* New York: Oxford University Press, 2004.

Hoffer, Eric. *Reflection on the Human Condition.* Titusville, NJ: Hopewell, 2006.

Hoffman, Jan. "Estimate of U.S. Transgender Population Doubles to 1.4 Million Adults." *New York Times,* June 30, 2016, 1–2. https://www.nytimes.com/2016/07/01/health/transgender-population.html.

Hruz, Paul., et al. "Growing Pains: Problems with Puberty Suppression in Treating Gender Dysphoria." *New Atlantis* 52 (2017) 3–36. https://www.thenewatlantis.com/publications/growing-pains.

Human Rights Campaign. *Growing Up LGBTQ in America: Youth Report of 2016.* 2016. http://www.hrc.org/youth-report.

———. "Resources." https://www.hrc.org/resources

———. "Sexual Orientation and Gender Identity Terminology and Definitions." 2019. https://www.hrc.org/resources/sexual-orientation-and-gender-identity-terminology-and-definitions.

———. "Our Victories." 2019. https://www.hrc.org/hrc-story/our-victories.

Hyde, Chris. "Follow-Up Studies of Post-Operative Transsexuals and Health Care Treatments for the National Health Service." Birmingham, UK: *University of Birmingham Aggressive Research Intelligence Facility (ARIF)* 2011. http://www.birmingham.ac.uk/Documents/college-mds/haps/projects/ARIF/completed-requests.pdf.

International Association of Athletics Federation. "2011 IAFF Regulations Governing Eligibility of Females with Hyperandrogenism to Compete in Women's Competitions" 2011. http://www.iaaf.org/mm/Document/AboutIAAF/Publications/05/98/78/20110430054216_httppostedfile_HARregulations(Final)-Appendices-AMG-30.04.2011.24299.pdf.

International Olympics Committee. "2012 IOC Regulations on Female Hyperandrogenism: Games of the XXX Olympiad in London, 2012." http://www.olympic.org/Documents/Commissions_PDFfiles/Medical_commission/2012-06-22-IOC-Regulations-on-Female-Hyperandrogenism-eng.pdf.

Intersex Society of North America (ISNA). *Consortium on the Management of Disorders of Sex Development: Handbook for Parents.* Rohnert Park, CA: ISNA, 2006.

———. "FAQ: Does ISNA Think Children with Intersex Should be Raised without a Gender, or in a Third Gender?" n/d. https://isna.org/faq/third-gender.

———. "How Can You Assign a Gender (Boy or Girl) without Surgery?" https://isna.org/faq/gender_assignment.

———. "How Common Is Intersex?" 2019. https://www.isna.org/faq/frequency.
———. "What Does ISNA Recommend?" http://wwww.isna.org/faq/what-does-isna-recommend?
———. "Why Doesn't ISNA Want to Eradicate Gender?" http://isna.org/faq/not_eradicating_gender.
James, S. E. et al., *The Report of the 2015 U.S. Transgender Survey*. Washington, DC: National Center for Transgender Equality, 2016.
Jellestad, J., et al. "Quality of Life in Transitioned Trans Persons: A Retrospective Cross-Sectional Cohort Study." *Biomedical Research International* (2018) 1–10. https://doi.org./10.1155/2018/8684625.
Jewett, Paul K. *Man as Male and Female: A Study of Sexual Relationships from a Biblical Point of View*. Grand Rapids: Eerdmans, 1990.
Johns, M.M., et al. "Transgender Identity and Experiences of Violence, Victimization, Substance Use, Suicide Risk, and Sexual Risk Behaviors among High School Students—19 States and Large Urban School Districts." *Morbidity and Mortality Weekly Report* 68 (2017) 67–71. http://dx.doi.org/10.15585/mmwr.mm6803a3.
Jolie, Angelina. "My Medical Choice." *New York Times*, May 14, 2013, 25. https://www.nytimes.com/2013/05/14/opinion/my-medical-choice.html.
Kallak, Theodora Kunovac, et al. "Maternal and Fetal Testosterone Levels are Associated with Maternal Age and Gestational Weight Gain." *European Journal of Endocrinology* 177 (2017) 379–88.
Karkazis, Katrina. *Fixing Intersex: Intersex, Medical Authority, and Lived Experience*. Durham, NC: Duke University Press, 2008.
Kay, Jonathan. "An Interview with Lisa Littman, Who Coined the Term 'Rapid Onset Gender Dysphoria.'" *Quillette* (March 2019). https://quillette.com/2019/03/19/an-interview-with-lisa-littman-who-coined-the-term-rapid-onset-gender-dysphoria.
Kessler, Suzanne. *Lessons from the Intersexed*. New Brunswick: Rutgers University Press, 1998.
Klein, C., and B. Boris. "Continuing Medical Education: Sexual Functioning in Transsexuals Following Hormone Therapy and Genital Surgery: A Review." *Journal of Sexual Medicine* 6(11) (2009) 2922–39.
Klein, Dianne. "Gender X: The Battle Over Boy or Girl." *Stanford Medicine* (Spring, 2011). http://sm.stanford.edu/archive/stanmed/2011spring/article4.html.
Kreukels, B. P., and P. T. Cohen-Kettenis. "Puberty Suppression in Gender Identity Disorder: The Amsterdam Experience." *National Review of Endocrinology* 7 (2011) 4666–72.
Kruijver, F. P., et al. "Male to Female Transsexuals Have Female Neuron Numbers in a Limbic Nucleus." *Journal of Clinical Endocrinology and Metabolism* 85 (2000) 2034–41.
Kuelfer, M. *The Manly Eunuch: Masculinity, Gender Ambiguity, and Christian Ideology in Late Antiquity*. Chicago: University of Chicago Press, 2001.
Kuhn, A., et al. "Quality of Life 15 Years after Sex Reassignment Surgery for Transsexualism." *Fertility and Sterility* 5 (2009) 1685–89.
Kuper, L. E. "Puberty Blocking Medications: Clinical Research Review." *IMPACT-LGBT Health and Development Program* 2 (2014) 1–10.
Ladin, Joy. "Torah in Transition." *TransTorah* (2014) 1–9. https://transtorah.com/joyladin/torah-in-transition.pdf.

Learn Genetics. "Epigenetics and Inheritance." *Learn·Genetics: Genetic Science Learning Center.* https://learn.genetics.utah.edu/content/epigenetics/.
Lee, P.A., et al., "Consensus Statement on Management of Intersex Disorders" *Pediatrics* 118.2 (August, 2006) e-488–e500. Doi: https://doi.org/10.1542/peds.2006-0738.
Lerner, Gerda. *The Creation of Patriarchy.* New York: Oxford University Press, 1986.
Lévinas, Emmanuel. *Alterity and Transcendence.* Translated by Michael B. Smith. London: Athlone, 1999.
Linker, Damon. "The Egregious Overreach of Transgender Activism." *The Week.com* (March 9) 2018. https://theweek.com/articles/759763/egregious-overreach-transgender-activism.
Lippa, Richard A. *Gender, Nature, and Nurture,* 2nd ed. London: Routledge, 2014.
Littman, Lisa. "Parent Reports of Adolescents and Young Adults Perceived to Show Signs of a Rapid Onset of Gender Dysphoria." *PLOS One* (August 16) 2018. http//journals.plos.org/plosone/article?id=10.1371/journal.pone.0202330. Corrected edition published March 19, 2019, *PLOS One* 13 e0202330.
Lohman, S., and E. Lohman. *Raising Rosie. Our Story of Parenting an Intersex Child.* London: Jessica Kingsley, 2018.
Longman, Jeré. "Understanding the Controversy Over Caster Semenya." *The New York Times* (August 18, 2016). https://www.nytimes.com/2016/08/20/sports/caster-semenya-800-meters.
Lorber, Judith. *Paradoxes of Gender.* New Haven: Yale University Press, 1995.
Louie, Sam. "Trauma and Transgender Identity." *Psychology Today,* December 31, 2019. https://www.psychologytoday.com/us/blog/minority-report/201912/trauma-and-transgender-identity.
Lucas-Stannard, P. *Gender Neutral Parenting: Raising Kids with the Freedom to Be Themselves,* Kindle Edition. Verity Press, 2013.
Luders, E., et al. "Regional Gray Matter Variation in Male-To-Female Transsexualism." *Neuroimage* 46 (2009) 904–7.
Luhrmann, Tanya A. "C. S. Lewis, Evangelical Rock Star." *New York Times Opinion,* June 25, 2013. https://www.nytimes.com/2013/06/26/opinion/luhrmann-c-s-lewis-evangelical-rock-star.html.
Lyons, Kate. "UK Doctors Prescribing Cross-Sex Hormones to Children as Young as 12." *The Guardian,* July 11, 2016. https://www.theguardian.com/society/2016/jul/11/transgender-nhs-doctor-prescribing-sex-hormones-children-uk.
Madueme, Hans. "Nip & Tuck: A Parable." *Dignitas* 16 (2009) 1.
Mahfouda, B.A., et al. "Puberty Suppression in Transgender Children and Adolescents." *The Lancet Diabetes and Endocrinology* 5 (2017) 816–26.
Manning, Sanchez. "How 800 Children as Young as 10 Have Been Given Sex Change Drugs: Huge Rise in Puberty-Blocker Jabs Revealed." *The Daily Mail,* July 2017. https://www.dailymail.co.uk/news/article-4743036/800-children-young-10-puberty-blockers.html.
Marchiano, Lisa. "Guidance for Parents of Teens with Rapid Onset Gender Dysphoria." *The Jung Soul,* October 27, 2016. http://thejungsoul.com.
Martínez-Patiño, María J. "Personal Account: A Woman Tried and Tested." *The Lancet Medicine and Sport* 366 (December 2005) 538.
Masterson, Mark, et al., eds. *Sex in Antiquity: Exploring Gender and Sexuality in the Ancient World.* Abingdon, UK: Routledge/Taylor & Francis, 2015.

Mayer, L. S., and P. R. McHugh. "Sexuality and Gender: Findings from the Biological, Psychological, and Social Sciences." *The New Atlantis* 50 (2016) 1–143.

McElwee, Joshua J. "Francis Explains 'Who Am I to Judge?'" *National Catholic Reporter* (January 2016). https://www.ncronline.org/news/vatican/francis-explains-who-am-i-judge.

McWhorter, J. *The Story of Human Language, Part I*. New York: The Teaching Company, 2004.

Melchior, Jillian Kay. "Peer Pressure and Transgender Teens." *The Wall Street Journal Online*, September 9, 2018. https://www.wsj.com/articles/peer-pressure-and-trandgender-teens-1536524718?mod=rsswn.

Metzger, Daniel. "The Endocrine Management of Transgender Youth." Paper presented at the Canadian Pediatric Endocrine Group 2012 Scientific Meeting, Winnipeg, MB, Canada. Feb. 9–11, 2012. (Also reported in *Endocrine Today*, "Pubertal Blockade Safe for Pediatric Patients with Gender Identity Disorder" [March] 2012. https://www.healio.com/endocrinology/pediatric-endocrinology/news/print/endocrine-today/%7B69c4c36a-37c3-4053-a856-22a27f8df62c%7D/pubertal-blockade-safe-for-pediatric-patients-with-gender-identity-disorder.)

Meyenburg, B. "Gender Dysphoria in Adolescents: Difficulties in Treatment." *Praxis in Kinderpsychologie und Kinderpsychiatrie* 63 (2014) 510–22.

Meyer-Bahlburg, et al. "Prenatal Androgenization Affects Gender-Related Behavior but Not Gender Identity in 5–12 Year Old Girls with Congenital Adrenal Hyperplasia." *Archives of Sexual Behavior* 33 (2004) 97–104.

Mieszczak, Jakub, et al., "Assignment of the Sex of Rearing in the Neonate with a Disorder of Sex Development." *Current Opinions in Pediatrics* 21.4 (2009) 541–47. https://www.ncbi.nlm.nih.gov/articles/PMC4104182/.

Mill, John Stuart. *The Subjection of Women*. 1st ed. London: Longmans, Green, Reader, & Dyer, 1869.

Mission of Israel to the United Nations in Geneva. "Jewish Sacred Texts." 2019. https://embassies.gov.il/UnGeneva/AboutIsrael/People/Pages/Jewish-Sacred-Texts.aspx.

Mollenkott, Virginia Ramey. "The Androgyny of Jesus." *Daughters of Sarah* 2 (March) 1976. http://www.virginiamollenkott.com/androgynyJesus.html.

Money, John, and Anke Ehrhardt. "Gender Dimorphic Behavior and Fetal Sex Hormones." In *Recent Progress in Hormone Research* 28, edited by E. B. Astwood, 367–91. New York: Academic, 1972.

———. *Man and Woman, Boy and Girl: Gender Identity from Conception to Maturity*. Rev. ed. New York: Aronson, 1996.

Money, John, and Patricia Tucker. *Sexual Signatures on Being a Man or a Woman*. Boston: Little Brown, 1975.

Money, John. *Gay, Straight, and In Between: The Sexology of Sexual Orientation*. New York: Oxford University Press, 1988.

———. "Gender: History, Theory and Usage of the Term in Sexology and its Relationship to Nature/Nurture." *Journal of Sex & Marital Therapy* 11 (1985) 71–79.

———. *Gendermaps: Social Constructionism, Feminism and Sexosophical History*. London: Bloomsbury Academic, 2016.

My Jewish Learning. "Ancient Israelitic Society and Lifestyle." *My Jewish Learning Journal Online* (2017). https://www.myjewishlearning.com/article/ancient_Israel/.

National Geographic Magazine. "Redefining Gender." *National Geographic Magazine Special Issue on the Shifting Landscape of Gender: Gender Revolution* 231 (January 2017).

Neto, R. R., et al. (2012). "Gender Reassignment Surgery—A 13 Year Review of Surgical Outcomes." *International Brazilian Journal of Urology* 38 (2012) 97–107.

North, Anna. "I Am a Woman and I Am Fast: What Caster Semenya's Story Says about Gender and Race in Sports." *Vox*, May 3, 2019. https://www.vox.com/identities/2019/5/3/18526723/caster-semenya-800-gender-race-intersex-athletes.

Oremus, Will. "Here Are All the Different Genders You Can Be on Facebook." *Slate*, February 14, 2014. http://www.slate.com/blogs/future_tense/2014/02/13/facebook_custom_ gender_ options_here_are_all_56_custom_options.html.

Pagonis, Pidgeon. Caster Semenya: Interview by Anna North in "I Am a Woman and I Am Fast" *Vox*, May 3, 2019. https://www.vox.com/identities/2019/5/3/18526723/caster-semenya-800-gender-race-intersex-athletes.

Parekh, Ranna. "What Is Gender Dysphoria?" *American Psychiatric Association Patients and Families*. 2016. https://www.psychiatry.org/patients-families/gender-dysphoria/what-is-gender-dysphoria.

Parkhurst, J. *The Politics of Evidence: From Evidence-Based Policy to the Good Governance of Evidence*. Abingdon, UK: Routledge, 2017.

Parler, Branson. "How Should Christians Navigate the Gender Revolution?" *ThinkChristian* (February 2017). https://thinkchristian.reframemedia.com/how-should-christians-navigate-the-gender-revolution.

Patel, Ilan. "Masculinities and Third Gender: Gendered Otherness in the Ancient Near East." *Ancient Near East Today* 5.2 (2017) 1–9. https://www.asor.org/anetoday/2017/02/masculinities-third-gender-gendered-otherness-ancient-near-east/.

Perry, Philip. "Does the Story of Adam and Eve Work Scientifically?" *BigThink* (January 2018). https://bigthink.com/philip-perry/does-the-story-of-adam-eve-work-scientifically.

Piacenza, Joanna, and Robert P. Jones. "Americans on Discrimination against and Social Contact with Transgender People." PRRI (Public Research and Regulation Initiative) 2017. https://www.prri.org/spotlight/transgender-military-ban-discrimination-social-contact/.

Poole, Matthew. *Commentary on the Holy Bible, Vols. 1–3*. Peabody, MA: Hendrickson, 1985.

Pope John Paul II. "Letter to Director of the Vatican Observatory." *Papal Addresses*, January 6, 1988, 300.

Pressin-Wheedbee, Brooke, and Naomi Bardoff. *Who Are You? The Kid's Guide to Gender Identity*. Philadelphia: Jessica Kingsley, 2016.

The Pulpit Commentary. Electronic Database, BibleSoft, 2010. https://www.biblehub.org.

Pyle, Nate. *Man Enough: How Jesus Redefines Manhood*. Grand Rapids: Zondervan, 2015.

Rachna, C. "Difference between Turner and Klinefelter Syndromes." *BioDifferences* (February 2018). https://biodifferences.com/?s=difference+between+Turner+and+Klinefelter+Syndrome+.

Rafferty, Jason. Committee on Psychosocial Aspects of Child and Family Health, AAP Committee on Adolescence. AAP Section on LGBT Health and Wellness. "Ensuring Comprehensive Care and Support for Transgender and Gender-Diverse Children and Adolescents." *Pediatrics* 142 (2018) 1–14. DOI: 10.1542/peds.e2018-2162.

Reilly-Cooper, Rebecca. "Gender Is Not a Spectrum." *Aeon*, January 28, 2016. https://aeon.co/essays/the-idea-that-gender-is-a-spectrum-is-a-new-gender-prison.

Richards, C., et al., "Non-binary or Genderqueer Genders." *International Review of Psychiatry* 28 (2016) 95–102.

Ringrose, K. M. *The Perfect Servant: Eunuchs and the Social Construction of Gender in Byzantium*. Chicago: University of Chicago Press, 2004.

Ritchie, Francis. "What If Jesus Had Been a Woman?" March 2013. https://www.francis-ritchie.com/what-if-jesus-had-been-a-woman?/

Robbins, Gary. "'Latino' Is Out, 'Latinx' Is In at UCSD." *Los Angeles Times*, December 3, 2018. https://www.latimes.com/local/lanow/la-me-latino-latinx-ucsd-20181202-story.html.

Roberts, Vaughan. *Transgender*. London: Good Book Company, 2016. http://thegoodbook.co.uk.talking-points-transgender/

Rosenberg, Noah A., et al. "Genetic Structure of Human Populations." *Science* 298 (2002) 2381–85.

Rosenberg, Stanley, and Michael Lloyd. *Finding Ourselves After Darwin*. Ada, MI: Baker Academic, 2018.

Rosenblum, Leonard A. "The Study of Masculinity/Femininity from a Comparative Developmental Perspective." In *Masculinity/Femininity: Basic Perspectives*, edited by June Maschover Reinisch et al., 150–56. New York: Oxford University Press, 1987.

Rousseau, Jean-Jaques. *The Social Contract. Principles of Political Right (1762)*. Translation in English by J. H. Tozier. London: Swan Sonnenschein, 1895.

Rude, May. "It's Time for People to Stop Using the Social Construction of 'Biological Sex' to Defend Their Transmysogyny." *Autostraddle*, June 6, 2014. https://autostraddle.com/its-time-stop-using-social-construct-biological-sex-to-defend-transmissogyny.

RxList. "Histrelin Acetate, *Supprelin LA*®," RxList.com. https://www.rxlist.com/supprelin-la-drug.htm.

Sabia-Tanis, J. *Trans-Gender: Theology, Ministry, and Communities of Faith*. Eugene, OR: Wipf and Stock, 2018.

Sakurai, Shige. "Ze-Hir." *MyPronouns.org. Resources on Personal Pronouns*, 2017. http://www.mypronouns.org/ze-hir.

Salazar, Lisa. *Transparently: Behind the Scenes of a Good Life*. Vancouver: Salazar, 2011.

Savin-Williams, R. C. "A Guide to Genderqueer, Non-Binary, and Gender Fluid Identities." *Psychology Today*, July 29, 2018. www.psychologytoday.com/us/blog/guide-to-genderqueer-nonbinary-genderfluid-identities.

ScienceDaily. "Estrogen: Not Just Produced by Ovaries." *ScienceDaily*, December 4, 2013. www.sciencedaily.com/releases/2013/12/131204181423.htm

Semenya, Caster. Interview by Jeré Jongman, in "Understanding the Controversy over Caster Semenya." *The New York Times*, August 16, 2016. https://www.nytimes.com/2016/08/20/sports/cster-semenya-800-meters.html.

Sharzer, Leonard. "Transgender Jews and Halakhah." Committee on Jewish Law and Standards of the Rabbinical Assembly. New York: The Rabbinical Assembly, 2017. https://www.rabbinicalassembly.org/sites/default/public/halakhah/teshuvot/2011-2020/transgender-halakhah.pdf.

Shoshana, Avraham. *Tosefta Megillah with Commentary on Toledot Yizhak*. Jerusalem: Koren, 2016.

Simon, Carolyn. "'Gender-fluid' Added to Oxford English Dictionary." *Human Rights Campaign* (September) 2016. https://www.hrc/blog/gender-fluid-added-to-oxford-english-dictionary.

Singal, Jesse. "Background Information on the Desistance Debate, and What Desistance-Deniers Often Get Wrong." *A Critique of the "Science Vs" Episode on Being Transgender, Part 2*. (Blog), March 29, 2019. https://jessesingal.substack.com/p/how-science-vs-accidentally-invented-a-gender-dysphoria-desistance-statistic.htm.

———. "What's Missing from the Conversation about Transgender Kids." *New York Magazine The Cut*, July 2016. https://www.thecut.com/2016/07/whats-missing-from-the-conversation-about-transgender-kids.html.

———. "When Children Say They're Trans." *The Atlantic*, July/August 2018. https://theatlantic.com/magazine/archive/2018/07/when-a-child-says-shes-trans/561749/.

Solomon, R. *The Impact of Labeling in Childhood on the Sense of Self of Young Adults*. MA thesis, Brock University, 2015. St Catherine's ON CAN: 2015. TC-STBCB.6252.pdf

Spack, N. P., et al. "Children and Adolescents with Gender Identity Disorder Referred to a Pediatric Medical Center." *Pediatrics* 5 (2012) 418–25.

Spansel, Mark. "How to Talk to Your Kids about Gender." *The Gospel Coalition*, April 2016. https://www.thegospelcoalition.org/profile/makr-spansel-2/.

Spence, H. D. M, and J. S. Exell, eds. *The Pulpit Commentary*. Peabody, MA: Hendrickson, 1985.

Steensma, T. D., et al. "Factors Associated with Desistence and Persistence of Childhood Gender Dysphoria: A Quantitative Follow-Up Study." *Journal of the American Academy of Child and Adolescent Psychiatry* 52 (2013) 582–90.

———. "How Should Physicians Help Gender-Transitioning Adolescents Consider Potential Itatrogenic Harms of Hormone Therapy?" *American Medical Association Journal of Ethics* 19 (2017) 762–70. https://journalofethics.ama-assn.org/article/how-should-physicians-help-gender-transitioning-adolescents-consider-potential-iatrogenic-harms/2017-08.

Stephens, Philip. Interview by Phillip Perry, "Does the Story of Adam and Eve Work Scientifically?" *BigThink*, January 2018, 3. https://bigthink.com/philip-perry/does-the-story-of-adam-eve-work-scientifically.

Stetzer, Ed. *Christians in the Age of Outrage: How to Bring Our Best When the World Is at Its Worst*. Carol Stream, IL: Tyndale Momentum, 2018.

Stevens, G. B., et al. *Homilies of St. John Chrysostom on the Epistle of St. Paul to the Romans*. Scotts Valley CA: CreateSpace, 2012.

Stiegler, Sam. "A Gender-Bending Look into GenEdge." *The Sound*, August 2018, 1–4. https://www.thesoundhq.com/2018/08/a-gender-bending-look-into-gen-edge/

Stoller, Robert. *Presentations of Gender*. New Haven: Yale University Press, 1985.

———. *Sex and Gender*. Abingdon, UK: Routledge, 1994.

———. *Sexual Excitement. Dynamics of Erotic Life*. Abingdon, UK: Routledge, 1986.
Swaab, D. F. "Sexual Differentiation of the Brain and Behavior." *Best Practice & Research in Clinical Endocrinology & Metabolism* 21 (September 2007) 431–44.
Tamar-Mattis. Interview by Susan Donaldson James in "Intersex Babies: Boy or Girl and Who Decides?" *ABC News*, March 16, 2011. www.abcnews.go.com/Health/intersex-children-pose-ethical-dilemma-doctors-parents-genital/story/id=13153068.
Taylor, L. M., et.al. "Labelling and Self-Esteem: The Impact of Using Specific vs. Generic Labels." *Educational Psychology* 30 (2010) 191–202.
Thompson, M. D. "A Theology of Gender and Gender Identity: A Report from the Sydney Diocesan Doctrine Commission." 2017. https://www.sds.asn.au/sites/default/files/ATheologyOfGenderAndGenderIdentity%28SydDoctrineCommission%29.Aug2017.pdf?doc_id=NTQ3NjM=
Thompson, S. K. "Gender Labels and Early Sex Role Development." *Child Development* 46 (1975) 339–47.
Throckmorton, W., and Mark A. Yarhouse. "Sexual Identity Therapy: Practice Framework for Managing Sexual Identity Conflicts." 2009. http://www.ewthrockmorton@gcc.edu. Also at https://sitframework.com/wp-content/uploads/2009/07/sexualidentitytherapyframeworkfinal.pdf.
Tomkins, Sylvan. *Exploring Affect: Selected Writings of Sylvan S. Tomkins*. Edited by Virginia Demos. Cambridge: Cambridge University Press, 1995.
Tornielli, Andrea. "To the Reader." Foreword in *The Name of God Is Mercy*, authored by Pope Francis, edited by Andrea Tornielli, and translated from the Italian by Oonagh Stransky. New York: Random House International Editions, 2016.
Tracy, Larissa, ed. *Castration and Culture in the Middle Ages*. Rochester, NY: Boydell & Brewer, 2013.
Trible, Phyllis. *God and the Rhetoric of Sexuality*. Philadelphia: Fortress, 1978.
Trotta, Daniel. "Born This Way? Researchers Explore the Science of Gender Identity." *Reuters Science News* (August) 2017. (Article quotes Dr. Paul McHugh.) https://www.reuters.com/article/us-usa-lgbt-biology/born-this-way-researchers-explore-the-science-of-gender-identity-idUSKBN1AJ0F0.
Ulmer, Rivka. "Rabbinic Judaism." *Oxford Bibliographies* (September 2016). https://www.oxfordbibliographies.com/view/document/obo-9780195393361/obo-9780195393361-0103.xml.
Unger, C. "Hormone Therapy for Transgender Patients." *Translational Andrology and Urology* 5 (2016) 877–84.
United Nations General Assembly (Human Rights Council). "Report of the Special Rapporteur on Torture and Other Cruel, Inhuman or Degrading Treatment or Punishment, Juan E. Mendez." (February 2013) A/HRC/22/53. https://www.ohchr.org/Documents/HRBodies/HRCouncil/RegularSession/Session22/A.HRC.22.53_English.pdf
University of Reading. "Gender in the Ancient World." University of Reading, Ure Museum of Greek Archaeology. Reading, Berkshire UK. https://www.reading.ac.uk/Ure/tour/citizenship/gender.php.
Urquhart, E., "What the Heck is Genderqueer?" *Slate*, March 24, 2015. http://www.slate.com/ blogs/outward/2015/03/24/genderqueer_what_does_it_mean_and_where_does_it_come_from.

US National Library of Medicine. "Androgen Insensitivity Syndrome." US National Library of Medicine, Genetics Home Reference, 2019. https://ghr.nlm.nih.gov/condition/androgen-insensitivity-syndrome.

USA Today. "Hyperandrogenism Explained and What It Means for Athletics" August 2, 2016. https://usatoday.com/story/olympics/2016/08/02/hyperandrogenism-explained-and-what-it-means-for-athletics/87944966.

Vaesen, Krist, et al. "Inbreeding, Allee Effects and Stochasticity." *PLOS|ONE* 14.1 (2019) 1–15. https://doi.org/10.1371/journal.pone.0225117.

van de Grift, Tim C., et al. "Surgical Satisfaction, Quality of Life, and Their Association After Gender-Affirming Surgery: A Follow-Up Study." *Journal of Sex and Marital Therapy* 44 (2018) 138–48. DOI: 10.1080/0092623X.2017.1326190.

Viloria, Hida. *Born Both: An Intersex Life*. New York: Hachette, 2017.

Volf, Miroslav. *Exclusion and Embrace: A Theological Explanation of Identity, Otherness, and Reconciliation*. Nashville: Abingdon, 1996.

Vrouenraets, Lieke J. J. J., et al., "Early Medical Treatment of Children and Adolescents with Gender Dysphoria: An Empirical Ethical Study." *Journal of Adolescent Health* 57 (April 2015) 367–72.

Walker, Andrew T. *God and the Transgender Debate*. London: Good Book Company, 2017.

Warfield, B.B. *The Inspiration and Authority of the Bible*. Philadelphia: Presbyterian & Reformed, 1948.

Warren, Rick. "What Does God Say about Your Body?" December 20, 2016. www.faithgateway.com.

Weisner-Hanks, M. *Gender in History: Global Perspectives Second Ed*. Hoboken NJ: Wiley-Blackwell, 2010.

Whitlow, B. J., et al. "First Trimester Diagnosis of Gender." *Ultrasound in Obstetrics and Gynecology* 13 (1999) 301–4.

Williams, Shawna. "Are the Brains of Transgender People Different from Those of Cisgender People? *The Scientist*, March 7, 2018. https://www.the-scientist.com/features/are-the-brains-of-transgender-people-different-from-those-of-cisgender-people-30027.

Wittgenstein, Ludwig. *Tractus Logico Philosophicus*. New York: Harcourt, Brace & Co., 1922.

World Professional Association of Transgender Health. *Standards of Care for the Health of Transsexual, Transgender, and Gender Nonconforming People*. 7th ed (2012). https://www.wpath.org/media/cms/Documents/SOC%20v7/SOC%20V7_English.pdf

Xavier, Neena A., and Janet B. Miller. "Hyperandrogenism and Intersex Controversies in Women's Olympics." *Journal of Clinical Endocrinological Metabolism* 97.11 (2012) 3902–7.

Yarhouse, Mark A. *Understanding Gender Dysphoria. Navigating Transgender Issues in a Changing Culture*. Downers Grove, IL: InterVarsity Academic, 2015.

Yarhouse, Mark, and Erica S. N. Tan. *Sexual Identity Synthesis: Attributions, Meaning-Making, and the Search for Congruence*. Lanham, MD: University Press of America, 2004.

Yong, Ed. "How Inbreeding Killed a Line of Kings." *National Geographic Science and Innovation*, April 2009. https://www.nationalgeographic.com/science/phenomena/2009/04/14/how-inbreeding-killed-off-a-line-of-kings/.

Zhou, J. N., et al. "A Sex Difference in the Human Brain and Its Relation to Transsexuality." *Nature* 378 (1995) 68–70.

Zucker, Kenneth J. "Children with Gender Identity Disorder: Is There a Best Practice?" *Neuropsychiatrie de l'Enfance et de l'Adolescence* 56 (2008) 327–408.

———. "Epidemiology of Gender Dysphoria and Transgender Identity." *Sexual Health* (August 2017) A-H. https://doi.org/10.1071/SHI17067.

———. "The DSM-5 Diagnostic Criteria for Gender Dysphoria." In *Management of Gender Dysphoria: A Multidisciplinary Approach*, edited by C. Trombetta et al., 33–37. Milan: Springer-Verlag Italia, 2015.

Zucker, Kenneth J., et al., "A Developmental, Biopsychosocial Model for the Treatment of Children with Gender Identity Disorder." *Journal of Homosexuality* 59 (2012) 369–97. https://doi.org/10.1080/00918369.2012.653309.

Index

A

AASECT, *See* American Association of Sexuality Educators, Counselors, and Therapists
accommodations, for gender differences, 7, 17, 35–36. 162, 193, 200, 208
accompagnateur, definition, 89, 177, 180
activism, gender-identity and, 198, 209
Adam, 69, 71, 139–42, 144, 147, 151, 162–63, 226, 228, 235, 237
adolescents, 3, 5, 25, 103–8, 110–11, 113–18, 120–21, 123–24, 126–29, 132, 201, 217–18, 228, 233–34, 236–37
adolescent trangender, 119, 227
adrenal glands, 73–74
Adrenal Hyperplasia, 226
age, and gender conflicts, 34–35, 45, 94, 97, 100, 113, 116, 119–20, 123–27, 129–30, 132, 202, 205
agender, 2, 15, 23–24, 98, 227
AGSN, *See* Ambiguous Genitalia Support Network
AIS, *See* Androgen Insensitivity Syndrome
Allison, Gregg T., 149–50, 152, 225
Ambiguous Genitalia Support Network (AGSN), 91
American Association of Sexuality Educators, Counselors, and Therapists (AASECT), 221

American Psycological Association, 15, 24–26, 43, 46, 116, 161, 225, 235
AMH, *See* Anti-Müllerian-Hormone
anatomy
  adult, 153
  child, 111
  reproductive, 9
  sexual, 76, 82, 101, 103, 111, 139, 153
Anderson, Ryan T., 17–18, 106, 110, 127, 196–97, 217, 225
Androgen Insensitivity Syndrome (AIS), 71, 98–99, 239
  complete (cAIS), 73
  partial (pAIS), 73, 99
androgens, 69, 73–75, 99
  adrenal, 73–74
andrôgînôs (Judaism), 78, 227
androgynous, 3, 24, 67, 71, 170, 227
androgyny, 152, 170, 172
Anti-Müllerian-Hormone (AMH), 69–70
Arnold, Arthur F., 67, 225
AOG, *See* Assemblies of God (denomination)
Assemblies of God (AOG), 153, 171, 173, 191, 209, 212–13, 225
  position on transgenderism, 173, 214.
athletes, 81–82, 235
athletic amenorrhea, 80
atrophy, genital/reproductive, 36, 67, 70, 122, 135–36
Augustine, St., 139, 225

ay'lonit (Judaism), masculine woman, 78

B

Bader, Lee, 79, 225
baldness, male pattern and FTM, 121
Baratz, Arlene, 100
Barlow, Dade, 226
Barrett, James, 118
Barth, Karl, 139, 226
Baudrillard, Jean, 184, 226
Beach, Shelly, 159
Beauchamp, Scott, 50, 226
Beemyn, Genny, 186, 226
behaviors
  body-rejecting, 45
  gender-concordant, 97
Ben-Noun, L., 142. 226
Benson, Joseph, 226
berdache (Native American), 17, 39
Berenbaum, Sheri A., 74–75, 226
Bergolio, Jorge María, *See* Pope Francis
Bertelloni, S., 120, 226
Bible, 1, 67–68, 84, 145, 151–53, 157–58, 163, 167, 228, 231, 239
  biblical foundation narratives, 67–68, 138, 223
bigender, 2, 24, 26
bilateral mastectomies, FTM, 125
binary sex model, binarism, 9, 22–27, 57, 83, 98, 146–47, 164, 202, 217–18
biological sex, 2–3, 18, 10–11, 15–17, 20, 29, 35, 44, 46, 149, 186, 197–98, 202–3, 206–7, 209, 214
biology, 6, 9, 18, 20, 66, 70–71, 75, 115, 118, 141, 145–46, 222, 225
  influence on gender, 75
birth, sex of, 77, 197–98, 208
bisexuality, 28, 60
Blackless, Melanie, 9, 71, 148, 226
Blackmore, S.J., 121, 226
blood clots, and hormonal therapy, 130
blood sugar, and hormonal therapy, 74

body, 36–37, 40–41, 43–44, 46–47, 51–56, 73, 76–77, 84, 95–103, 109–10, 117–20, 122–23, 136, 148–50, 153–56, 158–60, 162–68, 173, 181, 209–10
  anatomical, 103, 139
  developing, 77, 117
  female 13, 43
  gendered, 11, 101, 149, 173
  intersex, 70 (See also intersex)
  male, 34, 87, 99, 170–71
  physical, 79, 153, 158
  unformed, in utero, 66, 143
body/gender concordance, 101
body/gender incongruity, 117
body modifications, 124, 131, 138, 158
body politics, 95, 198
"body sex," 46, 70
body type, 11, 149
bone accretion, impaired by pausing puberty, 121, 124, 126, 135
boys, 12, 35, 39–40, 53, 57, 59, 72–73, 75, 99–100, 106, 119–21, 149, 229, 231–32, 234
Boylan, Jennifer Finley, 60, 226
brain, 44, 74, 99, 121, 155–56, 164, 231, 238–39
BRCA genes, 159
breast cancer, 134
breasts, 70, 72, 81, 121, 125, 131, 159–60
Brooks, John, 110, 226
Brown, Peter, 227
Bunge, Marcia, 145, 227
Butler, Judith, 195, 227 229

C

CAH *See* Congenital Adrenal Hyperplasia
  CAH girls, 102
cAIS *See* Complete Androgen Insensitivity Syndrome
Callahan, Gerald, 148
Camery-Hoggatt, Jerry, *Foreword*, 151, 162–63, 167, 227
Campbell, Douglas A., 227
cancers, 116, 130, 159

Index

cardiovascular diseases, 135
Carlson, Alison, 81
Carter, Joe, 227
castration, 157–58, 161, 227, 238
  male testicular, 130
  surgical, 124
CCCU, *See* Coalition of Christian Colleges and Universities
celibacy, 61–62, 157, 166
Chase/Cassandra's story, 35–36, 47–52
childhood gender dysphoria, 26
childhood gender nonconformity, 44
children and adolescents, 103, 106–8, 117, 124, 126–28, 132, 218, 225, 237, 239
Chrysostom, St. John, 154, 227, 237
Christ, 38, 54–55, 61–63, 138–39, 152, 164–66, 168–69, 188, 191, 199, 203, 205, 212, 226, 228
Christian civility and politeness, 184
Christian compassion and grace, 64
Christian critique of science, (*See also* science, Christian scientists), 146
Christian parents, 5, 56, 95, 106
Christian responses, stereotypical, 186
Christian theology, 140, 147, 149, 162, 164, 178, 228
Christian therapists (*See also* therapies, Christian therapy), 46, 107–8, 220–21
Christianity and Christian culture, 45, 85, 90, 108, 137–73, 204, 211, 226–28
chromosomes, 9, 19, 30–31, 39, 56–58. 66–76, 80–81, 87, 95–97, 102–3, 147
  normative parental contributions, 87
  parental contributions in syndromes, 87
Chu, Andrea Long, *See* Long Chu, Andrea
Church and transgender activism, 194–215
church civility, 192
church leadership (*See* clergy), 6, 174–93, 219–20
church ministries (*See* clergy), 220
church projects on gender, 220
cisgender, 2, 24, 32, 130, 208
  ideology, 22, 48, 77
clergy, xxii, 6, 93, 158, 174, 177–80, 184, 186–87, 189–91, 220
clitoris, 35, 39, 69, 102–3, 125
clothes,
  gender-affirming, 49
  gender neutral, 35, 45
Coalition of Christian Colleges and Universities (CCCU), 146
Cohen, A. 78, 227
Cohen-Kettenis, P.T., 119, 127, 227–28, 232
Collins, Francis S., 158, 222–23, 227
Colson, Charles (Chuck), 145, 228
complementarity, biological, 206
Complete Androgen Insensitivity Syndrome (cAIS), 73–74, 99
concealment model of gender rearing, 56–57
concordances, body, 77, 114, 139, 163, 199, 207
confirmation surgery/ies (*See* reassignment surgeries), 35, 111, 123–24, 129
Congenital Adrenal Hyperplasia (CAH), 73–75, 91, 102–3, 234
Conservative Judaism,
  positions on gender variances, 68, 160–62, 169, 209
Corinthians, quotes from epistles to, 153, 158, 211, 227
Cornwall, Susannah, 155, 168, 228
counseling, xxii, 33, 42, 89, 216, 221–22. (*See also* therapy, psychotherapies)
Cowdell, Scott, 140, 144, 228
Cox, J.A., 228
creation, 68, 71, 138, 141, 144–46, 148, 150, 152, 157, 163, 223, 227, 229
  human, 3, 13, 56, 68, 144, 172
Cretella, Michelle A., 121, 128, 228
cultural models of gender, 14, 173
cultural polarization on gender, 77

Index

culture, 11–14, 17, 50–51, 76–77, 79, 84, 92, 149, 152, 154, 157–58, 162–63, 171–72, 200–201
culture-bound syndrome, 27, 51, 200–201, 219, 230

D

David (psalmist), quotes from, 41–42, 58–59, 62, 65–66
David/Michelle's case, 41–42, 60–62, 228
Davidson, Gregg, 142, 22
Davis, Georgiann, 57, 96, 228
DBT, *See* therapies, dialectical behavior
Deaux, Kay, 228
DeFranza, Megan K., 140, 147, 162, 164, 178, 228
Denison, Jim, 228
DeVries, Annelou, 127, 228
demineralization, consequence of halting puberty, 134–35
denominational responses, gender issues, 137–38, 189–90, 212–13
desist/desisting from GD (*See also* Jesse Singal), 25, 46–47, 105, 107, 110, 113, 116, 118, 120, 123, 127, 133, 218, 226, 237–38
detransitioning, 25
diagnosis, 25, 27, 33, 43–44, 90, 103, 107, 110, 209
 and conditions, 64, 138, 219
Diagnostic and Statistical Manual of the American Psychological Association (DSM-5), 24–25, 31, 33, 43–44, 107, 113, 116, 161, 225
 criteria for gender dysphoria, 240
dialectical behavior therapies (DBT), 109
Diamond, Milton, 89, 228
disconnect, body-brain, 155–56, 160, 199
 as disjunctions, gender role-body, 109
 as disjunctions, identity-body, 25
disorders, 15, 25, 30–31, 82, 104, 113, 191, 225, 228, 230–32, 234

gender-identity, 117, 194
Disorders of Sexual Development (DSD), 15, 30, 82. *See also*, Klinefelter Syndrome, Androgen Insensitivity Syndrome, Turner Syndrome, Jacob Syndrome, Congenital Adrenal Hyperplasia, Triple X Syndrome
Docter, R.F., 31, 228
doctrine (Christian), in relation to gender, 6, 137, 151, 173, 177, 230
Donaldson James, Susan. 99, 209, 238
DNA (deoxyribonucleic acid), 80, 87, 139. 142, 222
Dreger, Alice, 56, 89, 229
Drescher, Jack, 61, 229
DSD, *See* Disorders of Sexual Development
DSM-5, *See* Diagnostic and Statistical Manual of the American Psychological Association (APA), Version 5
"Dutch Protocol," 127, 129
Dyer, W. Justin, 209, 229
dysphoria, gender 42–45, 51, 54–55, 59, 61–63, 102–5, 107–8, 115, 110, 123–24, 154, 156, 159, 161, 167, 194, 206
 dysphoria manifestations, 25, 55, 103, 111
dysphoric child, 44, 59, 119, 123, 156
 early-onset, 58

E

Ehrhardt, Anke, 75, 229, 234
endocrinologists, 10, 91, 118, 206, 232–33
Engelbart, Doug, 19
Eichler, Raanan, 163, 229
Erickson, Ives, 176, 229
estrogen, 69, 80, 99, 116, 118–19, 121, 123, 130, 134–35, 236
estrogen therapy in MTF patients, 117, 121, 134–36, 230
ethics, 101, 113–14, 128, 132, 229
 ethical issues in treatment, 113–14, 132, 229

Index

Eve, 71, 139–42, 144, 147, 162, 173, 203
exploration therapies, 109 (See also counseling, therapy, psychotherapy)
eunuchs, 78, 156–57, 160, 236
Evans, Rachel Held, 229
evidence-based medicine, and hormone treatments, 126, 128, 132, 209–10, 222, 230–31, 235
exegesis, biblical, in relation to gender, 151, 162–63, 223, 227

F

Facebook, as a gender identity platform, 2, 183, 198, 235
Farmer, Paul, 177
fat, body, and hormone therapy, 134
Fausto-Sterling, Anne, 9–10, 18, 20, 31, 44–45, 62–64, 74, 95–96, 121, 149, 20
Feinberg, Leslie, 159, 229
Feldman, Marcus, 147, 229
female body development, 101, 116
female characteristics, 24, 73, 121
female form, 17–18, 41, 52, 76, 79–80, 83, 99, 157, 206
female genetics, 171
female homosexuality, 30
female organs, 30, 40, 66–67
 reproductive, 13, 74, 77, 86 125
female to male (FTM) transgender, 60, 125, 131, 135–36, 226
females, 13–14, 30, 32, 50–51, 66, 69–72, 74, 84, 87, 99, 121, 149, 151–52, 170–72, 231–32
 and sexual bodies, 71
 and transgendered, 164, 210, 232
feminine roles, 2, 12, 31, 149, 154
femininity, 9, 12–13, 25–26, 36, 50–54, 58, 65, 72–73, 77–78, 81, 152, 155, 172–73
Ferris, Jaquelle (Crow), 201–2, 229
Fischer, M., 195, 201, 229
Flather, Curtis H., 142, 229
follicle stimulating hormone (FSH), 115–16, 118
foreskin, male, 69

Foucault, Michel, 196
Framework for Managing Sexual Identity Conflicts, 238
Francis, Pope, 169, 230, 236 See Pope Francis, José María Bergolio
friends, influences on gender, xx, xxii, 33, 35–37, 39, 41, 89, 93
FSH, See follicle stimulating hormone
FTM See Female to Male transgender individuals

G

Gardner, M., 95, 230
gay, xx–xxi, 18, 26–27, 29, 51, 60, 121–22, 234
GD, See Gender Dysphoria
Gender, xix–xxii, 1–20, 22–23, 25–29, 51, 60, 75, 121–22
 activism, 2, 138, 174, 195–96, 202, 206, 208, 212
 ambiguity, 71, 201, 232
 and identity, 1, 7, 17, 140, 144, 194, 228
 as performative, 195
 as a spectrum, 7, 16, 33, 48, 68, 143, 145, 198, 200, 208, 217
 assigned, 25, 57, 56, 100–101
 bending-gender, 15, 28, 33, 29, 155, 237
 binary, 48, 78, 210
 categories of, 15, 48, 98, 195, 197, 223
 confirmation of, 29
 confusion of, 3, 27, 200
 essentialism, 17, 194
 expression of, 2, 11, 18, 23, 58, 101, 197, 213
 incongruence with, 45, 58, 144, 209, 213
 labels, 7, 13, 15, 19, 23–24, 28, 198, 238
 language of, 2, 8–31
 neutral parenting, 100, 233
 nonconformity, xx, 44, 48, 51, 54, 114, 193
 politics, 195, 201, 206–7, 229
 pronouns, 2, 19, 27, 29, 34, 162, 165, 236

Gender *(continued)*
  rearing in a, 73, 93, 97–98, 100–102, 198
  reassignment *(see also confirmation)*, 22, 32, 59, 120, 129–31, 173, 190, 228, 230, 235
  rebellion, 200, 206.
  roles, 12, 14, 16, 22, 43, 46, 49, 119, 138, 192, 207
  role socialization, 11, 13
  self-identification, 77, 208–9
  schemas, binary, 162; nonbinary, 22
gender conflicts, 105–7, 110–11, 113, 174–75, 177, 180, 184, 188, 192–93, 198–200, 209
gender dysphoria (GD), xx–xxi, 15–16, 25–27, 32, 43–44, 62–63, 103, 106–8, 110, 114–16, 122, 127–29, 155–56, 189–91, 198–99, 209, 217–20, 225, 231–33, 239–40
genderfluid, 1–3, 15, 24, 26, 36, 48, 50–52, 98, 100, 201, 208, 210, 236–37
gender identity, 2, 4–5, 9–11, 16–18, 22, 24–32, 43–44, 48, 75–78, 102–3, 148–49, 153–56, 160–61, 192–93, 196–98, 208–10, 212–13, 230–32, 234–35, 238
  defined, 10
  conflicts with, 45, 52, 63, 108, 116, 118, 160, 169, 192–93, 197
  issues with, 2, 4, 6, 88–89, 174, 186, 189, 193, 216, 221
gender ideology, 15, 37, 217, 220
  in the ancient world, 238
genderqueer, 2–3, 22, 24, 26–28, 32, 36, 50–52, 100, 197, 236, 238
generalizations about gender, 5, 13, 103, 175–77
genes and genetics, 62, 66–70, 73, 83–84, 138, 141–42, 148, 164, 171, 178, 223, 228, 230, 233
  human, 66, 71,75, 90, 139–42, 152, 171
Genesis, references to, 47, 67–69, 83–85, 139–41, 143, 145, 147–48, 225, 227, 230

genitalia, 8–9, 19, 40, 57–58, 72–73, 93, 96, 100, 102
  ambiguous, 24, 39, 57, 72, 74, 94, 98, 156, 228
  external, 9, 70, 72
  intact, 97
  malformed, 58, 95, 102, 199
genital masculinization, 102
genital surgeries, 29, 95–96, 169, 232
  on girls with masculinized genitals, 12, 102
Gil, Vincent E., 51, 230
Gladd, Benjamin L., 227
GnRH, *See* Gonadotropin-Releasing Hormone (GnRH)
Gonadotropin Releasing Hormone (GnRH), 118–19, 226
GnRHas, *See* Gonadotropin-Releasing Hormone Agonist *analogs*
Goldberg, Steven, 152, 230
Gonadotropin-Releasing Hormone Agonist (GnRHas) *analogues*, 136
Goodman, M., 130, 230
Gorvett, Zaria, 142, 230
Green, Richard A., 233
Grohol, John M., 178, 230
Guarnaccia, Peter J., 51, 230
Guillaume, M., 226
Gurtner, Daniel M., 227
Gutierrez, M., 96, 230

H

Hayes, Kelsey, 132, 230
Hayton, Debbie, 210
Helmer, Christine, 151, 230
Hembree, W.C., 117, 121, 123, 134–36, 230
Heneghan, Carl, 124, 126, 231
Henry, Matthew, 164, 231
Herbert, J., 164, 231
Herek, G. M., 13, 231
Hess, J., 131, 231
heterosexual, 2, 26, 28, 30–31, 62, 81
Hines, Melissa, 75, 231
histrelin acetate, *(See also* hormone blockers), 116, 236.
Hoffer, Eric, xiii, xv, 231

Index

homosexuality, 62, 117, 153–54, 193, 217, 228, 240
hormonal therapy, 40, 116, 131
hormone blockers, 105, 114–15, 117, 123–24, 230
hormones, 66–67, 70, 73–76, 80, 83–84, 93, 95–99, 100, 116, 118, 121–23, 125–26, 128, 130, 136
effects of, 74, 101, 115, 121, 124
female, 73–75, 116
male, 73–75, 116
pituitary, 116
treatment of children/adolescents with, 132, 225
treatment of gender dysphoria with, 127–28, 134–36, 238,
HRC, *See* Human Rights Campaign
Hruz, Paul, 117, 119–20, 122, 231
Human Rights Campaign (HRC), 48, 196, 198, 231, 238
Hyde, Chris, 130
hyperandrogenism, 82, 231
hysterectomy, 125

I

identity, xix, xxii, 1–2, 11–12, 16–18, 22, 26, 29, 43–44, 76, 84, 104–6, 115, 117, 137–39, 153–55, 164–66, 168, 177–78, 196–99
body transition and, 161
genderfluid, 98
no-gender, 58
self-realized, 202
trauma and transgender, 132, 233
identity conflicts
in early childhood, 105
gender as cause of, 59, 108, 117, 155, 222
idic-Y/Idic-Y (Isodicentric-Y), xxix, xxx, 71
infants, 30, 73, 93, 96, 100, 145
intersex, 4, 9, 23–24, 30, 57–58, 72–74, 78–79, 88–92, 98, 128, 147–47, 156–60, 177, 191, 182–86, 193–94, 197–98, 206, 217–18, 220–21, 228, 231–32

infants, 1, 3, 5, 39–40, 78, 91, 96, 98–100, 128, 143, 148, 182, 229, 238
diagnosis, 94–95, 100, 111, 143, 233
genitalia, 71–72, 88, 91, 96, 218
Intersex Justice Project, 82
Intersex Society of North America (ISNA), 30, 57–58, 63, 72–74, 91, 97–100, 231–32
position on gender-based rearing, 100
intersexuality, 15, 20, 23, 186–87, 198–99, 206; 227–29
ISNA, *See* Intersex Society of North America (ISNA)
Israel, 78, 143, 172, 234

J

Jacob Syndrome, xxx, 23, 87. *See also* Disorders of Sexual Development
James, S.E., 3, 15, 47, 232
Jefferson, Tom, 126, 231
Jellestad, J. 130, 233
Jewett, Paul K., 14, 130, 232
John, gospel of, 6, 96, 171, 181, 204–5, 215, 223, 226, 230, 232, 234
Johns, M. M., 74, 232
Jolie, Angelina, 159, 232
Jones, R.P., 187

K

Kallak, Theordora K., 74, 232
Karkazis, Katrina, 99, 232
Kay, Jonathan, 201, 228, 232, 234
Kessler, Suzanne, 89, 232
Kingsley, Jessica, 233, 235–36
Klein, C., 100, 131, 232
Klein, Dianne, 100, 131, 232
Klinefelter Syndrome (KS), 23, 71–72, 87, 235
Kreukels, B.P., 127, 232
KS, *See* Klinefelter Syndrome
Kuelfer, M., 158, 232
Kuhn, A., 130, 232
Kuper, L.E., 119, 232

L

Lacey/Luke's story, 34–35, 43–45, 47
Ladin, Joy, 140–41, 166–67, 172, 232
laws, parenting and gender education, 78, 160–61, 164, 186, 209
Lee, P.A., 100, 233
Lerner, Gerda, 152, 233
lesbianism, 30, 53–54, 60
Lévinas, Emmanuel, 184, 233
LGBTQI persons, 29, 213
LH, *See* Luteinzing Hormone
Linker, Damon, 194, 233
Lippa, Richard, 74, 233
Littman, Lisa, 27, 201, 233, *See also* Rapid Onset Gender Dysphoria
Lloyd, Michael, 146, 236
Lohmans, S. and E., 91, 233
Long Chu, Andrea, 206
Longman, Jeré, 79, 82–83, 233–34
Lorber, Judith, 10–11, 233
Louie, Sam, 132
Luders, E., 186, 233
Luhrmann, Tanya, 183
Luke, gospel of, 34–35, 45–47, 169, 171, 188
luteinizing hormone (LH), 115–16, 118
Lynette/Kyler's story, 37–38, 53–55
Lyons, Kate, 118, 233

M

Madueme, Hans, 159, 233
Mahfouda, B.A., 122, 223
male to female transgender (MTF) women, 131
Mann, Paul K., 232
Manning, Sanchez, 127, 233
Marchinao, Lisa, 105–6, 233
masculinity, 9, 12, 32, 37–38, 50–51, 77, 149, 152, 154–55, 170–73, 228, 232
marriage, 26, 37, 441–42, 54, 59, 157, 173
Masterson, Mark, 157, 233
Mayer, L.S., 43–44, 46–47, 119, 122, 234
McElwee, Joshua, 169, 234
McHugh, Paul, 43–44, 46–47, 75, 117, 119, 234, 238
McWhorter, J., 19, 234
medical interventions, 90, 111, 119, 129
medical records, 57, 90
Melchior, Jillian, 201, 234
Mendez, Juan E., 96, 238
Metzger, Daniel, 119, 234
Meyenburg, B., 104, 234
Meyer-Bahlburg, Heino, 75, 101–2, 229, 234
MGD, *See* Mixed Gonadal Dysgenesis
Mieszczak, Jakub
Miller, Janet B., 239
Mill, John Stuart, *Foreword*
ministry to gender variant, 62, 177, 181, 199–200, 204, 212, 220. *See also* chapters 8, 9, complete.
Mixed Gonadal Dysgenesis (MGD), 23, 71–72
Mollenkott, Virginia R., 152, 172, 234
Money, John, 10, 18, 24, 75, 121–22, 149, 234
MTF, *See* male to female transgender women
Mullins, Robert A., 143
muscle mass, loss of in MTF, 120, 134–35
mutations, genetic, 73–74

N

Nash, Rebecca, 130, 230
National Center for Transgender Equality, (NCTE), 232
National Organization for Rare Diseases (NORD), 91
navigating surgical decision-making, 95, 230
Neto, R.R., 130, 235
North, Anna, 82, 235

O

omnigender, 22
optimum gender of rearing system, 56
Oremus, Will, 2, 235
outcomes,

of treatment for GD, 57, 63–64, 66–67, 69, 71, 73, 76, 114, 120, 122, 126, 129–30, 136
long-term surgical and emotional for GD, 9, 76, 111, 129, 136, 139, 219, 226
"outing," xx, 2, 47, 182, 220
ovaries, 67, 70, 72, 80, 94–95, 99, 118, 121, 125, 236

P

Pagonis, Pidgeon, 82–83, 235
pAIS, See Partial Androgen Insensitivity Syndrome
pangender, 2, 22, 26
Parekh, Ranna, 54, 235
Parkhusr, J., 107, 235
Parler, Branson, 188, 235
parents, 5–8, 35, 39, 41, 43, 56–57, 73–74, 87–115, 126, 131–33, 142, 192, 201–2, 209–10, 217–18
  help for, 130
  single parenting, 89
Parents and Friends of Lesbians and Gays (PFLAG), 98
Partial Androgen Insensitivity Syndrome (pAIS), 73, 99
Patiño, María, 79, 81–83, 233
pastoral care, 46, 89, 93, 188–89, 191, 213, 221 (See also clergy)
  roles and responsibilities, 34, 38, 40, 174, 177–78, 183, 186–89, 191
patriarchy, 152, 230, 233
Paul, apostle, references, 165, 211–12, 219, 153, 163, 165–66, 168, 172, 185–86, 191
pausing puberty, See puberty blockers, pubertal suppression, hormone blockers)
penis, 39, 45, 69, 95–96, 120
Perry, Phillip, 142, 235, 237
PFLAG, See Parents and Friends of Lesbians and Gays (PFLAG)
physical sex transition, 28, 38, 101, 166
Piacenza, Joanna, 235
polygender, 2, 26

Poole, Matthew (Poole's Commentary), 157, 235
Pope, Francis, See Francis, José María Bergolio
Pope, John Paul II, 222, 235
Prince, Virginia, 31, 228
procreation, 3–4, 70–71, 84, 139–41, 144, 147–48, 200, 202, 206
  as human reproduction, 84, 140, 148, 167
Psalms, quotes from, 65, 85, 93, 143, 145
psychologists, licensed Christian, 108
psychotherapies (See also therapies, therapists), 46, 108–11
  somatic 108
  dialectical, 109
  psychodynamic, 110
pubertal suppression, See puberty blockers/puberty suppression
puberty, hormonal, 98, 102, 116–17, 122
puberty blockers/puberty suppression, 2, 115–17, 120, 122–23, 126–27, 129, 136, 231
  guidelines advocating, 111, 117, 122
  medications to block puberty, 105, 115, 117–20, 122, 126–27, 228, 232
Pulpit Commentary, 157, 235, 237
Pyle, Nate, 170, 235

Q

quality of life in transitioned persons, 130, 232
queer, 26–27, 32, 49
queering (adjective), 2, 27, 32

R

Rachna, C., 71, 235
Rafferty, Jason, 236
Ranken, Susan, 186, 226
Rapid Onset Gender Dysphoria (ROGD), 27, 201, 233. See also Lisa Littman
reassignment surgeries (See also conformation surgeries), 56, 100 126

Reilly-Cooper, Rebecca, 16, 198, 208, 236
reproduction, 18, 22, 39, 71, 83–84, 203
Reinisch, June Machover, 228, 236
Richards, C., 236
Ringrose,, K.M., 157, 236
Ritchie, Francis, 172, 236
Robbins, Gary, 19, 236
Roberts, Vaughn, 236
ROGD, See Rapid Onset Gender Dysphoria
roles (See gender roles, role socialization)
  female, 52, 207
  male, 152
Rogler, Lloyd H., 51, 250
Romans, epistle references, 147, 153–54, 157, 165, 167, 169, 181–82, 185–86, 191, 219, 226–27
Rosenberg, Noah A., 246
Rosenberg, Stanley, 146, 236
Rosenblum, Leonard A., 75, 236
Roussean, Jean-Jaques, 207, 210, 236
Rude, May, 20

S

Sakurai, Shige, 236
Salazar, Lisa, 170, 236
Sam[antha's] story, 39–41, 56–58
Savin-Williams, R.C., 236
saris, feminine men, (Judaism), 78
Schaff, Philip, 227
schools, role of in teaching gender, 3, ,8, 49, 53, 205, 209, 218
science,
  views by Christian scientists, 6, 75–76, 96, 146, 222, 239
  views by conservative Christians, 4–6, 14, 16, 68–69, 107, 113, 144–46, 155–56, 222–23, 228–29.
scripts, body and gender, 6, 10, 12, 108, 128, 150, 163, 222
self-diagnosis, a child's GD, 104, 106
self-identification, of gender, 16, 23, 27, 42, 51, 77, 84, 195, 209–10

Semenya, Caster, 79, 81–83, 233, 235–36
sex, 4–5, 8–11, 16–20, 22, 24, 26–27, 29–31, 40, 66–67, 69, 76–78, 101, 162–64, 172, 195–200, 202, 210–11, 227–28, 233–34, 236–37
  assigned, 11, 22, 43, 77, 197
  biologic, 18, 22, 28, 58, 71, 139
"sex adjunctive," 18, 149
sex glands, 9, 67, 72, 86, 95, 118, 121
sex hormones, 9, 86, 115, 118, 123–24
sexual biology, 16, 24, 86, convert149, 197
sexual body, 4, 10–11, 18, 28–29, 78, 84, 164
sexual orientation, 27–28, 30, 36, 46, 51, 55, 62, 75, 144, 229, 234
Sharzer, Rabbi Leonard, 160
Singal, Jesse, 47, 127, 237 (*See also* desistance)
Sister Mihcelle, *See* David/Michelle's story 61–62, 166
Smith, Michael B., 233
Solomon, R., 3, 237
socialization, role and gender, 10–14, 75, 77, 84, 101, 149–50, 172, 176, 197
Spack, N.P., 127, 237
Spansel, Mark, 202
Spence, H.D.M., 237. *See also* The Pulpit Commentary
sports, xxi, 12, 80, 83, 227, 233, 235
  and gender/identity, xxi, 12, 80, 83, 227, 233, 235
Steensma, T.D., 43, 126, 237
Stephens, Philip, 142, 237
stereotypes, and gender, 13, 152, 175–77, 186, 188, 207, 213
Stetzer, Ed, 205
Stephens, Philip, 142, 237
Stevens, G.B. 154, 237
Stiegler, Sam, 49, 237
Stoller, Robert, 9, 121, 155, 230, 237
Stuart, John, 234
Swaab, D.F., 156, 238
surgeries, 123
  aesthetic, 159
  confirmation, 111, 123, 161

Index

corrective, 99
cosmetic, 96, 159, 226
infant, 100
minimal, 40, 102
needless, 96

T

Tamar-Mattis, Anne, 128, 238
Taylor, John Hammond, 225
teens, and gender, 2, 34, 106, 109, 135, 202–3, 233
testicles, 40, 67, 69, 73, 80, 94, 99, 116, 118, 120, 158
testosterone, 60, 70, 73–74, 80, 82, 99, 116, 118–21, 123, 135, 226
absorption issues, 80
ovarian "T," 74
production, 69, 73, 80, 130, 134
testosterone therapy on FTM patients, 117, 121, 125, 135–36, 230
initiating T therapy, 38, 135
theological interpretations of gender, 6, 156, 167, 169–70, 178, 211, 214
theology, and biblical doctrine, 14, 84, 151, 155, 164, 206, 216, 227
therapies, (*See also* psychotherapies, hormone therapy)
"conversion" (wrongly identified), 117, 225
desisting, 46, 117
gender-affirming, 116, 130
gender-exploration, 46, 107, 109, 117, 221, 238
therapists
behavioral, 180
Christian, 35, 40, 45–46, 113, 107–8, 124, 128, 221–22.
selecting, 107
training, 222
"third genders," 58, 79, 98, 225, 231, 235
Thompson, M.D., 13, 160, 238
Throckmorton, W., 107, 221, 238
Throckmorton-Yarhouse Practice Framework, 107, 221, 238
tissue re-use, in gender surgeries,
clitoral, 125, 131
labial, 125
penile, 125
scrotal 125
Tomkins, Sylvan, 156, 238
Torah, and references to gender, 78, 160–61, 229
Tornielli, Andrea, 188, 238
transgender, xx, 22, 28, 30, 44, 58–59, 61, 105, 130–31, 160, 168, 186–87, 191–93, 215, 236
activism, 139, 144–45, 148–49, 156, 194–215, 233, 239
Christian's experience as, 166, 170, 236
as identity, 43, 47, 106, 153, 232, 240
transgenderism, 38, 43, 153, 156, 160, 186–87, 191–92, 196, 209, 212–13, 225–26, 235, 239
transitioning gender, 130, 136, 180, 187, 193
transphobia, 48, 194, 207
transsexual, 26–28, 31, 42, 131, 171, 173, 191, 193, 195, 209, 212–13, 232, 239–40
tumtum (Judaism), 78, 227
Tucker, Patricia, 10, 234
Turner Syndrome, 71–72, 235

U

Ulmer, Rivka, 143, 238
Unger, C., 134–37, 238
urination issues, and intersex organs, 99

V

Viloria, Hida, 186, 239
Volf, Miroslav, xx, 165, 166, 181–82, 204–5, 213, 239
Vrouenraets, Lieke, 239

W

Walker, Andrew T., 139, 141, 144–45, 148–49, 156, 236
Warren, Rick, 158, 239
Weinser-Hanks, M., 157, 239

Whitlow, B.J., 56, 239
Williams, Shawna, 156, 239
Wittgenstein, Ludwig, 19, 239
woman, 36–37, 42, 52, 60–61, 65, 68–69, 75, 77, 80–83, 139, 141, 149–50, 154, 171–72, 234–36
  feminine, 12
  heterosexual, 12, 81
  masculine, 78
women
  gay, 154
  transgender, 134
Women's Olympics
  gender controversies in, 82, 231, 239
World Professional Association for Transgender Health (WPATH), 117, 123
WPATH *See* World Professional Association for Transgender Health)

X

Xavier, Neena, 83, 239
XO karyotype, xxx, 23, 71–72, 87, 143
XX karyotype, xxx, 66, 87
XY karyotype, xxx, 9, 39–40, 52, 56, 67, 71–73, 80–81, 87, 139, 144
XYY karyotype, xxx, 23, 87, 143

Y

Yarhouse, Mark, 104, 107, 110, 200, 214, 221, 238–39
YO karyotype, xxviii, 87
Yong, Ed, 142, 239
YouTube, as gender exploration vehicle, 48, 60

Z

Ze/zir, 27, 29, 236
Zucker, Kenneth J., 44–46, 240

www.ingramcontent.com/pod-product-compliance
Lightning Source LLC
Chambersburg PA
CBHW022001220426
43663CB00007B/911